"As for me, I will dwell at Mizpah …": The Tell en-Naṣbeh Excavations after 85 Years

Gorgias Studies in the Ancient Near East

9

This series of monographs and edited volumes explores the societies, material cultures, technologies, religions and languages that emerged from the Levant, Mesopotamia, and Egypt.

"As for me, I will dwell at Mizpah ...": The Tell en-Naṣbeh Excavations after 85 Years

Edited by

Jeffrey R. Zorn

Aaron J. Brody

gorgias press

2014

Gorgias Press LLC, 954 River Road, Piscataway, NJ, 08854, USA

www.gorgiaspress.com

Copyright © 2014 by Gorgias Press LLC

2014   ,

ISBN 978-1-4632-0416-7

Library of Congress Cataloging-in-Publication Data

A Cataloging-in-Publication record is available from the Library of Congress.

Printed in the United States of America

This volume is dedicated to the memories of Betsy Badè Bacon and Bill Badè, long serving Advisory Board members of the Badè Museum of Biblical Archaeology, children of William F. and Elizabeth M. Badè.

TABLE OF CONTENTS

LIST OF FIGURES AND TABLES

FIGURES

Zorn — 20th–21st Centuries

Brody — Memories

Fig. 2.1. Bill Badè and Palestinian boy by Room 493 on south slope of tell, Tell en-Naṣbeh 1935 excavation season. Badè Museum photograph #1287 (Courtesy of Badè Museum of Biblical Archaeology, Pacific School of Religion).

Fig. 2.2. Bill Badè and Palestinian boy modeling similarity between modern clay canteen (R) and ancient pilgrim flask (L), Tell en-Naṣbeh 1935 excavation season (Badè Museum photograph #1534. Courtesy of Badè Museum of Biblical Archaeology, Pacific School of Religion).

Fig. 2.3. Bill Badè's 11th birthday costume party, Tell en-Naṣbeh dig house in Ramallah, May 29, 1935. Standing, left to right: Robert Branstead, J. Philmore Collins, Boulos el-'Araj, William F. Badè, Joe Carson Wampler, Nicias P. Reckas, Labib Sorial; seated left to right: Betsy Badè, Elizabeth Le Breton Marston Badè, Bill Badè. Badè Museum photograph #1421 (Courtesy of Badè Museum of Biblical Archaeology, Pacific School of Religion).

Boutin — Life and Death

Fig. 3.1. Commingled hand phalanges, metacarpals, and metatarsals of at least three individuals from Cistern 173.

Fig. 3.2. Mineralized cranium (B) of probable female adult from Tomb 52.

Fig. 3.3. Charred left tibia from an adolescent of unknown provenience.

Fig. 3.4. Jar burial of a 3–5 year old child from Tomb 52. Mandible with teeth indicated by arrow.

Fig. 3.5. Mandible of 12-10782 from Tomb 54. Of note: linear enamel hypoplasia on incisors and canines; severe chipping of right first incisor; rounding and porosity of alveolar margin, indicative of periodontal disease; antemortem loss of first molars.

Brody — Ammonite Pottery

Fig. 4.1. Ammonite painted wares from Tell en-Naṣbeh. See table 4.1 for descriptions (Illustrations by Christin Engstrom).

Brown — Iron

Fig. 5.4. Photo of iron agricultural implements from McCown 1947: pl. 96. Objects 11 and 17 in this photo correspond to this study's Objects 21 and 20 respectively (Courtesy of Badè Museum of Biblical Archaeology, Pacific School of Religion).

Fig. 5.5. Object 22 (Photograph by Stephanie Brown).

Fig. 5.6. Map of Tell en-Naṣbeh with iron agricultural implement find spots indicated: a = Rm 97, b = Rm 297, c = Rm 328, d = Rm 363, e = Rm 386, f = Rm 407, g = Rm 409, h = Rm 430, i = Rm 436, j = Rm 443, k = Rm 463, l = Rm 467, m = Rm 476, n = Rm 515, o = Rm 587, p = Rm 625A, q = Ci 159, r = Ci 176.

Adapted from the 1:400 Tell en-Naṣbeh site plan (Courtesy of Badè Museum of Biblical Archaeology, Pacific School of Religion).

Fig. 5.7. View of southwest portion of Tell en-Naṣbeh: g = Rm 409, h = Rm 430, i = Rm 436, k = Rm 463, l = Rm 467, n = Rm 515, o = Rm 587, p = Rm 625A,. Adapted from the 1:400 Tell en-Naṣbeh site plan (Courtesy of Badè Museum of Biblical Archaeology, Pacific School of Religion).

Fig. 5.8. Four-room house Building 142.05 and adjoining courtyard Building 142.06; Room 625a is where the cache of iron tools was found (Image courtesy of Jeffrey R. Zorn; adapted from the 1:100 Tell en-Naṣbeh site plan. Used with the permission of the Badè Museum of Biblical Archaeology, Pacific School of Religion).

Foster — Collection Management

Fig. 6.1. Outside the excavation house local workmen pack artifacts into crates for shipment to Berkeley, CA. Badè Museum photograph #108 (Courtesy of Badè Museum of Biblical Archaeology, Pacific School of Religion).

Fig. 6.2. Interior view of the Badè Museum in its original location on the northwest side of Holbrook Hall, circa 1940's. Badè Museum photograph #1561 (Courtesy of Badè Museum of Biblical Archaeology, Pacific School of Religion).

Fig. 6.3. Preventive conservation interventions in the storage area include upgraded drawer liners and inert foam and shaped paper object supports (Courtesy of Badè Museum of Biblical Archaeology, Pacific School of Religion).

Zissu — Roman–Byzantine Necropolis

Zorn — Water

TABLES

Boutin — Life and Death

TELL EN-NAṢBEH IN THE 20TH AND 21ST CENTURIES[1]

JEFFREY R. ZORN
DEPARTMENT OF NEAR EASTERN STUDIES
CORNELL UNIVERSITY

INTRODUCTION

The present volume grew out of the editors' long term involvement with the study, publication and curation of the archaeological remains and records from Tell en-Naṣbeh (Zorn since 1986, Brody since 2002), and also from the desire to promote additional interest in and study of this important site through an academic session at the American Schools of Oriental Research Annual Meeting held in San Francisco (across the bay from Berkeley where the Tell en-Naṣbeh materials are located) in November, 2011. A special evening reception celebrating William F. Badè's work at the site was held at the Badè Museum. That year also marked the 85th anniversary of the beginning of the excavation of Tell en-Naṣbeh in 1926. The necessary session time and room were secured and papers were solicited from various scholars currently working on Tell en-Naṣbeh material. Papers were read by Boutin, Foster, Larkum, Zissu and Zorn. It was subsequently decided to seek publication of these conference papers. Additional papers were then solicited, resulting in submissions from Brody, Brown, and Sussman. Unfortunately, as the volume was in preparation, William "Bill" G. Badè, the son of William F. Badè, the excavation director, passed away.

---

[1] Unless otherwise noted all illustrations are courtesy of the Badè Museum of Biblical Archaeology, Pacific School of Religion.

He was 11 years old in 1935 when he and his sister Elizabeth accompanied their parents for the final season at the site. He was the
last known living member of the excavation. We had hoped to interview him about his remembrances of that excavation season and
his other work with the Tell en-Naṣbeh artifacts (it was Bill who
discovered the famous fragmentary bronze cuneiform circlet while
cleaning and conserving the metal artifacts from the site; McCown
1947: pl. 55:80). The observations of an American boy of the "dig
experience" would have provided a novel view not found in other
excavation retrospectives of the Mandate Era. Still, we are grateful
to be able to include the comments of his family who heard of his
time at the site. His passing truly marks the end of living memory
of that period at the site. A bibliography of all works dealing with
Tell en-Naṣbeh in a significant way rounds out the present collection. We are grateful that Gorgias Press was willing to publish the
resulting volume.

Tell en-Naṣbeh is located on a Cenomanian limestone ridge
848 m (2762') above sea level. It is about 12 km (eight miles) north
of the Old City of Jerusalem (31°53'6.00"N, 35°12'59.00"E; New
Israel Grid 220559.86E – 643543.35N; Old Israel Grid 1706.1144;
Fig. 1.1). It also lies immediately south of the modern Palestinian
city of Ramallah. Indeed, parts of Ramallah's southern suburbs
now surround the site and some houses are built in the areas of the
site's cemeteries; in some cases individual homes are encroaching
on the tell itself (Fig. 1.6). The site, not including surrounding cemeteries, is about 250 m north to south and 160 m east to west. It
covers an area of 3.2 hectares (ca. 8 acres), though the area inside
the fortifications only amounts to about 2.4 hectares and the actual
area occupied by houses is only a bit over 1.7 hectares. At its height
in Iron Age II it probably had a population of about 900.

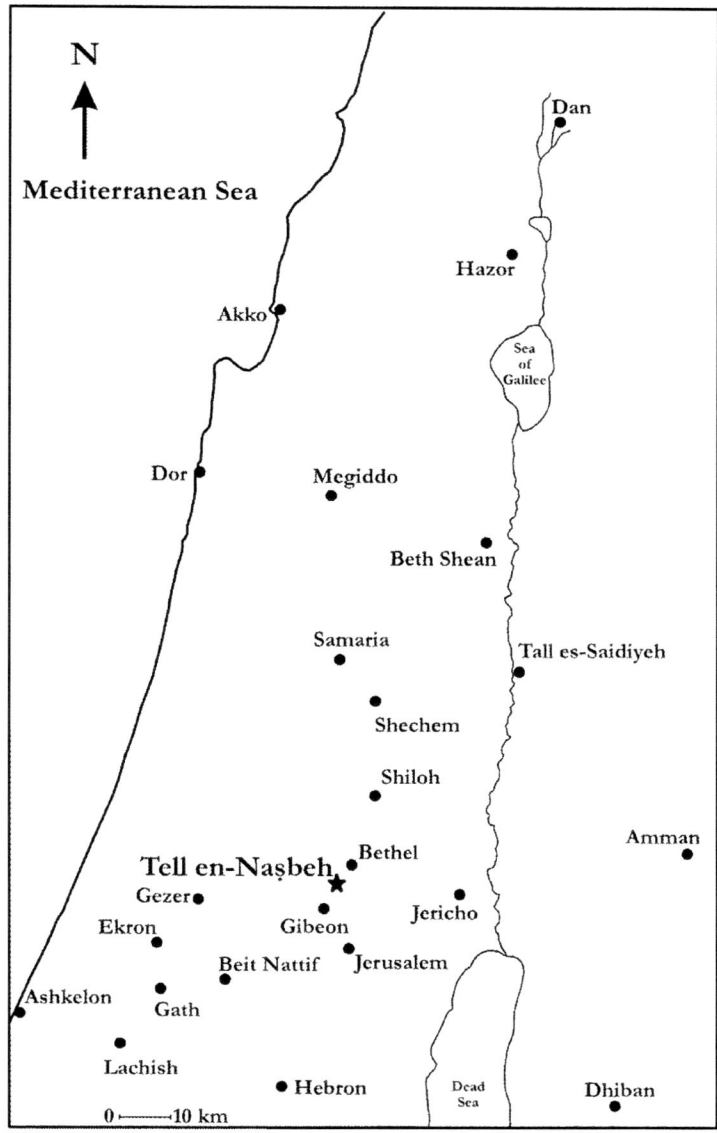

Fig. 1.1 Map showing location of Tell en-Naṣbeh in relation to local southern Levantine sites.

WILLIAM F. BADÈ AND THE HISTORY OF WORK AT TELL EN-NAṢBEH

Fig. 1.2. William Frederic Badè, director of the Tell en-Naṣbeh excavations, in a staged photograph exiting Cistern 369 during the 1935 season (Badè Museum photograph #1245. Courtesy of Badè Museum of Biblical Archaeology, Pacific School of Religion).

William Frederic Badè (Fig. 1.2), of what is now Pacific School of Religion, excavated the site in five lengthy seasons (1926, 1927, 1929, 1932, and 1935), eventually uncovering about two thirds of the site. A variety of preliminary reports were published during and after this period. Badè died in 1936, a year after the conclusion of the excavation. His death, the Great Depression, and the advent of World War II delayed the publication of the final report until 1947 (however, 12 years is less than the publication delays for many current excavations under far less difficult circumstances; for example, the third volume of Wright's excavations at Shechem appeared 29 years after the last excavation season). The two volume final report (McCown 1947; Wampler 1947) was brought to completion by Badè's seminary colleague, Chester C. McCown (Fig. 1.3), and his chief assistant during the last three years of the excavation, Joseph C. Wampler (Fig. 1.4). McCown dealt largely with the site's architecture and certain of the small finds, including late period lamps, while Wampler was mainly responsible for the publication of the pottery and certain aspects of the stratigraphy. Other chapters of special note were contributed by Muilenburg on the identification of Tell en-Naṣbeh with biblical Mizpah of Benjamin and the history of Mizpah, and a concise report on the Greek pottery produced by von Bothmer. The site plans were largely the work of Labib Sorial, the excavation's Egyptian surveyor and architect (Fig. 1.5). Sorial was the only member of the staff, besides Badè, to participate in all five seasons of the excavation.

Fig. 1.3. Chester Carlton McCown, who took on the task of publishing the results of Badè's excavations, hiking in the Galilee ca. 1921 (Courtesy of Pacific School of Religion).

Fig. 1.4. Joseph Carson Wampler (on right), the excavation's chief recorder who also published the majority of the ceramics, repairing pottery with Mahmoud in 1932 (Badè Museum photograph #A816. Courtesy of Badè Museum of Biblical Archaeology, Pacific School of Religion).

Fig. 1.5. Labib Sorial, the Egyptian architect responsible for most of the excavation's plans, working on the 1:100 map sheet 93 in 1932; this plan depicts most of the outer two-chamber gate (Badè Museum photograph 1009. Courtesy of Badè Museum of Biblical Archaeology, Pacific School of Religion).

When the final report was published it was hailed as a great and valuable achievement in advancing knowledge of the archaeology of ancient Israel (Albright 1948; May 1948; Perkins 1948; Sellers 1948; Simmons 1948; Vincent 1948; Wright 1948). Criticisms at this point tended to be minor, often focusing on Wampler's statistical method for determining dates for pottery types, and then the dates of the features in which they were found. However, it was not long before Kenyon's harsher appraisal appeared (1950). She faulted the excavators for not digging stratigraphically (i.e. according to debris layers, not according rooms), a common problem at the time. She also noted the lack of full cross-referencing which, for example, prohibited anyone from determining all the pottery types found in a specific tomb. Wright, who originally had much good to say of the report, later (1969: 126–29) was more critical of Badè's efforts in comparison to the work of his own mentor, Albright, at Tell Beit Mirsim. However, as others have subsequently noted, Albright did struggle with stratigraphy when he did not have the luxury of destruction layers sealing in situ ceramic assemblages, as in his Stratum B (e.g. Green 1987: 56), which is precisely the situation Badè faced at Tell en-Naṣbeh. Possibly Albright would have done a better job with Tell en-Naṣbeh than Badè, but how much better is debatable. For example, in the site's environs Badè located several cemeteries and 70 tombs. This contrasts with Albright who failed to find any tombs at Tell Beit Mirsim, though subsequent looters found them in abundance close by the site (Ben-Arieh 2004).

PROBLEMS WITH THE 1947 REPORT

Despite McCown and Wampler's exemplary efforts to produce a final site report after Badè's death there is no doubt that the 1947 report does contain some severe problems that have greatly limited its usefulness to scholars. Some of these same issues are found in other reports of the period (and in some from long after) and so are not unique to Tell en-Naṣbeh. Some derive from the nature of archaeological work in Mandate Era Palestine, some arise from choices made in how the data would be presented in the report, and some result from the interpretations of those who produced the report.

The first problem involves the lack of published detailed site plans and plans which group the site's architectural features into distinct strata. Most of the site's remains, though not all, were published on a single 1:400 plan (fig. 10.1 is a reduced and adapted version of this plan). Some areas are presented in more detail in text figures, and some features are not shown on the 1:400 plan, but only in the figures. A series of more detailed 1:100 plans were prepared, and some were published in McClellan's article (1984), but were not reproduced in the 1947 report. Similarly, hundreds of photographs were taken of the excavation in progress, but only a sample was included in the report. Unfortunately, many features were not documented by even a single photograph and excavation areas were usually not photographed in as clean a state as in modern excavations. Section drawings are few and schematic, which is not surprising since debris layer oriented archaeology was largely unpracticed at the time. Relatively few of the 1000+ excavated architectural features are discussed at all in the 1947 report; most are treated only in a few summary lists. All this has limited scholars in their ability to understand the stratigraphy proposed in the 1947 report, or to reanalyze it.

Similarly daunting problems face those wishing to restudy the site's pottery and other small finds. From the way in which the pottery types are described it is impossible to determine the specific find spots for virtually all of the ceramics. Such details are only provided for the type piece itself and a few examples from select other contexts, usually tombs and cisterns. All other representatives of a type are grouped under broad stratigraphic categories. For example, for pot Type 89 it is reported that 19 rims came from Stratum I contexts, but not which specific contexts. Coverage of other small finds is equally problematic. For example, pl. 105 in Vol. 1 of the report shows seven bone "spatulas" and the text mentions them only in passing; however, record cards for the excavation document a total of 94 spatulas. Only a few cisterns and tombs come anywhere close to full reporting. Two examples will suffice. From Cistern 370, 97 vessels are cited and illustrated, but 281 objects of all classes were recorded; thus citations attest to only 35% of the total number of recorded finds. From Tomb 32, 119 vessels are reported, but 792 objects were recorded; thus only 15% are mentioned in the 1947 report. Because of this incomplete reporting and indexing of artifacts it is impossible to reconstruct the contents of any given feature.

A final problem, not related to the nature of the publication itself, hampers efforts to use the site's artifacts. The recording method used at Tell en-Naṣbeh was adopted from the system used by Clarence S. Fisher, an early adviser of Badè. If no floor level could be determined for a room all artifacts from the tops of the room's walls, to the base of its walls were reported as coming from one homogenous unit. If some indication of a floor could be determined for a room artifacts from below that level would be given a separate designation within the room. For this reason it is usually impossible to determine which sherds (and most of the ceramics from the rooms are sherds, not complete forms) were floating in debris high above floor level in redeposition, which were found on or at least close to a floor, and which came from below a floor. Such an approach to recording makes any chronological or contextual study of the artifacts virtually impossible.

THE IDENTIFICATION OF TELL EN-NAṢBEH

Perhaps the most important reason Badè chose to excavate at Tell en-Naṣbeh was to determine whether the archaeological remains uncovered there could shed any light on the possible identification of the site with biblical Mizpah of Benjamin, a topic of much debate up to that time (ably discussed by Muilenburg in the 1947 report and again in 1954–55). The only other site today which some consider a rival candidate for this identification is nearby Nebi Samwil. Both sites have reasonable claims to this identification based solely on textual data. Unfortunately later occupation at Nebi Samwil removed virtually all architectural remains and in situ deposits from the Iron Age (Magen 2008; Magen and Dadon 2003; Magen and Har-Even 2007). Thus, it is very difficult to characterize the site's occupation during that period. However, while Iron Age II pottery was found in redeposited fills, apparently nothing from Iron I was found there. This is a period that should be represented at any site identified with Mizpah, and such material is found at Tell en-Naṣbeh. Similarly, no remains from the Babylonian period of the 6ᵗʰ century were uncovered at Nebi Samwil (though remains from the subsequent Persian period are reasonably abundant). Material of this period should be well-attested at any site identified with Mizpah and is found at Tell en-Naṣbeh. Finally no trace of the famous wall associated with Asa of Judah's building campaign (1 Kings 15: 22) was found at Nebi Samwil. Could an entire settlement's wall disappear and leave no trace? Tell en-Naṣbeh was surrounded by a massive set of fortifications that could well be those associated with Asa. Thus, on the basis of the surviving archaeological data Tell en-Naṣbeh is still the best candidate for the Iron Age Mizpah of Benjamin.

A NEW ERA IN TELL EN-NAṢBEH STUDIES

Because of the various problems outlined above Tell en-Naṣbeh was the subject of relatively few scholarly works after the publication of the 1947 report, appearing mostly in works related to Israelite architecture and town planning (e.g. Shiloh 1970). Work undertaken by Zorn in his dissertation (1993) considerably revised and clarified the stratigraphy presented by McCown and Wampler. The revised stratigraphy uses Arabic numerals in order to avoid confusion with the Roman numerals used in the 1947 report.

Some Chalcolithic remains were recovered, but the first real settlement is Stratum 5 in Early Bronze Age I (ca. 3200 BC). After that, the site was abandoned until the Iron Age I (ca. 1200 BC) when Stratum 4 was established. This was followed by Stratum 3, which was continuously occupied and rebuilt from the tenth to the beginning of the sixth century. Stratum 3, which initially represents a modest rural agricultural settlement but came to take on the role of a Judean border fortress as well, is divided into three sub-phases. The original 3C settlement of three- and four-room houses was protected by a casemate-like wall. Subsequently in 3B a massive offset-inset wall with an inner-outer gate complex was constructed slightly down slope from the 3C town, most likely in the ninth century. Stratum 3A represents additional modifications to the town plan subsequent to the construction of the fortifications. Stratum 2 witnessed a complete change in the site's layout, in accord with the site's new role as a Babylonian administrative center following the destruction of Jerusalem in 586 BCE (Zorn 2003). Stratum 2 seems to last through the Babylonian period into the Persian period, until the late fifth, perhaps early fourth century. A few in situ deposits suggest a violent end to the site, but the agent of the destruction is not known. After a gap the site was occupied, but more sparsely, apparently around the beginning of the second century BCE into the Roman period. Remains of a Byzantine era church and tombs were found off the main site. The two most important results of the reevaluation of the site stratigraphy include the documentation of the presence of a massive Inner (four-chamber) and Outer (two-chamber) gate system in Stratum 3 (reduced to just the two-chamber gate in Stratum 2), along with the identification of the until then unsuspected remains from the Babylonian period which helped foster additional research into that previously largely unknown era.

The presentation of a revised stratigraphy in general fostered renewed interest in the site. This is especially evident in the increased number of publications using the site material beginning around 1990, as found in this volume's master site bibliography.

FUTURE ARCHAEOLOGICAL WORK ON TELL EN-NAṢBEH

Because of the current political climate the chance for future archaeological work at Tell en-Naṣbeh, at least in the near term is slim. The site lies close to the border between the West Bank (the Palestinian Territories) and the municipal boundary of Jerusalem. It is located in Zone C, the area still largely controlled by Israel, but which eventually is to be turned over to the Palestinians. For a while an Israeli checkpoint stood just east of the tell on the road running north from Jerusalem (it is now located south of the site). Except for work done by the Israel Antiquities Authority (IAA) most archaeological work in Israel is carried out by, and financed by, volunteers, mostly from abroad, under the direction of staff from an academic institution (usually an Israeli university in partnership with foreign institutions, many from the United States). This has allowed large, reasonably funded projects to flourish. Work in the Palestinian controlled areas is conducted at present primarily by the Palestinian Department of Antiquities and Cultural Heritage (PDACH). There have been attempts at joint archaeological projects with some foreign governments/institutions but these have been relatively few so far. Because of the site's location, and the often times unpredictable nature of local politics, which has included violent confrontations between Israelis and Palestinians, an archaeological project involving foreign institutions and volunteers on their mutual border in the near future is not likely. Few foreign institutions would allow their staff and volunteers (often primarily college students) to participate in a research project in a potentially dangerous area, even if the actual chance of violence is relatively small. Even one such incident would be a legal, financial, and public relations nightmare for an American university.

It also has to be admitted that politically the Palestinians have little reason to excavate an Iron Age Israelite site such as Tell en-Naṣbeh. Publicizing the presence of what was once the Judean capital, albeit briefly, on the very doorstep of their own current capital runs counter to their own efforts to bolster national heritage in the area.

However, if/when new work could be undertaken at the site it is worth asking what could such an excavation achieve? First, as noted above, Badè was quite successful at locating cemeteries and tombs in the area around the tell. It seems likely that since his day other tombs have been discovered around the site by looters and then plundered of their materials for sale on the antiquities market. Renewed work at the site should attempt to document the specific location of the tombs Badè excavated relative to the main site (which was not done in the 1947 report) and also plot the locations of subsequently looted tombs; in addition, an effort should be made to locate any additional undiscovered tombs around the site. Because the site is in the Palestinian territories studies of human remains from such tombs might well be possible, something which is currently impossible in Israel due to the out-sized importance of religious parties in Israel's Knesset.

The area in which Tell en-Naṣbeh has played the greatest role over the years is in understanding Judean town planning. The reason for this is obvious. The published 1:400 site plan gives the impression that most of the tell was excavated. Indeed, about two thirds of it was excavated, much of it down to bedrock. However, there are areas on the site that were not excavated, or apparently not excavated down to bedrock. For example, much of the area in the north central part of the site bounded by grid squares R15–R21 on the north to Z13–22 on the south was never touched, much of it because of the presence of large rubble heaps created over the centuries by local farmers clearing the tell's top soil of stones in order farm the tell (Badè had to rebury the excavated portions of the site at the end of each season so that farming could continue). Similar large rubble heaps are found in the south central and southeastern parts of the site. Clearing away these rubble heaps would open large areas for further excavation. Such excavation would likely reveal a great deal more information about the site's plan and road system and add to the corpus of Israelite domestic architecture. The only caveat to this is that due to erosion remains along the central spine of the hill on which the town was built tend to be more fragmentary than those located toward the periphery of the site. Re-excavation of some of the squares between the inner four-chamber gate and outer two-chamber gate would likely clarify issues regarding their construction and integration as a single architectural unit.

One of the current archaeological fads in the Levant is household archaeology. That is, archaeological endeavors which attempt to elucidate the behaviors of the occupants of a dwelling's various rooms. It is even hoped that the functions of sub-spaces within individual rooms can be determined. The vast number of entire, or nearly entire buildings that were excavated at Tell en-Naṣbeh, and which belong to the main Iron Age II phase (Stratum 3 of the revised stratigraphy), might seem to make the site a perfect candidate for household archaeology on a massive scale. However, there is a major problem that negates any hope of such a program. Of the hundreds of Stratum 3 rooms excavated none of them contained in situ deposits left as a result of the room's destruction, and such deposits are the very foundation of household archaeology. Without such snapshots of the last moments of a building's existence it is impossible to create even a satisfactory approximation of the activities that were undertaken in the various spaces inside a dwelling just before it came to an end. This lack of in situ assemblages is not an artifact of the excavators' methods for they did uncover a few such deposits in Stratum 2 of the Neo-Babylonian to Persian periods, proving that they were capable of identifying them. Instead, it is a result of the nature of the end of Stratum 3. It seems that in order to construct the new Judean administrative center of Stratum 2 the previous settlement was leveled, filled in, and built over. In other words, Stratum 3 was "destroyed" as a result of a program of peaceful urban renewal, not sudden destruction by some enemy. This means that the inhabitants had sufficient time to remove any of their possessions that they wanted to take with them. Installations cut into the bedrock, such as cisterns and silos, or sunk into debris such as stone-lined storage bins, or which were otherwise unmovable, such as ovens or heavy stone presses and basins used for olive oil extraction are the primary materials found that hint at the inhabitant's activities. There are also occasional ground stone implements, such as complete saddle querns or mortars, that might reasonably be expected to reflect some, but not all,

of the functions of a specific room. What are largely lacking, besides the ceramics, are the clusters of small objects that suggest
certain activities. For example, there are no in situ groupings of
loom weights to suggest weaving, nor religiously affective items
that might suggest household cult. Only Room 625A and its cluster
of iron tools (see the article by Brown in this volume) suggests a
specific functional role for a space. Renewed excavations would
likely turn up additional unmovable installations, but not major
clusters of in situ artifact assemblages. The occasional cluster might
be uncovered, again like Room 625A, but such finds will not provide the sort of comprehensive data needed for a successful program of household archaeology. Because of the nature of archaeology in Palestine of the 1920s and 1930s there are no floral or faunal
assemblages recorded from the site. Careful excavation with modern methods might be able to recover floral and faunal remains
imbedded in the floors of specific rooms, but it will remain uncertain whether these reflect the final use of such spaces, or merely
reflect the totality of the room's functions throughout its existence.

Renewed excavations might be able to clarify certain aspects
of the chronology of the site's stratigraphy. As noted above, in situ
deposits are lacking from most of the site's architectural features. A
few Stratum 2 rooms containing such assemblages were found,
which allowed that stratum to be assigned a date from the beginning of the sixth century to the end of the fifth century. It is possible that other assemblages of Stratum 2 might be uncovered. The
dates for the beginning of Stratum 2 provide a date for the end of
Stratum 3, around the beginning of the sixth century. Excavations
in the previously unexcavated areas listed above would certainly
provide more examples of Stratum 3 architecture, though, for the
reasons mentioned above, probably no in situ ceramic assemblages.
Using modern methods it would be possible to isolate materials
above and below living surfaces/floors. Sherd data from below the
floors of Stratum 3 would provide a *terminus post quem* for the construction of those buildings. Similar careful excavation and collection of sherd material from within building walls might suggest
some dates for structural modifications. Remains of Stratum 4 are
very fragmentary and difficult to date. It is possible though that
rock cut features originating in Stratum 4, such as silos, crossed
over by walls of Stratum 3 might be found and provide finer dating
for that period. Stratum 5 of the Early Bronze I is even more poor-

ly preserved than Stratum 4, though tombs of this period might be uncovered.

Another area where renewed excavations could help clarify chronological issues involves the site's massive offset-inset wall. Until the last two decades it was generally believed that the site's fortifications were those constructed for Mizpah by King Asa of Judah in the early ninth century, as recounted in 1 Kings 15:22. Recently, however, here have been attempts to redate the walls to other periods: Katz suggested a period post-dating the eighth century (1998: 132); Finkelstein has argued for a date in the time of King Jehoash at the end of the ninth century (Finkelstein 2012: 24–25). For Finkelstein such a redating is required by his Low Chronology scheme that posits that there was no significant state in Judah until the post-Omride era. If there was no state to build massive fortifications, then the walls of Tell en-Naṣbeh, which match the solid wall of Megiddo in size, could not possibly be dated to the early ninth century (Finkelstein 2012: 22–23). However, this dating is based primarily on his reconstruction of Israelite and Judean history, not on conclusive archaeological data from Tell en-Naṣbeh itself. The material data needed to settle the issue, a stratigraphic excavation of the debris layers piled up against the wall, a cut through the walls, along with the collection any sherd material recovered from the wall itself, and any sherd material from below the base of the wall, is lacking. Badè did make a cut through the wall at the north end of the site, but apparently did not record the ceramics he found inside the wall. He also excavated adjacent to the city wall at several points, but material from these cuts (such as the deep sounding made between the south face of the four-chamber gate and the adjacent 4-room house) were not conducted or recorded in a stratigraphic manner, and so are worthless for dating the wall. Stratigraphically excavated trenches in the debris adjacent to the city wall in the area between the two gates (where Badè apparently did not reach bedrock in several places), below the walls of the four-chamber gate (which are built on the fill piled against the inner face of the town wall, and which Badè left in place), and perhaps on the western side of the site in Y11–13 (where again Badè does not seem to have excavated deeply), could, with a cut through the wall at some point, provide the data necessary to put the chronology of the construction of the fortifications on a firmer footing.

TELL EN-NAŞBEH IN THE 21ST CENTURY

However, since it seems unlikely that there will be renewed excavations at Tell en-Naṣbeh anytime in the near future an important issue is whether scholars can expect anything new to be said about the site based on the currently available records and artifacts? As is evident from the papers presented in this volume, and other studies published over the last two decades, the answer is a resounding yes. The essays by Zissu and Klein and Zorn attest to the insights still to be gained on the site's architectural remains. Those by Brody and Sussman show the important role that the site's ceramics can continue to play. The papers by Brown, Boutin et al., and Larkum document how the use of modern scientific analytic techniques on the curated artifacts can shed welcome light on Israelite life ways. Finally, Foster's paper highlights the important interplay between modern museology and the Badè Museum that houses many of the Tell en-Naṣbeh artifacts and all the site records. It also attests to the importance of making these records available online.

As for possible future studies, only a few examples can be suggested here. One possibility would be to examine the Tell en-Naṣbeh pottery (both typologically and petrographically) on a regional scale, with sites on both sides of the border of the kingdoms of Judah and Israel. How common were northern forms and fabrics at this border town, and how does the relative quantity of northern forms at Tell en-Naṣbeh compare to assemblages at other northern Judean/Benjaminite sites? Was the area relatively open to contacts with the north (at least as far as ceramics can suggest) or relatively closed? As noted above, major features were not well-documented in the 1947 report. For example, a full publication of the abundant material from Tomb 32 would provide data on burial practices in the early part of the Iron Age II era. The Early Bronze I material is still in need of systematic study. As more forms of scientific analysis are developed and become inexpensive enough to use on a large scale Tell en-Naṣbeh may have much to offer on Israelite diet, health, trade and commercial activities, and so on.

Fig. 1.6. Satellite image of immediate environs of Tell en
Naṣbeh (kidney shape feature near center of image). The road
on the right connects Jerusalem with the Nablus/Shechem region to the north. Note the encroachment of modern buildings
in the vicinity of the site. The buildings to the west (left) and
north (top) of the site are built over two of the settlement's ancient cemeteries (Image: © 2014 Google Earth).

Badè had hoped to undertake a study of the fingerprints found on
the site's ceramics. With today's scanning and computing technologies such a study, including other sites in Israel, might yield interesting results. Source analysis of various ceramics from Tell en-
Naṣbeh has already been undertaken by various scholars, but, as
suggested above, more could be done (Mommsen, Perlman, and
Yellin 1984; Zorn, Yellin, and Hayes 1994; Gunneweg et al. 1994).
For example, the wedge- and circle-decorated pottery, found so
abundantly at Tell en-Naṣbeh and other sites in Israel, has also
been found in Jordan and northern Arabia (Zorn 2001). From
where does this pottery originate and what would such a study reveal about international connections in the later Babylonian-Persian

periods? In many ways the list of possible projects involving extant Tell en-Naṣbeh material hinges only on the imagination of archaeologists working in the area, and on the availability of modern scientific analytical testing techniques. Hopefully other scholars will take up the fascinating challenges and opportunities offered by this site.

REFERENCES

Albright, W. F.
1948   Review of Tell en-Naṣbeh: Excavated Under the Direction of the Late William Frederic Badè, Vol. 1, Archaeological and Historical Results by Chester Charlton McCown; Vol. 2, The Pottery by Joseph Carson Wampler. *Journal of Near Eastern Studies* 7: 202–05.

Ben-Arieh, S.
2004   *Bronze and Iron Age Tombs at Tell Beit Mirsim*. Israel Antiquities Authority Report 23. Jerusalem: Israel Antiquities Authority.

Finkelstein, I.
2012   The Great Wall of Tell en-Nasbeh (Mizpah), The First Fortifications in Judah, and 1 Kings 15:16–22. *Vetus Testamentum* 62: 14–28.

Greenberg, R.
1987   New Light on the Early Iron Age at Tell Beit Mirsim. *Bulletin of the American Schools of Oriental Research* 265: 55–80.

Gunneweg, J.; Asaro, F.; Michel, H. V.; and Perlman, I.
1994   Interregional Contacts between Tell en-Nasbeh and Littoral Philistine Centres in Canaan during Early Iron I. *Archaeometry* 36: 227–40.

Katz, H.
1998   A Note on the Date of the 'Great Wall' of Tell en-Naṣbeh *Tel Aviv* 25: 131–33.

Kenyon, K. M.
1950   Palestinian Excavations. *Antiquity* 24: 196–200.

Magen, Y.
2008   Nebi Samwil: Where Samuel Crowned Israel's First King. *Biblical Archaeology Review* 34.3: 36–45, 78–79.

Magen, Y., and Dadon, M.
2003   Nebi Samwil (Montjoie). Pp. 123–38 in *One Land - Many Cultures: Archaeological Studies in Honour of Stanislao Loffreda OFM*, ed. G. C. Bottini, L. Di Segnie, and L. D. Chrupcala. Collectio Maior 41. Jerusalem: Franciscan Printing Press.

Magen, Y. and Har-Even, B.
2007   Persian Period Stamp Impressions from Nebi Samwil. *Tel Aviv* 34: 38–58.

May, H. G.
1948   Review of *Tell en-Naṣbeh: Excavated Under the Direction of the Late William Frederic* Badè, Vol. 1, *Archaeological and Historical Results* by Chester Charlton McCown; Vol. 2, *The Pottery* by Joseph Carson Wampler. *Journal of Religion* 28: 134–35.

McClellan, T. L.
1984   Town Planning at Tell en-Naṣbeh. *Zeitschrift des Deutschen Palästina-Vereins* 100: 53–69.

McCown, C. C.
1947   *Tell en-Naṣbeh*, Vol. 1: *Archaeological and Historical Results*. Berkeley, CA: The Palestine Institute of Pacific School of Religion.

Mommsen, H.; Perlman, I.; and Yellin, J.
1984   The Provenience of the *lmlk* Jars. *Israel Exploration Journal* 34: 89–113.

Muilenburg, J.
1954–55 Mizpah of Benjamin. *Studia Theologica* 8: 25–42.

Perkins, A. L.
1948   Review of *Tell en-Naṣbeh: Excavated Under the Direction of the Late William Frederic* Badè, Vol. 1, *Archaeological and Historical Results* by Chester Charlton McCown; Vol. 2, *The Pottery* by Joseph Carson Wampler. *Journal of the American Oriental Society*, 68: 196–99.

Sellers, O. R.
1948   Review of *Tell en-Naṣbeh: Excavated Under the Direction of the Late William Frederic* Badè, Vol. 1, *Archaeological and Historical Results* by Chester Charlton McCown; Vol. 2, *The Pottery* by Joseph Carson Wampler. *Journal of Biblical Literature* 57: 392–93.

Shiloh, Y.
1970   The Four-Room House: Its Situation and Function in the Israelite City. *Israel Exploration Journal* 20: 180–90.

Simons, J. J.
1948   Review of *Tell en-Naṣbeh: Excavated Under the Direction of the Late William Frederic* Badè, Vol. 1, *Archaeological and Historical Results* by Chester Charlton McCown; Vol. 2, *The Pottery* by Joseph Carson Wampler. *Bibliotheca Orientalis* 7: 104–07.

Tufnell, O.
1948   Review of *Tell en-Naṣbeh: Excavated Under the Direction of the Late William Frederic* Badè, Vol. 1, *Archaeological and Historical Results* by Chester Charlton McCown; Vol. 2, *The Pottery* by Joseph Carson Wampler. *Palestine Exploration Quarterly* 80: 145–50.

Vincent, L. H.
1948   Review of *Tell en-Naṣbeh: Excavated Under the Direction of the Late William Frederic* Badè, Vol. 1, *Archaeological and Historical Results* by Chester Charlton McCown; Vol. 2, *The Pottery* by Joseph Carson Wampler. *Revue biblique* 55: 287–97.

Wampler, J. C.
1947   *Tell en-Naṣbeh*, Vol. 2: *The Pottery*. Berkeley, CA: The Palestine Institute of Pacific School of Religion.

Wright, G. E.
1948   Review of *Tell en-Naṣbeh: Excavated Under the Direction of the Late William Frederic Badè*, Vol. 1, *Archaeological and Historical Results* by Chester Charlton McCown; Vol. 2, *The Pottery* by Joseph Carson Wampler. *American Journal of Archaeology* 52: 470–72.
1969   Archaeological Method in Palestine – An American Interpretation. *Eretz Israel* 9 (W. F. Albright Volume): 120–33.

Zorn, J. R.
1993   Tell en-Nasbeh: A Re-evaluation of the Architecture and
        Stratigraphy of the Early Bronze Age, Iron Age and Later
        Periods. Ph.D. dissertation, University of California,
        Berkeley.
2001   Wedge- and Circle-Impressed Pottery: An Arabian Con-
        nection. Pp. 689–98 in *Studies in the Archaeology of Israel and
        Neighboring Lands in Memory of Douglas. L. Esse* ed. S. R.
        Wolff. Studies in Ancient Oriental Civilizations 59. Chica-
        go: Oriental Institute.
2003   Tell en-Naṣbeh and the Problem of the Material Culture of
        the 6th Century. Pp. 413–47 in *Judah and the Judeans in the
        Neo-Babylonian Period,* ed. O. Lipschits and J. Blenkinsopp.
        Winona Lake, IN: Eisenbrauns.

MEMORIES FROM TELL EN-NAṢBEH

AARON J. BRODY
PACIFIC SCHOOL OF RELIGION
BADÈ MUSEUM OF BIBLICAL ARCHAEOLOGY

When plans for this volume were taking shape, Jeffrey R. Zorn suggested that I interview Bill Badè (William George Badè) about his experiences at Tell en-Naṣbeh in 1935, when he was a ten-eleven year old boy. As the son of the excavator, Bill accompanied his parents, William Frederic Badè and Elizabeth Le Breton Marston Badè, and sister, Elizabeth "Betsy" Le Breton Badè, on what would prove to be the final season of the excavation project at Tell en-Naṣbeh. To our knowledge, Bill was the only one left, at least in the United States, with any first-hand memories of the dig. Tragically, Bill passed away quite suddenly on August 10, 2012, before I had the opportunity to capture some of his memories directly. What follows is an amalgamation of Bill's reminiscences, based on an interview with his wife Elly (Eleanor Jane Barry Badè); stories that his sister, Betsy, shared with me before she died in 2008; and details from a diary that Betsy kept from the travels to, and from, the British Mandate of Palestine. The Badè family has generously donated Betsy's diary to the Badè Museum at Pacific School of Religion.

The Badè family left San Francisco on December 28, 1934 aboard the S. S. President Hoover ocean liner. As Betsy remarked to me many decades later, their departure from the San Francisco Bay predated the time when the iconic Golden Gate Bridge spanned the entryway to the Pacific Ocean. The bridge would be completed several years later. Accompanying the family was Joseph (Joe) Wampler, a student of W. F. Badè's at Pacific School of Religion and valued member of the Tell en-Naṣbeh project team. Wampler would go on to author the second final report volume on the pottery from Tell en-Nasbeh and several chapters in the first volume. Joe was nominally Betsy and Bill's tutor, primarily, I was later told, because this position allowed him to travel aboard the ship at a discount. Joe did do some tutoring with the children, however, especially Arabic language instruction. Ironically the only other travelers with their own tutor onboard ship, which Bill and Betsy mentioned, were DuPonts, which must have made the Badè children feel a bit posh.

New Year's Eve was celebrated on the S. S. President Hoover en route to Honolulu. The ship arrived in Hawaii, then an American protectorate, early in the morning of January 2, 1935. The Badè's were met by a cousin living there, and were able to enjoy a few hours of rest and relaxation on the island. W. F. Badè lectured at the Honolulu Academy of Arts after lunch, and the family boarded the ship later that day before it departed for Japan. The ocean liner arrived in Yokohama on January 11, and the Badè family and Joe Wampler spent the next two weeks in Japan. Besides sightseeing in Tokyo, Kyoto, Nara, Kobe, and in the countryside, W. F. Badè visited with former students, who had studied with him at Pacific School of Religion, and delivered several talks while in country. They departed Japan on board a different ship, the S. S. President Johnson, on January 25 and arrived in Shanghai on the 28th. Time in Shanghai was brief, although there was a bit of sightseeing and a lecture delivered at the Asiatic Society. They arrived in Hong Kong by February 1st where they spent some time on shore, overnighted on the ship, and left the next morning for Manila. The ship arrived in the Philippines on February 4th, where a former student met the family and W. F. Badè gave a formal talk. The ship departed the next morning, arriving in Singapore on the 9th, Penang (Malaysia) on the 12th, and Columbo on the 18th. In her diary, Betsy mentions visiting several gem stores while in Columbo, Ceylon (now Sri Lanka), and details her father purchasing some lapis lazuli. Bill remembered his father searching for onyx in these shops, which W. F. Badè acquired in order to make replicas of the Ja'azaniah seal, discovered in the excavations at Tell en-Nasbeh in 1932. The ocean liner reached Bombay on February 20th, left on the 22nd, and arrived in Suez on March 3rd. On the 4th the ship travelled up the Suez Canal arriving in Port Said just after midday, which completed their sea voyage more than three months after leaving California.

Fig. 2.1. Bill Badè and Palestinian boy by Room 493 on south slope of tell, Tell en-Naṣbeh 1935 excavation season. Badè Museum photograph #1287 (Courtesy of Badè Museum of Biblical Archaeology, Pacific School of Religion).

From Port Said, the group took the train down to Kantara and then on to Jerusalem, arriving on March 5th. The Badès and Joe Wampler settled in at the newly built Y. M. C. A., now an iconic Jerusalem building, and were able to travel out to Ramallah that afternoon to inspect the house that they would live in during the dig season. The move to this house in Ramallah, close to the dig site of Tell en-Naṣbeh, took place on March 12th. From Betsy's diary and remarks she made decades later in Berkeley, it seems clear that she did not spend much time at the archaeological site. There is one entry that mentions helping spread the *shekef* (pottery sherds) at the tell, another that details going to the site for pay-day, and one time she helped with shellacking numbers on pottery.

Fig. 2.2. Bill Badè and Palestinian boy modeling similarity between modern clay canteen (R) and ancient pilgrim flask (L),
Tell en-Naṣbeh 1935 excavation season (Badè Museum photograph #1534. Courtesy of Badè Museum of Biblical Archaeology, Pacific School of Religion).

Otherwise, Betsy spent most of her time off-site in Ramallah, helping her mother with duties that kept the dig-house running smoothly. She remarked to me something to the effect that "It wasn't considered proper in those days for women or girls to be at the site." Bill seems to have spent more time at the tell, as we find him in several of the excavation's photos (Figs. 2.1–2).

Fig. 2.3.Bill Badè's 11th birthday costume party, Tell en-Naṣbeh dig house in Ramallah, May 29, 1935. Standing, left to right: Robert Branstead, J. Philmore Collins, Boulos el-'Araj, William F. Badè, Joe Carson Wampler, Nicias P. Reckas, Labib Sorial; seated left to right: Betsy Badè, Elizabeth Le Breton Marston Badè, Bill Badè. Badè Museum photograph #1421 (Courtesy of Badè Museum of Biblical Archaeology, Pacific School of Religion).

For the Badè children there were trips to Jerusalem for food or dig supplies, play with each other or other children, sightseeing, visits to other digs (including Garstang's excavation at Jericho), holiday celebrations like Palm Sunday, and viewings of British army parades. Betsy recorded being invited to the American School (now Albright Institute) in Jerusalem by Dr. (Clarence S.) Fisher to watch the military parade commemorating King George V's Silver Jubilee, on May 6, 1935. Fisher had been a consultant for the Naṣbeh excavation project for many years. She also mentions building a "house" with Bill out of stones, a kind of playhouse, in their yard in Ramallah. On May 29 the group celebrated Bill's 11th birthday with a costume party, captured in a photograph (Fig. 2.3). In her diary, Betsy detailed the costume of each individual who came to the party, many of which had been purchased on the long voyage to Palestine.

On June 17 the family visited Tell el-Fukhar (Tel Akko) near Acre (Akko). W. F. Badè was interested in seeing the site to determine if it would be a good choice for a future excavation, since the Tell en-Naṣbeh project was coming to a close. This would never come to be, as Badè passed away six months after the family's return to California. Ironically, Pacific School of Religion has been part of the current excavations at Tel Akko that began in 2010, as a consortial member of the Total Archaeology at Tel Akko project, co-sponsored by Penn State University and the University of Haifa.

Other notable instances from Betsy's diary include a visit, along with the excavation staff, to the new museum in Jerusalem (the Rockefeller Museum). She mentions the fishpond in the courtyard of the Museum, and the cork flooring. The Palestine Archaeological Museum (now Rockefeller) did not officially open to the public until 1938, so this must have been a special, behind-the-scenes tour. Earlier, representatives from the Museum had come to the site to make the "division," taking an agreed upon percentage of the season's finds from the Tell en-Naṣbeh excavation season back to Jerusalem. Several hundred items from Naṣbeh remain in the Rockefeller Museum collection until today.

The family left Ramallah the morning of July 21st, after almost four months in Palestine. The train took them back to Kantara, and then on to Port Said to begin the return voyage to the United States. They met up with Joe Wampler, who had left Palestine before the Badès, on board the S. S. President Van Buren and left Port Said on July 23rd with a stop in Alexandria the next day. Bill told the story of visiting the suq in Alexandria and bargaining in Arabic for a string of prayer beads that he fancied. The seller would not drop what Bill considered an outrageous price, so Bill said in Arabic something like "I will not pay that price because in Jerusalem (*Al-Quds*) they would only cost X." Having an eleven-year-old American boy chastise the seller in Arabic amused neighboring shopkeepers and Bill's father to no end, and shamed him into dropping his price, so Bill made the purchase. Betsy's diary does not detail this incident, but mentions that Bill bargained hard for beads in the suq in Port Said to go with an Arab costume he had, and that he purchased a second set of beads in Alexandria. It is possible that this story's setting was in Port Said, despite Bill's memory of the event transpiring in Alexandria. The Badè family has very kindly donated both of these prayer beads to the collection of the Badè Museum as a legacy of the 1935 excavation and voyage.

The ship sailed through the Straits of Messina and passed the island of Capri before landing in Naples on July 27th. In Naples the family visited the museum, Betsy mentions seeing objects from Pompeii in her diary. On the 29th they arrived in Genoa where they visited Christopher Columbus' house. On July 31st, the ship docked in Marseille where W. F. Badè took ill, suffering a stroke. Travel plans then changed, and after a few days in the French port the Badè family left for Frankfurt, Germany on the train. On August 8th, presumably after consulting medical specialists, the Badès went on to a spa town to the north of Frankfurt, Bad Nauheim, whose waters were renowned for the treatment of heart conditions and presumably strokes.

Decades later, Betsy mentioned to me how eerie it was to be in Nazi Germany in 1935 with all the Hitler Youth and Brownshirts around. This is reflected in several passages in her diary, where she detailed going out one evening to see a Nazi movie and how propagandistic it was; or seeing a group of around 200 Hitler youth boys rehearsing for a pageant; or Hitler youth girls dressed in old fashioned clothes dancing and doing gymnastics. These jarring experiences are balanced out by time having fun in Bad Nauheim: biking, rowing and kayaking on the lake, swimming, taking day trips to visit castles and museums, and attending a kinderfest. By the end of August the family left Bad Nauheim for Marburg, where they spent a few days sightseeing before traveling on to Göttingen on September 2nd. W. F. Badè must have felt recouped as he lectured in Göttingen, and the family spent over a week there visiting with German friends and colleagues.

On September 10th the Badès left for Hamburg, where they boarded the S. S. Washington for the voyage back to the United States. En route they stopped in Le Havre, France; Southampton, England; and Cobh, Ireland; arriving in New York City on September 20th. The family spent a few days in New York taking in the sights and watching a few Shirley Temple movies. Betsy mentions how crowded their hotel was prior to their departure on September 23rd because of the Max Baer-Joe Louis boxing match, which took place the following day in Yankee Stadium. That evening they boarded a train that arrived in California on September 27th. The Badè family returned to Berkeley almost exactly nine months after their departure, having circumnavigated the globe.

Within six months of their homecoming, W. F. Badè passed away from a stroke, the condition that began to manifest itself in Marseille on their voyage home. The world was on the verge of global transformations manifested through the events leading up to, and through, World War II. Many of these events were centered at locations that the Badè family visited during the Tell en-Naṣbeh excavation season of 1935 or their travels to, and from, the British Mandate of Palestine. In addition, Palestine was impacted by the Arab uprising of 1936–1939 that began not long after their visit. Had the final excavation season been planned for 1936 it seems doubtful that the children would have been brought along. The adventures of 1935 clearly had major impacts on the lives of Betsy and Bill Badè, memories of the experiences on that expedition and travels continued to influence them throughout their rich and productive lives.

LIFE AND DEATH AT TELL EN-NAṢBEH: A BIOARCHAEOLOGICAL ANALYSIS

ALEXIS T. BOUTIN
DEPARTMENT OF ANTHROPOLOGY
SONOMA STATE UNIVERSITY

WHITNEY R. MCCLELLAN
DEPARTMENT OF ANTHROPOLOGY
SONOMA STATE UNIVERSITY

DANIEL A. CUSIMANO
DEPARTMENT OF ANTHROPOLOGY
CALIFORNIA STATE UNIVERSITY, EAST BAY

ABSTRACT

The Tell en-Naṣbeh Bioarchaeology Project was started in 2010 to study human skeletal remains that had been excavated from the site some 75 years earlier. Now housed at two museums in Berkeley, California, the remains had never been analyzed systematically. We collected standard osteological data to document the minimum number of individuals in the assemblage and to reconstruct age, sex, and health profiles. These efforts were challenged by the inconsistent recovery, recording, and curatorial practices to which the human skeletal material had been subjected, which caused the loss of contextual data for nearly half of the remains. For those individuals whose provenience was known, we coupled information from published reports and unpublished museum records with osteological data to shed new light on life and death at Tell en-Naṣbeh.

31

INTRODUCTION

This chapter presents a bioarchaeological analysis of human remains from Tell en-Naṣbeh. After explaining the origins of our research project, we provide an overview of the burials' mortuary contexts; describe the methods and findings of osteological analysis, focusing on age, sex, pathologies, and dental non-metric traits; share some of the challenges that taphonomic conditions posed to conducting a comprehensive and holistic bioarchaeological analysis; and conclude with case studies of skeletal remains from provenienced contexts, which shed new light on life and death in this ancient town.

A HISTORY OF THE HUMAN SKELETAL ASSEMBLAGE EXCAVATED FROM TELL EN-NAṢBEH

As described in Foster's chapter in this volume, much of the material excavated from Tell en-Naṣbeh was brought to the U.S. and now forms the core collection of the Badè Museum of Biblical Archaeology at Pacific School of Religion in Berkeley, California. Just over one third of the extant assemblage of human skeletal remains (15/41 individuals) is still housed at the Badè, while the remainder is at the Phoebe A. Hearst Museum of Anthropology at the University of California, Berkeley. How did the skeletal materials become split between the two museums? It seems that Chester C. McCown (Professor of New Testament at Pacific School of Religion) transferred the bones to his son, Theodore D. McCown, an archaeologist and physical anthropologist on the Anthropology faculty at the University and curator at the Lowie (now the Hearst) Museum, a mere mile away. Based on the accession file kept in the Hearst Museum's archives, the human remains currently stored there were discovered in Professor T. McCown's office in September 1973, some four years after his death, and were subsequently identified as having originated from the Tell en-Naṣbeh expedition. In a letter written that same month, Dave D. Herod (Senior Curatorial Anthropologist at the Lowie) provided a detailed description of the remains to Mary Kimber, a staff member of the Badè. Shortly thereafter, they were recorded in the Hearst's doorbook, and the accompanying documents added to the accession file, with the Badè Museum's apparent knowledge and consent.

We initiated the Tell en-Naṣbeh Bioarchaeology Project in 2010, as part of a renewed research agenda commemorating the 75th anniversary of the conclusion of the site's excavation. Osteological data were collected during the summers of 2011 and 2012. The human remains at the Hearst had undergone some preliminary analysis, including separation into distinct individuals and cursory age/sex estimation, sometime during the past 30 years. On the other hand, there was no record of any analysis of the human remains stored at the Badè Museum. These included the fragmentary skeleton of a child in a jar burial on permanent display in the museum gallery and three heavily mineralized crania. Additional commingled human remains were distinguished from animal bones by Mary Larkum during her analysis of the faunal assemblage, which suggests that many of the human remains at Tell en-Naṣbeh had been disarticulated and commingled in situ and that the excavators' knowledge of human skeletal anatomy was limited. Despite Badè's stated interest in the "vanished generations of human beings" (1931: 39) who once populated the site, he and his excavation team seem to have been unaware of the insights that osteological data could provide. To be fair, they were not alone in this regard. Comprehensive osteological analyses of human skeletal remains from ancient Near Eastern sites (e.g., Buxton 1920; Buxton and Rice 1931; Keith 1927, 1934) were the exception rather than the rule in the first decades of the 20th century. Synthetic interpretations of osteological and archaeological data, akin to the bioarchaeology of today (e.g., Macalister 1912), were even more rare.

When estimating the minimum number of individuals (MNI) necessary to account for all of the elements in the extant assemblage, we relied on the curation methods used by the Badè and Hearst museums. That is, if a museum stored a set of remains separately from others, and/or gave them unique registration numbers, presumably this reflects their recovery from distinct archaeological contexts (for a comparable situation, see Sheridan 2002). On this basis, we estimated that the MNI for the Tell en-Naṣbeh skeletal assemblage (housed at both museums) is 41. This number may be somewhat inflated: when we calculated MNI using a single non-repeating bone (in this case, the frontal bone), the best estimate is 19 individuals. Nevertheless, given the numerous mortuary features of various types excavated at Tell en-Naṣbeh, as well as their vast temporal span, we feel confident that the higher MNI estimate

(n=41) is more representative of the extant skeletal assemblage. As is so often the case with archaeological skeletal assemblages, this number accounts for only a small number of the people who lived and died at Tell en-Naṣbeh due to taphonomic processes, ephemeral mortuary treatments, and extramural burials that have not been located.

MORTUARY CONTEXTS

The same principles described for MNI approximation apply when reconstructing from how many unique mortuary features the 41 individuals derive. Our best estimate is 21: four tombs (re-used between the Early Bronze I and Byzantine periods), two cave tombs (dating exclusively to Early Bronze I), five cisterns (all apparently from inside the settlement, and dating to Iron Age II or later), and ten features of unknown provenience.

Serious challenges are faced when attempting to understand the individuality of the burials. As curated currently, there appear to be almost equal numbers of single (n=5), double (n=6), and multiple (n=5) burials. However, a closer investigation of the excavators' methods suggests that the extant assemblage represents only a small fraction of the remains originally unearthed. For example, McCown (1947: 82) describes Tomb 54 thus: "It contained a large number of human bones, but unfortunately they had so far disintegrated as to be of little anatomical value. Mandibles of 54 individuals were counted. One well preserved skull was saved for description." This skull was indeed well-preserved and is described further below, along with the bones of another individual from the same tomb. Photographs taken of Tomb 54 during its excavation (McCown 1947: pl. 18) reveal dozens, if not hundreds, of commingled bones; articulated remains and undisturbed grave goods that were the exception (e.g., pl. 18.6). It now becomes apparent that each type of mortuary feature could have held any number of people: the curation of only two individuals' remains from the populous communal Tomb 54 exemplifies the highly selective preservation methods that Badè's expedition employed. Nevertheless, we can posit that it was normative for the deceased at Naṣbeh to be buried with the remains of at least one other person. This is consistent with an established preference for communal tombs in the southern Levant, which presumably housed extended family groups (Burke 2011: 901–03).

One last aspect of burial contexts that may be ascertained from the curated Naṣbeh assemblage is the form of disposal, that is, whether the burials are primary or secondary. Again, our direct evidence is frustratingly meager. Only the jar burial can be confirmed as primary, based on the in situ articulation of the child's bones. Conversely, the commingled remains of multiple individuals in two of the Iron Age cisterns strongly suggest secondary burial (Fig. 3.1). These cisterns were originally hewn for on-site water storage, but eventually came to be a place for disposal of a variety of goods, judging by the pottery, weights, metal objects, and animal bones that were found in Cistern 370 alone (Wampler 1941: 25–31). Finally, although the disposal of the tombs' occupants at Naṣbeh cannot be confirmed, they were likely primary. In both the Bronze and Iron Ages, communal tombs associated with highland settlements usually housed primary burials (Bloch-Smith 1992; Gonen 1992: 13), although secondary mortuary rituals for the remains of defleshed ancestors may have accompanied the interment of new occupants (Osborne 2011).

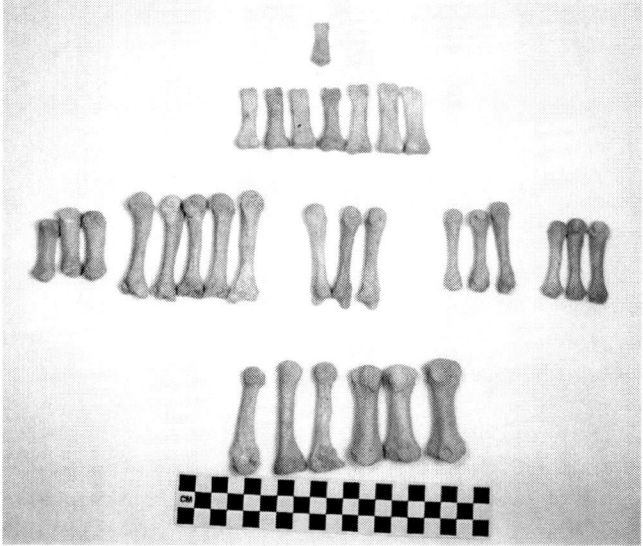

Figure 3.1. Commingled hand phalanges, metacarpals, and metatarsals of at least three individuals from Cistern 173.

OSTEOLOGICAL ANALYSIS

Methods

Detailed skeletal and dental inventories were created, and morphological and metric data collected, from the Tell en-Naṣbeh skeletal assemblage. Buikstra and Ubelaker's forms (1994: Attachment 1–2), completeness codes (1994: 7), and age and sex classes (1994: 9) were used. These procedures have facilitated an estimate of MNI, each individual's extant completeness, and an analysis of population and demographic attributes (e.g., age, sex, health and nutritional status).

The morphology of the pelvic girdle and cranium, and the size and robusticity of post-cranial bones, were used to assess sex. Standards followed were derived from Ascádi and Nemeskéri (1970), Buikstra and Ubelaker (1994), France (1998), and White et al (2012). The age of subadults was estimated through several methods, including dental development, bone size and length, and the developmental morphology of ossification centers (Kósa 1989; Liversidge and Molleson 2004; Scheuer and Black 2004; Ubelaker 1999: 64–69). Due to poor preservation, the progressive union of cranial sutures was used for aging the vast majority of adults (Meindl and Lovejoy 1985), hence the coarse resolution of the adult age profile. Steckel and colleagues' (2002) health index for skeletal remains was used to evaluate patterns of morbidity and mortality. The index includes three attributes that primarily reflect malnutrition, infectious disease, and anemia suffered during childhood: stature, linear enamel hypoplasia (lines caused by deficiencies in the formation of dental enamel), and porotic hyperostosis/cribra orbitalia (localized porous lesions on the skull vault or roofs of the eye orbits). Two attributes relate primarily to adult health, diet, and habitual activity: dental pathologies (e.g., caries, periodontal disease, and antemortem tooth loss) and degenerative joint disease (which includes osteoarthritis). The final two attributes, traumatic injury and periosteal reactions (infection-induced inflammation of the membrane that covers a bone's outer surface), are relevant to the health and behavior of both adults and subadults.

Results

Because we are uncertain of recovery methods and the provenience of many remains, the small assemblage from Tell en-Naṣbeh cannot be considered representative of its population during any one time period, nor throughout the site's occupation. Even when provenience has been documented, many communal tombs at Tell en-Naṣbè were reused over not just centuries, but millennia (Badè 1934: 57). Our ability to track changes in population demography, health, and behavior across time is severely hindered. For this reason, frequency data are not presented, as they would have no utility for comparative temporal analyses.

Of the 41 individuals present, roughly one third (*n*=14) are subadults, and two thirds (*n*=27) are adults (Table 3.1). The majority of the subadults are children, with smaller numbers of infants (including two possible late-term fetuses) and adolescents. The resolution of these adult age estimates is fairly coarse: the majority could be categorized as older than 20 years at the time of death, although four individuals fell between 20–50 years and two more between 20–35 years.

Age		%	n
Fetus/Infant	(prenatal up to 3 years)	4.9	2
Infant	(0–3 years)	2.4	1
Child	(3–12 years)	17.1	7
Child/Adolescent	(3–20 years)	2.4	1
Adolescent	(12–20 years)	7.3	3
Young Adult	(20–35 years)	2.4	1
Young/ Middle Adult	(20–50 years)	9.8	4
Adult	(20+ years)	53.7	22
Total		**100.0**	**41**

Table 3.1. Age Estimations

Of the 30 individuals who were sufficiently mature for sex estimation, only 15 of them could be analyzed (i.e., preservation of sexually dimorphic elements was adequate). The resulting breakdown by sex (Table 3.2) is remarkably even, with six probable/definite females and seven probable/definite males, as well as two individuals of sexually ambiguous skeletal morphology.

Sex	%	*n*
Female	7.3	3
Probable Female	7.3	3
Ambiguous	4.9	2
Probable Male	4.9	2
Male	12.2	5
Unknown	63.4	26
Total	**100.0**	**41**

Table 3.2. Sex Determinations

Several individuals exhibited one or more skeletal or dental pathologies. The latter included linear enamel hypoplasia ($n=3$ individuals affected), caries ($n=5$), periodontal disease ($n=3$), and antemortem tooth loss ($n=7$), while the former included cribra orbitalia ($n=2$) and porotic hyperostosis ($n=1$). The health implications of some of these conditions will be considered below.

Dental Non-metrics

Analysis of non-metric traits has long been used to identify biological affinities within and between past populations (Buikstra et al. 1990). Establishing genetic profiles for skeletal assemblages allows a rough determination of relatedness between individuals and populations, as well as larger cultural constructs. These studies of biological distance, or biodistance, have aided in mapping episodes of gene flow, genetic drift, and founder effects (Pacelli and Márquez-Grant 2010; Scott and Turner 1997). Due to the heritable nature of morphological variances in the tooth crown and root, osteologists and odontologists are able to identify well-established epigenetic markers that distinguish ancestral affinities. Teeth are often the most abundant elements recovered from archaeological skeletal assemblages, and their size and morphology are under strong genetic control. Thus, dental non-metric analyses are considered one of the most effective methods for assessing biodistance (White et al. 2012).

Trait	Tooth	# of Teeth Observed	# with Positive Expression	Frequency (nearest tenth)
Winging	I¹	2	0	0%
Shoveling	I¹	2	0	0%
	I²	1	0	0%
Double-shoveling	I¹	2	0	0%
	I²	2	0	0%
Interruption groove	I¹	2	0	0%
	I²	2	1	50%
Mesial ridge	C	1	0	0%
Accessory cusps	P¹	3	0	0%
	P²	2	0	0%
Hypocone	M¹	6	6	100%
	M²	5	3	60%
Carabelli's trait	M¹	6	4	67%
	M²	5	0	0%
	M³	3	0	0%
Cusp 5	M¹	4	1	25%
	M²	5		0%
	M³	3	1	33%
Enamel extension	M¹	7	1	14%
	M²	6	1	17%
	M³	4	2	50%
Parastyle	M²	5	1	20%
	M³	3	1	33%

Tables 3.3. Non-Metric Traits Observed on Maxillary Dentition

Non-metric data from the Tell en-Naṣbeh assemblage was record-ed at the Hearst Museum for 65 permanent teeth (both in and out of occlusion) from 12 individuals. Standards set by the Arizona State University Dental Anthropology System were used to assess 21 traits (Scott and Turner 1997; Turner et al. 1991). Variances in tooth morphology appear in both the tooth crown and root and often can be identified simply as present or absent. These variances include ridges, grooves, and the extension of enamel, as well as the position in occlusion and the number of cusps and roots. The re-sulting data are presented in Tables 3.3 and 3.4. Because the sample is so small and some of the individuals observed lack a known pro-venience, it is unlikely that this information will hold any merit on its own when determining biodistance patterns for Tell en-Naṣbeh. Furthermore, much of the observed dentition exhibited heavy attrition and/or postmortem damage, which hindered the observation of non-metric traits. Thus the raw data are presented here, in hopes that they may be used for future studies and add to a larger population analysis for the region.

Trait	Tooth	# of Teeth Observed	# with Positive Expression	Frequency
Double-rooted	C	1	1	100%
Tomes's root	P_1	1	0	0%
Cusp 6	M_1	3	0	0%
Cusp 7	M_1	3	0	0%
Deflecting wrinkle	M_1	1	0	0%
Groove pattern Y	M_1	2	1	50%
	M_2	4	2	50%
	M_3	4	0	0%
Groove pattern +	M_1	2	1	50%
	M_2	4	1	25%
	M_3	4	0	0%
Groove pattern X	M_1	2	0	0%
	M_2	4	1	25%
	M_3	4	4	100%
Enamel extension	M_1	5	0	0%
	M_2	6	2	33%
	M_3	4	2	50%
Protostylid	M_1	7	0	0%
	M_2	5	0	0%
	M_3	5	1	20%

Table 3.4. Non-Metric Traits Observed on Mandibular Dentition

TAPHONOMIC CONDITIONS

The current condition of the Tell en-Naṣbeh skeletal assemblage is the result of manifold taphonomic processes, which have been enacted by physical and biological agents between the time of death and curation (White et al. 2012). We have used inventory data to estimate the completeness of the individuated skeletons ($n=29$; those that are commingled or are represented by an isolated element were excluded). Five categories of completeness, each reflecting the relative completeness of dentition, cranial, and post-cranial elements, respectively, have been employed (after Selinsky 2009: 44–50). Skeletal completeness is based exclusively on the percentages of the cranial (22 bones, auditory ossicles excluded) and post-cranial skeleton (178 bones) that were extant, without special regard for the presence of diagnostic elements. Dental completeness (32 permanent teeth) has been evaluated for adult individuated skeletons only ($n=17$), to control for completion of tooth development and eruption. Looking at the results (Table 3.5), fragmentary (less than 25% of all elements/teeth preserved) is by far the most common completeness category for the skeleton and dentition. A notable exception is the high proportion of partially complete crania (7/17 with cranial bone present): this may be due to the excavators' preference for recovering skulls.

Completeness	Cranial		Post-Cranial		Dental	
	%	*n*	%	*n*	%	*n*
None Present	41.4	12	27.6	8	52.9	9
Fragmentary (<25%)	27.6	8	72.4	21	35.3	6
Partial (26–50%)	24.1	7	0.0	0	5.9	1
Fairly Complete (51–75%)	6.9	2	0.0	0	5.9	1
Mostly Complete (>75%)	0.0	0	0.0	0	0.0	0
Total	100.0	29	100.0	29	100.0	17

Table 3.5. Completeness of Individuated Skeletons

Physical agents

Despite their fragmentation, the condition of the bone itself from Tell en-Naṣbeh is, overall, quite good. Erosion and exfoliation of the bony cortex is minimal, and plant root etching is largely absent. This is somewhat surprising, as Badè (1931:12) commented on the "rapidly disintegrating effect" that the karstic limestone soils had on both bone and pottery in the tombs. Thus, we may be observing the best-preserved remains recovered from Tell en-Naṣbeh, which were considered worthy of curation for this very reason.

Three articulated crania from Tomb 52 are held together by a light brown mineralized matrix (Fig. 3.2). The remains of five other individuals are stained dark brown and partially mineralized (12-10779, 12-10780, 12-10780A, 12-10783, 12-10787). Many of the remains were recovered from cave tombs on the tell slope that would fill up with water and debris every rainy season. Calcium carbonate salts and other minerals would have been transported from the surrounding sediment and precipitated on the bone surface, eventually causing many of them to mineralize over the millennia (Lyman 1994: 420).

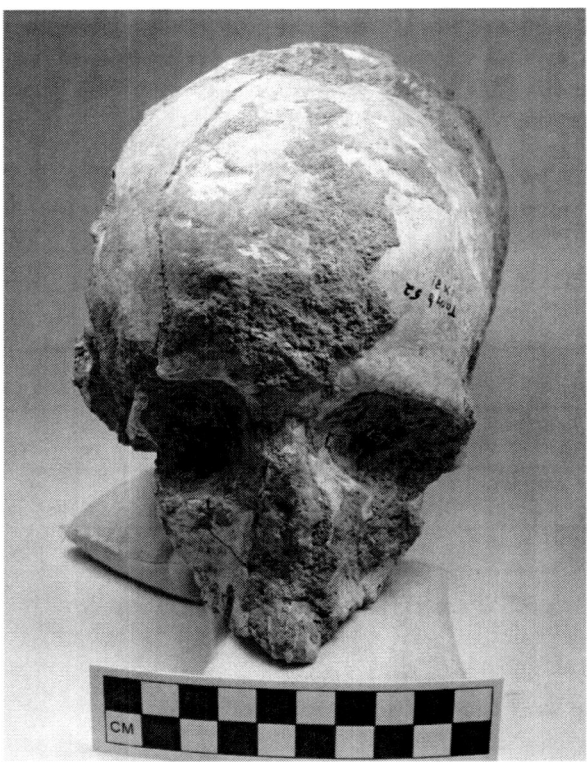

Fig. 3.2. Mineralized cranium (B) of probable female adult from Tomb 52.

Other remains have clearly undergone a different set of taphonomic processes. The bones of two individuals (12-10786, 12-10786B, provenience unknown) are black and dark gray in color, and this color penetrates the bones' cortex in many places (Fig. 3.3). This is suggestive of charring, that is, exposure to a fire of moderate heat (over 700 degrees Centigrade) for a fairly short duration (less than 20 minutes) (Ubelaker 2009). Cremation is unlikely to have caused these changes, as it usually results in at least partial calcination of the bone (nor was it a normative Israelite mortuary practice; de Vaux 1997: 57). More likely, the exposure of these bones to fire was unintentional, and may have occurred during re-use of a communal tomb.

Fig. 3.3. Charred left tibia from an adolescent of unknown provenience.

Organic agents

If we consider humans as organic agents of taphonomic processes, then mortuary traditions, modern recovery methods, and curatorial practices can all be explored as sources of alteration between death and curation. For an early 20th century excavation, the recovery methodology proposed and executed by Badè and his team was remarkably similar to modern techniques. Burials were reportedly excavated "carefully with knife and brush in successive six-inch layers in order to determine whether a series of periods were represented" (McCown 1947: 68). Unfortunately, lack of in situ analysis and inconsistent numbering of artifacts and features has caused much of the mortuary data to become lost or mixed up with other records.

For example, in the 1926 and 1927 excavation seasons, Tombs I and II were described as containing a wide array of skeletal remains from the Early Bronze I period. Later in the publication process, these same tombs were re-numbered Cave Tombs 5 and 6 (McCown 1947: 70, n. 5), probably to distinguish them from the tombs found in the various cemeteries surrounding the site. Over years of museum transfers and changing catalog systems, the human remains from Cave Tombs 5 and 6 appear to have been eventually attributed to Tombs 5 and 6, which date to the Iron Age and Hellenistic to Roman periods, respectively. This is problematic because the literature on Tombs 5 and 6 mentions little or no human remains being recovered (McCown 1947: 83, 110). The result of this sort of mix-up is bones with no home, no context, and no personal history. However, based on similar taphonomic processes, comparison of mortuary feature usage dates, and re-inspection of the museum accession file, we propose that these particular human remains come from Cave Tombs 5 and 6, which date to the Early Bronze I, rather than Tombs 5 and 6.

Of the minimum 41 individuals represented in the Tell en-Nasbeh skeletal assemblage, just over half (*n*=22) have a known provenience (Table 3.6). For the remainder, their original location has disappeared somewhere in the process of recovery, renumbering, and/or curation. Important opportunities for holistic bioarchaeological analysis and meaningful interpretation have been lost due to this absence of contextual data. Nevertheless, for those burials whose provenience is known, important insights into life and death at Tell en-Nasbeh can be gained. We conclude this chapter with several case studies for which both rich archaeological and osteological information is available.

Grave #	Date	Museum	Museum #/ Description
Cave Tomb 5	Early Bronze I†	Hearst	12-10779
Cave Tomb 6	Early Bronze I†	Hearst	12-10780
		Hearst	12-10780A
Tomb 2	Roman-Byzantine‡	Hearst	12-10776
		Hearst	12-10776A
		Hearst	12-10777
Tomb 14	Iron Age-Hellenistic-Roman‡	Badè	"Individual B" (frontal)
			"Individual E" (mandible)
			"Individual G" (mandible)
Tomb 52	Early Bronze I‡	Hearst/Badè	12-10781/Articulated, mineralized cranium (A)
		Badè	Articulated, mineralized cranium (B)
		Badè	Articulated, mineralized cranium (C)
		Hearst/Badè	12-10781A/Jar Burial
Tomb 54	Early Iron Age II‡	Hearst	12-10782
			12-10782A
Cistern 173	Late Iron Age II- Persian†	Badè	
			Left MC5
			Left MC5
			Left MC5
Cistern 183	Iron Age II-Hellenistic‡	Badè	
			Left MC2
			Left MC2
Cistern 231	Iron Age II-Roman†	Badè	Permanent molar
Cistern 370	Late Iron Age II†	Hearst	12-10784

Table 3.6. Bioarchaeological Data for Burials of Known Provenience (continued on following page).

Grave #	MNI	Sex□	Age♦	Age in Years	Pathologies*
Cave Tomb 5	1	M	A		None extant
Cave Tomb 6	1	M	A		None extant
	1	Unk.	A		None extant
Tomb 2	1	F	A		AMTL
	1	Unk.	C	7–9 years	None extant
	1	Amb	Y/MA		None extant
Tomb 14	3	M	A		Cribra orbitalia
		PF	A		AMTL
		Unk.	A		AMTL
Tomb 52	1	F	A	25+	None extant
	1	PF	A		None extant
	1	PM	A	30+	None extant
	1	Unk.	C	3–5 years	None extant
Tomb 54	1	Amb	Y/MA		Cribra orbitalia, porotic hyperostosis; LEH, periodontal disease; AMTL, caries
	1	Unk.	F/I		None extant
Cistern 173	3				None extant
		Unk	A		
		Unk.	A		None extant
		F	A		None extant
Cistern 183	2	Unk.	A		None extant
		M	A		None extant
Cistern 231	1	Unk.	C	5–6 years	None extant
Cistern 370	1	M	YA		Caries, AMTL

†: Zorn 1993.
‡: McCown 1947.
□ F: female; Unk.: unknown; Amb.: ambiguous; M: male, PF: probable female; PM; probable male.
♦A: adult; C: child; Y/MA: young/middle adult; F/I: fetus/infant; Adol.: adolescent; YA: young adult
*AMTL: antemortem tooth loss; LEH: linear enamel hypoplasia

Table 3.6. (continued).

CASE STUDIES OF PROVENIENCED BURIALS

Tomb 52 was located in the northeast necropolis and dated to the Early Bronze I by the large volume of pottery that it contained. McCown (1947: 74) described some of its contents as follows: "Three partly mineralized skulls were found and, in the bottom of a large, flat-bottomed pithos when cleaned, there were discovered the bones of an infant, along with a shallow flat-bottomed plate with incurved rim and a small painted juglet. There were also other bones in a large flat-bottomed bowl." Indeed, almost all of these skeletal remains are still housed at the Badè. The three crania are so thoroughly encased in a limestone matrix that our attempts to analyze them were impeded. One cranium belonged to a female who was at least 25 years old when she died, another to a probable female adult (see Figure 2), and the last to a probable male who was at least 30 years old at death. The "other bones" in the bowl may refer to the fragmentary post-cranial remains of at least one adult now stored at the Hearst (12-10781). These arm and hand, leg and foot bones are quite possibly associated with one or more of the crania, although it is impossible to tell with which. They are arbitrarily presented with Cranium A in Table 3.6 for the purpose of accurate MNI representation. The jar burial (Fig. 3.4; see also McCown 1947: pl. 28.23) still contains the shallow plate and juglet, although now we know that its occupant was not an infant, but a child who died between the ages of 3 and 5 years. This age was estimated through ossification and fusion of a cervical vertebra and development of the deciduous and permanent dentition.

Cistern 183 was located ca. 25 m inside the city wall. It displays two phases of use, the late Iron Age II (dated by a *lammelekh* seal impression) and Hellenistic periods, based on copious amounts of pottery found therein (McCown 1947: 132–33). It is unknown during which period the human remains were deposited. These consist of three metacarpals belonging to at least two individuals, one of whom was a male. To estimate sex, stature was obtained from metacarpal length (Meadows and Jantz 1992) and then compared with post-cranial metric data from ancient Near Eastern populations (Boutin 2008: 116–18). The same method was used to identify the female sex of one of at least three individuals represented in Cistern 173. This feature, whose last use dates to the late Iron Age II, contained 17 metacarpals, three hand phalanges, and

six metatarsals. Whether the presence of human remains in these
disused cisterns was a matter of accident, illicit disposal, or meaningful deposition is uncertain (but see Pollock 2012: 50–51 for an
interesting comparandum from Halaf-period Fısıtklı Höyük).

Figure 3.4. Jar burial of a 3–5 year old child from Tomb 52.
Mandible with teeth indicated by arrow.

As mentioned above, Cistern 370 (late Iron Age II in date) contained numerous objects, including two *lammelekh* seal impressions
and "a human skull and other skeletal remains" (Wampler 1941:
29). These include an articulated cranium, a disarticulated but well-

preserved pelvis, and one hand phalanx. They belong to a male, based on morphology of the pelvis and cranium. His was the only skeleton that could be aged using modal changes on the auricular surface of the ilium (Buckberry and Chamberlain 2002); he proved to be a Young Adult. Of seven extant teeth, one mandibular molar had occlusal surface caries. Another mandibular molar had been lost not long before death, judging by the alveolus's initial stage of remodeling. Attrition ranged from light to heavy, and none of the teeth displayed calculus deposits.

Tomb 54 was found in the northeast necropolis, and its period of use was the early Iron Age II. The extant skull comes from an individual with sexually ambiguous skeletal morphology who died between the ages of 20 and 50. This person was the least healthy in the Tell en-Naṣbeh skeletal assemblage. A childhood beset by environmental and physiological stress—most likely caused by infectious disease, malnutrition, or some combination of the two—is indicated by healed cribra orbitalia and porotic hyperostosis of moderate severity (Stuart-Macadam 1985), as well as multiple linear enamel hypoplasia. Nineteen extant teeth demonstrate that as an adult, s/he suffered from multiple dental afflictions (Fig. 3.5). Attrition was heavy on all teeth. The enamel of several teeth was chipped, ranging in severity from grades 1–3 on Bonfiglioli and co-authors' (2004) three point scale. Tooth chipping can be caused by both masticatory activities (e.g., consumption of fruit pits, shell, bone) and extra-masticatory activities (e.g., use of teeth as tools). Fourteen teeth bore calculus deposits, ranging from mild to moderate. Only one tooth (left maxillary first molar) exhibited caries, but these were so massive that the surface of origin could not be identified. This individual also suffered the pain and gingival inflammation of periodontal disease: both maxillary and mandibular alveolar margins exhibited rounding and exposure of porous cancellous bone. Significant horizontal bone loss can also be attributed to periodontal disease: the resultant weakening of the tooth's anchoring in the alveolus doubtless contributed to the antemortem loss of three molars (Clarke and Hirsch 1991; Hillson 1996: 262–66). Two bones from a late-term fetus or young infant were also recovered from this tomb.

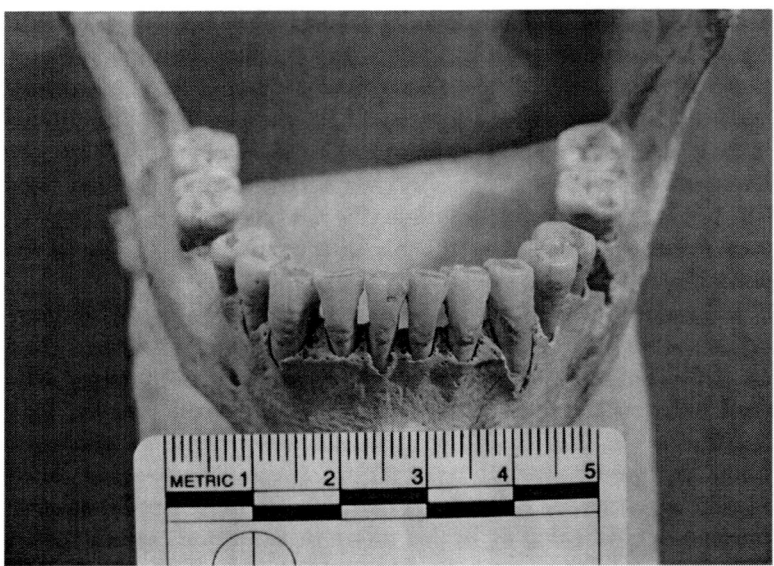

Figure 3.5. Mandible of 12-10782 from Tomb 54. Of note: linear enamel hypoplasia on incisors and canines; severe chipping of right first incisor; rounding and porosity of alveolar margin, indicative of periodontal disease; antemortem loss of first molars.

It is helpful to contextualize living conditions during the Iron Age II by drawing on Zorn's 1994 publication, "Estimating the Population Size of Ancient Settlements." He estimates that in this period, Tell en-Naṣbeh would have had only 1.72 hectares of living space. Between 800 and 1000 people lived there, in houses "packed close together along narrow roads" (1994: 36). Cribra orbitalia, porotic hyperostosis, and linear enamel hypoplasia—such as were observed on the occupant of Tomb 54—are part of the limited repertoire of skeletal and dental responses to a suite of environmental and physiological stressors. High frequencies of these pathologies may reflect episodes of infectious disease, metabolic and nutritional stress, and consequent growth disruptions suffered during childhood (Goodman and Rose 1991; Walker et al. 2009). Such patterns of poor health proliferate in conditions of increased sedentism, large and dense populations, poor sanitation and hygiene, and close contact with domesticated animals—all of which are associated with an agricultural subsistence strategy (see the chapter by Zorn in this volume; Cohen and Crane-Kramer 2007; Kent 1986; Larsen 1995). These conditions may well have characterized Tell en-Naṣbeh during parts of the Iron Age.

SUMMARY AND CONCLUSIONS

The transport of the Tell en-Naṣbeh skeletal assemblage across continents, only to be divided up by two institutions a mile apart, exemplifies Near Eastern archaeologists' attitude toward human remains in the first part of the 20th century—for the most part, one of benign neglect (Porter and Boutin 2014). Never having undergone systematic analysis, the human remains from Tell en-Naṣbeh have much to add to this important site's legacy as it is re-evaluated 75 years after excavation ended. The remains of at least 41 individuals are represented in the extant skeletal assemblage. Standard osteological methods were employed to collect age, sex, health, and non-metric data. The assemblage's generally poor contextual information and small size prevents the use of these data in meaningful diachronic analyses. Nevertheless, the human remains from Tell en-Naṣbeh constitute a rare addition to the available corpus of osteological material from the Judean hills.

Selective and inconsistent methods of recovery and curation challenge our attempts to reconstruct mortuary contexts. Many of the burials, however, appear to be consistent with regional patterns favoring primary interment in extramural communal tombs. Perhaps less expected is the significant number of commingled human remains in abandoned intramural cisterns. One intriguing (albeit much larger-scale) parallel may be found in Jeremiah 41:9, in which Ishmael and his followers dispose of dozens of corpses in a large cistern, following their attempted coup at Mizpah. Nevertheless, a direct connection cannot be drawn between the bioarchaeological evidence and biblical events, as primary and secondary disposal of human remains in cisterns is documented cross-culturally (e.g., Aviam 2002: 129–31; Cotter et al. 1993: 118; Little and Papadopoulos 1998). Despite being subjected to taphonomic processes both environmental and human-initiated in nature, several sets of remains with known provenience provide particularly well-contextualized glimpses into life and death at Tell en-Naṣbeh.

In conclusion, we have shown that the bioarchaeological analysis of long-curated skeletal assemblages, like that from Tell en-

Nasbeh, is a worthwhile task despite interpretive challenges. Through a holistic methodology of osteological data collection and archival research, lost stories of lives and deaths can resurface. Badè wrote that his goal was a "human story of the mound when the excavation is completed" (1931: 39). We hope that the Tell en-Nasbeh Bioarchaeology Project has provided some of the answers that he originally set out to find.

ACKNOWLEDGEMENTS

We would like to thank the staff of two museums for making this research project possible: at the Badè, Aaron Brody, Rebecca Hisiger, and former staff member Catherine Foster; and at the Hearst, Mari Lyn Salvador, Tim White, and Leslie Freund. We are grateful to the School of Social Sciences at Sonoma State University for providing research funds. Finally, we thank Jeffrey R. Zorn and Aaron Brody for inviting us to participate in this volume and in the conference session that inspired it, as well as for their extremely helpful editorial feedback.

REFERENCES

Aviam, M.
2002   Yodefat/Jotapata: The Archaeology of the First Battle. Pp. 121–33 in *The First Jewish Revolt: Archaeology, History, and Ideology*, ed. A. M. Berlin and J. A. Overman. London: Routledge.

Ascádi, G., and Nemeskéri, J.
1970   *History of Human Life Span and Mortality*, trans K. Balas. Budapest: Akadémiai Kiadó.

Badè, W. F.
1931   *Some Tombs of Tell en-Nasbeh Discovered in 1929: A Special Report*. Berkeley: Palestine Institute Publications.
1934   *A Manual of Excavation in the Near East: Methods of Digging and Recording of the Tell en-Nasbeh Expedition in Palestine*. Berkeley, CA: University of California Press.

Bloch-Smith, E.
1992   *Judahite Burial Practices and Beliefs about the Dead*. JSOT/ASOR Monograph Series 7. Sheffield: Sheffield University Press.

Bonfiglioli, B.; Mariotti, V.; Facchini, F.; Belcastro, M. G.; and Condemi, S.
2004   Masticatory and Non–masticatory Dental Modifications in the Epipalaeolithic Necropolis of Taforalt (Morocco). *International Journal of Osteoarchaeology* 14: 448–56.

Boutin, A. T.
2008   Embodying Life and Death: Osteobiographical Narratives from Alalakh. Ph.D. dissertation, University of Pennsylvania.

Buckberry, J. L., and Chamberlain, A. T.
2002   Age Estimation from the Auricular Surface of the Ilium: A Revised Method. *American Journal of Physical Anthropology* 119: 231–39

Buikstra, J. E.; Frankenberg, S. R.; and Konigsberg, L. W.
1990   Skeletal Biological Distance Studies in American Physical Anthropology: Recent Trends. *American Journal of Physical Anthropology* 82: 1–7.

Buikstra, J. E., and Ubelaker, D. H. ed.
1994   *Standards for Data Collection from Human Skeletal Remains: Proceedings of a Seminar at the Field Museum of Natural History, Organized by Jonathan Haas.* Arkansas Archeological Survey Research Series 44. Fayetteville, AR: Arkansas Archaeological Survey.

Burke, A. A.
2011   The Archaeology of Ritual and Religion in Ancient Israel and the Levant, and the Origins of Judaism. Pp. 895–907 in *Oxford Handbook of the Archaeology of Ritual and Religion*, ed. T. Insoll. Oxford Handbooks. Oxford: Oxford University Press.

Buxton, L. H. D.
1920   The Anthropology of Cyprus. *The Journal of the Royal Anthropological Institute of Great Britain and Ireland* 50: 183–235.

Buxton, L. H. D., and Rice, D. T.
1931   Report on the Human Remains found at Kish. *The Journal of the Royal Anthropological Institute of Great Britain and Ireland* 61: 57–119.

Cohen, M. N., and Crane-Kramer, G. M. M.
2007   Editors' Summation. Pp. 320–43 in *Ancient Health: Skeletal Indicators of Agricultural and Economic Intensification*, ed. M. N. Cohen and G. M. M. Crane-Kramer. Bioarchaeological Interpretations of the Human Past: Local, Regional, and Global Perspectives. Gainesville: University Press of Florida.

Clarke, N. G., and Hirsch, R. S.
1991   Physiological, Pulpal, and Periodontal Factors Influencing Alveolar Bone. Pp. 241–66 in *Advances in Dental Anthropology*, ed. M. A. Kelley and C. S. Larsen. New York: Wiley-Liss.

Cotter, J. L.; Roberts, D. G.; and Parrington, M.
1992   *The Buried Past: An Archaeological History of Philadelphia*. Philadelphia: University of Pennsylvania Press.

France, D. L.
1998   Observational and Metrical Analysis of Sex in the Skeleton. Pp. 163–86 in *Forensic Osteology: Advances in the Identification of Human Remains*, 2nd ed., ed. K. J. Reichs. Springfield, IL: Charles C. Thomas.

Gonen, R.
1992   *Burial Patterns and Cultural Diversity in Late Bronze Age Canaan*. ASOR Dissertation Series 7. Winona Lake, IN: Eisenbrauns.

Goodman, A. H., and Rose, J. C.
1991   Dental Enamel Hypoplasias as Indicators of Nutritional Status. Pp. 279–93 in *Advances in Dental Anthropology*, ed. M. A. Kelley and C. S. Larsen. New York: Wiley-Liss.

Hillson, S.
1996   *Dental Anthropology*. Cambridge: Cambridge University Press.

Keith, A.
1927   Report on the Human Remains. Pp. 214–40 in *Ur Excavations*, Vol 1: *Al-ʿUbaid*, ed. H. R. Hall and C. L. Woolley. Oxford: Oxford University Press.

1934 Report on Human Remains. Pp. 400–09 in *Ur Excavations*, Vol 2: *The Royal Cemetery*, ed. C. L. Woolley. London: Publications of the Joint Expedition of the British Museum and of the Museum of the University of Pennsylvania to Mesopotamia.

Kent, S.
1986 The Influence of Sedentism and Aggregation on Porotic Hyperostosis and Anaemia: A Case Study. *Man* 21: 605–36.

Kósa, F.
1989 Age Estimation from the Fetal Skeleton. Pp 21–54 in *Age Markers in the Human Skeleton*, ed. M. Y. İşcan. Springfield, IL: Charles C. Thomas.

Larsen, C. S.
1995 Biological Changes in Human Populations with Agriculture. *Annual Review of Anthropology* 24: 185–213.

Little, L. M., and Papadopoulos, J. K.
1998 A Social Outcast from Early Iron Age Athens. *Hesperia* 67: 375–404.

Liversidge, H. M., and Molleson, T.
2004 Variation in Crown and Root Formation and Eruption of Human Deciduous Teeth. *American Journal of Physical Anthropology* 123: 172–80.

Lyman, R. L.
1994 *Vertebrate Taphonomy*. Cambridge Manuals in Archaeology. Cambridge: Cambridge University Press.

Macalister, R. A. S.
1912 *The Excavation of Gezer 1902–1905 and 1907–1909*, 3 vols. London: Murray.

McCown, C. C.
1947 *Tell en-Naṣbeh*, Vol. 1: *Archaeological and Historical Results*. Berkeley, CA: The Palestine Institute of Pacific School of Religion.

Meadows, L., and Jantz, R. L.
1992 Estimation of Stature from Metacarpal Lengths. *Journal of Forensic Sciences* 37: 147–54.

Meindl, R. S., and Lovejoy, C. O.
1985   Ectocranial Suture Closure: A Revised Method for the De-
        termination of Skeletal Age at Death Based on the Lateral-
        Anterior Sutures. *American Journal of Physical Anthropology* 68:
        57–66.

Osborne, J. F.
2011   Mortuary Practice and the Bench Tomb: Structure and
        Practice in Iron Age Judah. *Journal of Near Eastern Studies*
        70: 35–53.

Pacelli, C. S., and Márquez-Grant, N.
2010   Evaluation of Dental Non–metric Traits in a Medieval
        Population from Ibiza (Spain). *Bulletin of the International As-
        sociation for Paleodontology* 4.2: 16–28.

Pollock, S.
2012   Making a Difference: Mortuary Practices in Halaf Times.
        Pp. 29–53 in *Breathing New Life Into the Evidence of Death:
        Contemporary Approaches to Bioarchaeology*, ed. A. Baadsgaard,
        A. T. Boutin, and J. E. Buikstra. School for Advanced
        Research Advanced Seminar Series. Santa Fe, NM: School
        for Advanced Research Press.

Porter, B. W., and Boutin, A. T.
2014   Introduction: Bringing Out the Dead in the Ancient Near
        East. Pp. 1–26 in *Remembering the Dead in the Ancient Near
        East: Recent Contributions from Bioarchaeology and Mortuary Ar-
        chaeology*, ed. Benjamin W. Porter and Alexis T. Boutin.
        Boulder: University Press of Colorado.

Scheuer, L., and Black, S.
2004   *The Juvenile Skeleton*. London: Elsevier/Academic Press.

Scott, G. R., and Turner II, C. G.
1997   *The Anthropology of Modern Teeth: Dental Morphology and Its
        Variation in Recent Human Populations*. Cambridge Studies in
        Biological Anthropology. Cambridge: Cambridge Universi-
        ty Press.

Selinsky, P.
2009   Death a Necessary End: Perspectives on Paleodemography and Aging from Hasanlu, Iran. Ph.D. dissertation, University of Pennsylvania.

Sheridan, S. G.
2002   Scholars, Soldiers, Craftsmen, Elites? Analysis of French Collection of Human Remains from Qumran. *Dead Sea Discoveries* 9: 199–248.

Steckel, R. H.; Sciulli, P. W.; and Rose, J. C.
2002   A Health Index from Skeletal Remains. Pp. 61–93 in *The Backbone of History: Health and Nutrition in the Western Hemisphere*, ed. R. H. Steckel, and J. C. Rose. Cambridge: Cambridge University Press.

Stuart-Macadam, P.
1985   Porotic Hyperostosis: Representative of a Childhood Condition. *American Journal of Physical Anthropology* 66: 391–98.

Turner II, C. G.; Nichol, C. R.; and Scott, G. R.
1991   Scoring Procedures for Key Morphological Traits of the Permanent Dentition: The Arizona State University Dental Anthropology System. Pp. 13–31 in *Advances in Dental Anthropology*, ed. M. A. Kelley and C. S. Larsen. New York: Wiley-Liss.

Ubelaker, D. H.
1999   *Human Skeletal Remains: Excavation, Analysis, Interpretation*, 3rd ed. Manuals on Archeology 2. Washington, DC: Taraxacum.
2009   The Forensic Evaluation of Burned Skeletal Remains: A Synthesis. *Forensic Science International* 183: 1–5.

Vaux, R. de
1997   *Ancient Israel: Its Life and Institutions*. The Biblical Resource Series. Grand Rapids: Eerdmans.

Walker, P. L.; Bathurst, R. R.; Richman, R.; Gjerdrum, T.; and Andrushko, V. A.
2009   The Causes of Porotic Hyperostosis and Cribra Orbitalia: A Reappraisal of the Iron-Deficiency-Anemia Hypothesis. *American Journal of Physical Anthropology* 139: 109–25.

Wampler, J. C.
1941   Three Cistern Groups from Tell en-Naṣbeh. *Bulletin of the American Schools of Oriental Research* 82: 25–43.
1947   *Tell en-Naṣbeh*, Vol. 2: *The Pottery*. Berkeley, CA: The Palestine Institute of Pacific School of Religion.

White, T. D.; Black, M. T.; and Folkens, P. A.
2012   *Human Osteology*. 3rd edition. San Diego: Elsevier/Academic Press.

Zorn, J. R.
1993   Tell en-Nasbeh: A Reevaluation of the Architecture and Stratigraphy of the Early Bronze Age, Iron Age and Later Periods. Ph.D. Dissertation, University of California, Berkeley.
1994   Estimating the Population Size of Ancient Settlements: Methods, Problems, Solutions, and a Case Study. *Bulletin of the American Schools of Oriental Research* 295: 31–48.

TRANSJORDANIAN COMMERCE WITH NORTHERN JUDAH IN THE IRON II– PERSIAN PERIOD: CERAMIC INDICATORS, INTERREGIONAL INTERACTION, AND MODES OF EXCHANGE AT TELL EN-NAṢBEH

AARON J. BRODY
PACIFIC SCHOOL OF RELIGION
BADÈ MUSEUM OF BIBLICAL ARCHAEOLOGY

ABSTRACT

The economies of southern Levantine societies are defined primarily as agropastoralist, yet archaeological finds and ancient texts testify to a breadth of interregional and international commerce during the Iron II–Persian periods. Recent publications of bronze bangles from these periods at Tell en-Naṣbeh suggest that one source of their copper was the Feinan mines in Edom, and that this copper was alloyed with tin and lead in Edom before it was traded as bronze rings to Naṣbeh. Is it possible that other goods were exchanged from Transjordan in addition to, or along with, these bangles? In the present research I visually identify several ceramic forms and wares uncovered at Tell en-Naṣbeh as Transjordanian. The pottery imports are primarily painted wares and black wares that are ceramic hallmarks of the region of Ammon, from the Iron II-Persian period. These ceramics will be reviewed in detail in order to better understand interregional interactions between Ammon and northern Judah. The distribution patterns of these Ammonite pottery vessels at Naṣbeh will be presented and inter-

*preted as representative of a local marketing mode of ex-
change at the site.*

INTRODUCTION

The economy of southern Levantine societies in the Iron II–
Persian periods is classified primarily as agropastoralist, focused on
subsistence farming and householding and not wide-ranging commerce. Yet archaeological finds and ancient texts indicate a breadth
of interregional and international commerce during these periods
(Sherratt and Sherratt 1993; Thompson 2007; Stremlin 2008; Tyson
2011). Textual sources, especially the few focusing on commerce in
the Hebrew Bible and epigraphic writings, are typically skewed towards royal sponsored or controlled ventures, but are too scant to
reconstruct a full picture of southern Levantine interregional interactions (Hopkins 1996; King and Stager 2001; Master 2010; Nam
2012). One must turn to archaeological evidence to fill in gaps in
our understanding of ancient commerce and interconnections,
both at the elite and non-elite level (Aznar 2005; Bienkowski and
Van der Steen 2001; Daviau and Chadwick 2007; Daviau and Dion
2002; 2007; Edens and Bawden 1989; Faust and Weiss 2005; Holladay 2006; Katz 2004; Kletter 1998; Knauf-Belleri 1995; Levine
2008; Master 2003; Singer-Avitz 1999; Steiner 1999; 2002; Thompson 2007; Tyson 2011). Various archaeological research methods,
including contextual, stylistic, statistical, and comparative analysis,
material science sourcing, and spatial patterning allow for a reconstruction of interregional and long-distance trade networks. Material cultural evidence may help shed light on economic contact with
other cultures, while contextual analysis of imports may inform us
about economic stratification and modes of economic exchange.

Recent studies on bronze bangles from these periods at Tell
en-Naṣbeh, conducted by Elizabeth Friedman and myself, suggest
that one source of their copper was the Feinan mines in Edom
(Brody and Friedman 2007; Friedman et al. 2008). Further, we
propose that Feinan copper was alloyed with tin and lead in Edom
before it was traded in the form of bronze rings to Naṣbeh and
elsewhere in the southern Levant. Is it possible that other artifacts
uncovered at Naṣbeh were exchanged from Transjordan in addition to, or along with, these bronze rings?

In the present essay I identify several ceramic forms and wares
uncovered at the site of Tell en-Naṣbeh as imports from Transjor-

dan. These pottery imports are of two types: painted wares (Fig. 4.1) and black wares (Fig. 4.2). Both types are considered ceramic hallmarks of the region of Ammon (Herr 1999; Herr and Najjar 2008), the painted wares are generally dated more broadly to the Iron II through the Persian period, while the black wares are more narrowly placed in the Iron IIC–early Persian period, or the seventh–fifth centuries BCE (Herr 1991; 2006: 526–27; Daviau and Dion 2007: 304–05; Groot 2007: 99).

When the painted wares and black wares from Tell en-Naṣbeh are analyzed contextually, their patterning highlights aspects of the local economy in northern Judah. In the Iron II phase at the site, the imported Ammonite wares are relatively evenly distributed throughout the settlement irrespective of house size or location. These attributes are hallmarks of a market exchange economy (Smith 1990; Hirth 2010; Feinman and Garraty 2010; Stark and Garraty 2010). In the Babylonian–Persian phase, the Ammonite wares are much more limited and are only found associated with two buildings by the entrance to the settlement. This patterning suggests a marked decrease in interconnections with Ammon in the sixth–fifth centuries BCE, while contemporary Greek imports to Naṣbeh demonstrate more robust exchange to the west with emporia on the Mediterranean coast. The interpretations for both phases give refined understandings of interregional interactions and localized modes of exchange for the Iron II and Babylonian–Persian periods in northern Judah.

Tell En-Naṣbeh

The site of Tell en-Naṣbeh was excavated in five seasons from 1926 to 1935 by a team from Pacific School of Religion, under the direction of W. F. Badè. The settlement is located 12 km northwest of Jerusalem and is a prominent tell site in the region. The project uncovered two thirds of the approximately 3 ha site, along with two extramural cemeteries. Two final reports were published in 1947 that were good by the standards of the day, but are difficult to use now because of the lack of stratigraphic control at the site, the general excavation and recording standards of the 1920–30's, and the conventions used for ceramic illustration (McCown 1947; Wampler 1947).

Fortunately, the Badè Museum at Pacific School of Religion houses all of the original notes, photographs, and architectural plans from the Naṣbeh project, together with numerous objects from the site. Use of this documentation, together with the final reports and the invaluable stratigraphic work of J. R. Zorn allows for contextual study of the materials from the site, with the caveat that the material was excavated and recorded according to some very different standards than are commonly in use in modern excavations (Badè 1934; Zorn 1993a; 1993b). It must be emphasized that the notions of context when these finds were excavated and recorded in the 1920–30's were very different than they are currently. So the association of an artifact with a room did not take into account the relationship of that artifact to the matrix in which it was found, let alone the relationship of that matrix to one of the walls or features that defined the room. Thus a pottery sherd attributed to a room may have been part of a sub-floor fill, a floor, occupational debris above a floor, collapsed materials from a superstructure or roof, could have belonged to an unidentified pit within the room, etc. These limitations, however, may be balanced out by the breadth of the excavations, which provide one of the most complete exposures of an Iron II and a Babylonian–Persian site from the southern Levant.

Zorn re-analyzed all of the phases of occupation at the site, from the Early Bronze I through the Roman period, utilizing the project's original field notes, photographs, and plans (1993a). He established that Naṣbeh has five main strata: Stratum 5, Early Bronze I pits and tombs cut into the bedrock; Stratum 4, Iron I features, such as silos and cisterns, cut into the bedrock; Stratum 3, an Iron IIA–IIC village or town made up primarily of pillared houses and several phases of fortification systems; Stratum 2, Babylonian–Persian period four-room buildings; and Stratum 1, an ill-defined phase from the Hellenistic–Roman periods (Zorn 1993a; 1993b). Zorn has subsequently published numerous articles on Tell en-Naṣbeh, especially on aspects of the Iron II and Babylonian–Persian Stratum 3 and 2 at the site (see Zorn 1997–2003, current volume). It is in these two strata, Stratum 3 and 2 or the Iron II to Persian periods, that the ceramics imported to the site from Transjordan are found.

Since these ceramic imports span the Iron II–Persian periods in their region of origin, comparative stratigraphic information from other sites with more refined stratigraphy may not be used as a tool for improving our understanding of their deposition at

Naṣbeh. For example, I was able to use this technique with imported Phoenician pottery, some types of which have a much shorter chronological span in well stratified deposits from their home region (Brody 2014). Stratum 3 at Naṣbeh likely ends in the Iron IIC and Stratum 2 spans the Babylonian—early Persian period (Zorn 1993a; 1993b; 2003). Thus the entire temporal horizon of black-burnished wares in Ammon and a good portion of that of the Ammonite painted ware tradition are paralleled by the chronology of Stratum 3 and 2 at Naṣbeh. Given the aforementioned caveat regarding questions surrounding depositional attributions of artifacts in room contexts at the site, it is unfortunate that we cannot use external chronologies linked to either black-burnished or Ammonite painted wares to correct stratigraphic attributions between Stratum 3 and 2 at Tell en-Naṣbeh. We must rely on a critical assessment of the chronology of loci with Transjordanian imports at Naṣbeh based on the ceramic chronologies of J. C. Wampler, modified by the architectural stratigraphic analysis of J. R. Zorn (Wampler 1947: 120–25; Zorn 1993a).

AMMONITE CERAMICS

The ceramics that I am identifying visually as Ammonite fall into two broad categories: painted wares and black wares (Figs. 4.1–2). These black wares are slipped and burnished in different fashions (Figs. 4.3–5). Both types stand out from local contemporary Judean ceramics, which are known for their general lack of surface decoration (this was already recognized by Badè, who referred to the importance of "polished black ware" in his field manual; Badè 1934: 43). Very little painting, if any, was used on Judean pottery, and red slip and burnish dominated the Judean decorative tradition (Wampler 1947: 54; Amiran 1970: 200). The vast majority of Judean ceramics, however, remained undecorated, lacking any painting, slip, or burnish. Thus both painted wares and black burnishing are visually distinct from locally produced pottery.

Within the group of Ammonite painted wares from Naṣbeh are several vessel types. These include a small bowl, large bowls or kraters, a jug, an amphariskos, and juglets (perhaps better termed "bottles") (Fig. 4.1, Table 4.1). The black ware group is made up primarily of small bowls and variations on bowls, such as chalices and a tripod bowl (Fig. 4.2, Table 4.2). There is one black ware perforated lid (Fig. 4.2.25, Table 4.2.25). In general, the group of both painted and black wares is made up primarily of open vessels, which indicates that the ceramics were exchanged as products themselves and not for their contents, which could be argued for the few closed vessels.

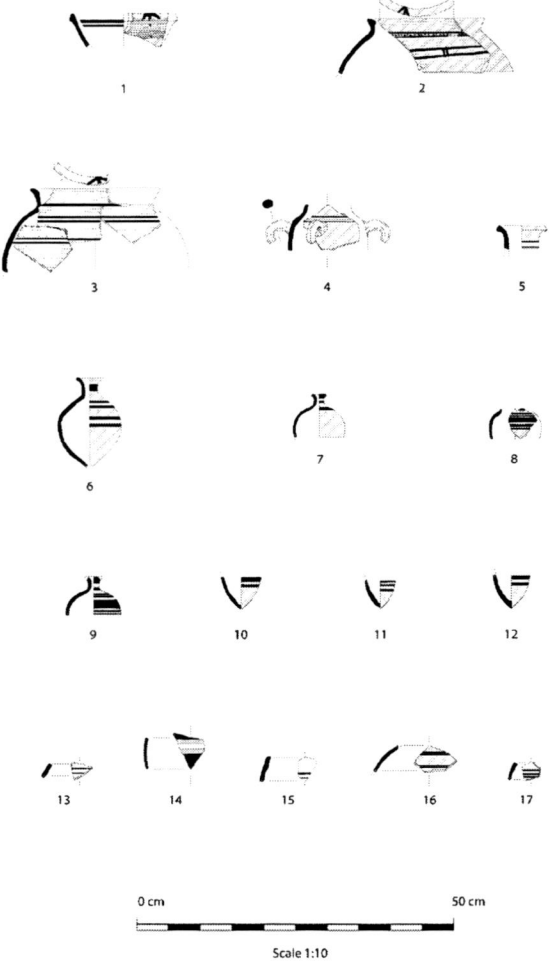

Fig. 4.1. Ammonite painted wares from Tell en-Naṣbeh. See table 4.1 for descriptions (Illustrations by Christin Engstrom).

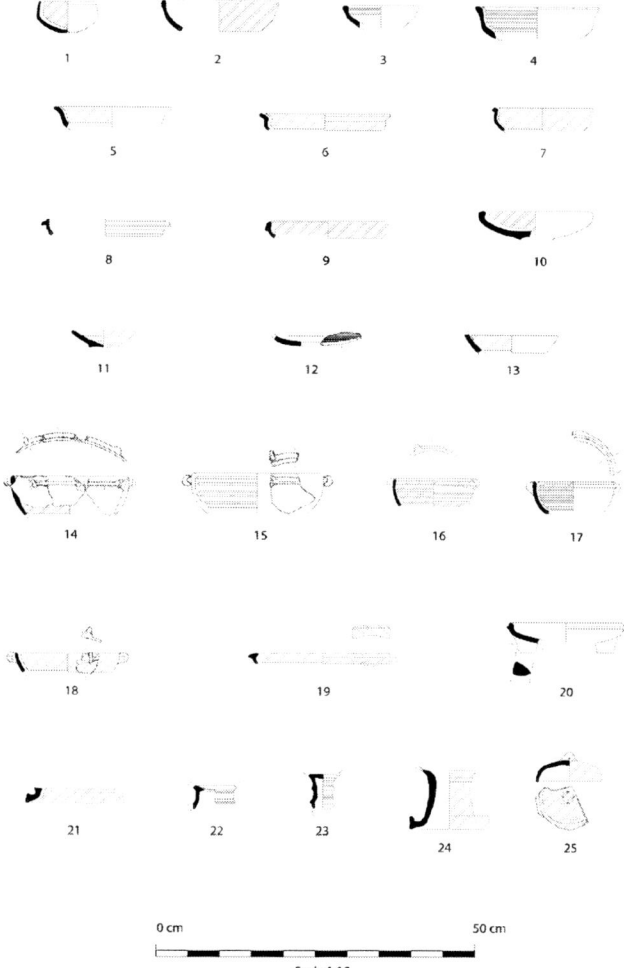

Fig. 4.2. Ammonite black wares from Tell en-Naṣbeh. See table 4.2 for descriptions (Illustrations by Christin Engstrom).

There appears to be a slight distinction between the ceramics I am labeling black wares and those defined as black-slipped and burnished wares or black burnished bowls. These specialized wares have been the focus of recent studies by L. Herr (2006), G. London (1991; 1999; London et al. 2007), P. M. M. Daviau and A. J. Graham (2009), and N. Groot (2007; 2009; 2011). They may differ from the Naṣbeh finds in terms of the fineness of their clay and care with which their burnish was applied. Unfortunately I have not had the opportunity to handle these black-slipped and burnished wares from Umayri, Hisban, Tall Jawa, or Deir 'Alla. However, I have personally handled black wares from Khirbat Marbat Badran, the Amman Citadel, the Meqabelein tomb assemblage, Tall es-Saidyeh Stratum IV, and Hisban survey material and find the parallels with similar wares from Naṣbeh compelling.

Fig. 4.3. Large bowl or krater, black slipped and burnished. AG28 I x42, drawing fig. 4.2.21 (Photograph by Rebecca Hisiger and Aaron J. Brody).

J. A. Sauer described a ware from Tall Hisban as decorated with black slip and widely spaced wheel burnishing marks (1994: 247; Lugenbeal and Sauer 1972: 33–34). R. Dornemann describes similar pottery sherds from the Amman Citadel as decorated with "… wheel burnish, but in some cases the burnish lines have become broad and/or have unburnished areas between them," (1983: 107). In a more recent study on black-burnished bowls from Umayri, Herr notes that a majority of the examples from the site "… have spaces of up to a few millimeters between the burnishing lines," (2006: 540). These descriptions of surface treatment and decoration by Sauer, Dornemann, and Herr are perfect parallels for several of the black ware finds from Tell en-Naṣbeh (Figs. 4.4–5).

It seems that ceramics that are black slipped and wheel burnished with widely spaced marks should be considered within the Ammonite black burnished ceramic tradition.

Fig. 4.4. Bowl? Black slipped with streaky burnish. Q18 II x21, drawing fig. 4.2.12 (Photograph by Rebecca Hisiger and Aaron J. Brody).

Comparative studies suggest that the Naṣbeh black ware ceramics were fired in a reduced atmosphere to achieve their black color (London 1991; 1999; London et al. 2007; Groot 2011: 183). Most of the Naṣbeh examples have black slip and burnish, and numerous small white inclusions (limestone?) intentionally added to the clay (Fig. 4.6). There are parallels for the addition of pulverized limestone to black-slipped and burnished clays found in examples of the ware from Umayri, Jawa, and Deir 'Alla (Herr 2006: 526; Daviau and Graham 2009: 49; Groot 2011: 202).

Fig. 4.5. Bowl, bar handled, black slipped with streaky burnish. "Rock outcrop, peninsula," probably a surface find from south end of site; drawing fig. 2.17 (Photograph by Rebecca Hisiger and Aaron J. Brody).

Fig. 4.6. Close-up of black ware fabric, note numerous small white inclusions typical of ware in general regardless of surface treatment. Q18 II x21, drawing fig. 4.2.12 (Photograph by Rebecca Hisiger and Aaron J. Brody).

The best parallels for the painted wares are from sites on the Ammon plateau and in the Jordan Valley. These include the Iron II–Persian period repertoire from the Amman region tombs, the Amman Citadel, Umayri, Hisban, Tall Jawa, Sahab, Nimrin, Tall es-Saidiyeh, and Deir Alla (Lugenbeal and Sauer 1972: 61; Dornemann 1983: 76–78, 100–02; Pritchard 1985: 46; Daviau 2003: 473; Groot 2007: 99). Groot even refers to this localized decorative tradition as "Ammonite bands," (2011: 242, 252; Fig. 4.7, Fig. 4.1.5).

Fig. 4.7. Jug, faint red slipped and burnished, painted bands on neck. AF16 I x19, drawing fig. 4.1.5 (Photograph by Rebecca Hisiger and Aaron J. Brody).

A vessel very similar to an Ammonite krater from Naṣbeh (Fig. 4.1.2, Table 4.1.2), a painted, red slipped and burnished krater from Jericho's seventh century material that is a unique imported vessel, helps us to suggest a path that some of these ceramics took from east to west (Franken 1974: 148, fig. 14.48; Kenyon and Holland 1982: 512, H.III.e, fig. 210.29; for further discussion of late Iron Age II routes see Ji 1998: 602; 2001: 386; Bienkowski 2001: 268–69). Franken even comments "It is not at all surprising that Transjordanian pottery occasionally migrated to Jericho in the 7th century B.C." (1974: 86). While the red slip and burnish of several of the pieces is a decorative feature with a long history in the Iron Age on both sides of the Jordan River, the cream colored slip and burnish on another painted krater from Naṣbeh (Fig. 4.1.3, Fig. 4.8, Table 4.1.3) has its counterparts in the Iron IIC repertoire from the Amman Citadel, as detailed by Dornemann (1983: 107–10).

Fig. 4.8. Krater, cream slipped and burnished, painted bands. AH20 x12, drawing fig. 4.1.3 (Photograph by Rebecca Hisiger and Aaron J. Brody).

The best parallels for the black wares are from the Meqabelein tomb assemblage, the Amman Citadel, Hisban, Umayri, Khirbat Marbat Badran, Tall Jawa, Sahab, Tall es-Saidiyeh, and Deir Alla (Lugenbeal and Sauer 1972: 33–38; Dornemann 1983: 107–10; Pritchard 1985: 46, figs. 15.8, 17.28; Abu Shmais 2005: 414; Herr 2006: 525–40; Groot 2007: 100; 2011; Daviau and Graham 2009: 41–58; for another black ware import to Cisjordan see Mazar and Panitz-Cohen 2001: 52; for further black ware vessels in Cisjordan but skepticism that they are all imports see Singer-Avitz 2007: 188–90). Material science testing on black burnished wares by G. London has shown that there were a minimum of three distinct clay sources for the ware, two on the Ammon plateau and one in the Jordan Valley (1999: 94; London, Shuster, and Jacobs 2007: 84). Until similar testing is conducted on the black wares imported to Nasbeh, we will not be able to distinguish possible regionality among Ammonite wares identified through visual analysis.

CONTEXTS OF THE IMPORTED CERAMICS

I have visually identified forty-two vessels or vessel fragments from Nasbeh as Transjordanian. Seventeen are painted wares, and twenty-five are black wares (Tables 4.1–2). Only one piece was uncovered in a tomb, the black ware pierced lid (Fig. 4.2.25, Table 4.2.25). All of the other examples came from the settlement itself or from Cave 193, located just east of the city wall in Square AG28.

Of the painted wares, ten vessel fragments were found in stratified contexts on the tell (Table 4.1). Of the black wares, twelve fragments came from good contexts on the site (Table 4.2). The remaining examples of both wares were found in unstratified surface layers of the settlement, or lack provenience but are known to have come from Tell en-Nasbeh. The provenience of finds from surface layers was recorded by the 10 x 10 meter square from which they were excavated, otherwise we can say very little about their original contexts except that they were from the tell and not from extramural burials (Fig. 4.9).

No.	Object	Field #	Locus	Stratum	Description
1	Bowl	R 378 I x34	Room 378, Square T23 4-Room building (Zorn 1993a: 538-40, 1534)	2, Babylonian-Persian	Direct, externally thickened, triangular rim. Paste is red on exterior, brown interior, small gray and white inclusions. Wheel burnished on exterior with gaps in burnishing. Painted black bands on interior, painted trident on rim.
2	Krater	Ci 191 I x19	Cistern 191, Square AG25	3 or 2, ca. 625–500 BCE	Direct, internally thickened, triangular rim. Paste is red on exterior, brown interior, small to medium white inclusions. Red slip and wheel burnished on exterior over top of rim. Red slip continues down 2.5 cm into interior. Painted parallel black bands just below neck with row of dots painted in between, below on shoulder are two more parallel black bands with pair of vertical bands connecting horizontal bands, trident on rim.
3	Krater	AH20 x12	Surface fill Square AH20	Unstratified	Flared, externally thickened, oval rim. Paste is salmon pink on the exterior, grey brown interior, few small white inclusions. Cream slip and wheel burnished on exterior over top of rim. Painted black band at base of neck, two parallel black lines on shoulder, and two more parallel black lines on waist, trident on rim.
4	Amph-ariskos	R 571 I x13	Room 571, Square AD19 4-Room building (Zorn 1993a: 784, 1579)	3, Iron II	Rim not preserved. Paste is salmon pink on exterior, pinkish buff interior very few small white inclusions. Red slip on exterior. Painted parallel black lines above shoulder with broad white band painted between (mostly gone).

Table 4.1. Ammonite Painted Wares from Tell en-Naṣbeh in Fig. 4.1 (continued on following pages).

No.	Object	Field #	Locus	Stratum	Description
5	Jug	AF16 I x19, and dump from AF16, AG16 I x5 [two sherds join]	Surface fill Square AF16	Unstratified	Flared, indeterminate, rectangular, slightly rounded rim. Paste is dark salmon pink on exterior and interior, very few small white and grey inclusions. Very slight red slip on exterior up to top of rim, vertical burnishing on neck. Painted parallel black lines on neck with broad white band painted between.
6	Juglet	Si or Ci 152 x5 = Museum #334	Silo or Cistern 152, Square AJ22	3, Iron II	Flared, indeterminate, rectangular, slightly rounded rim. Globular body, base missing. Paste is brown to light brown on exterior, grey interior, numerous small to medium white inclusions. Painted parallel red lines, one on neck, one pair on shoulder with white band between, one pair on waist with white band between.
7	Juglet	R 366 I x36	Room 366, Square R22, S22 4-Room building (Zorn 1993a: 501, 1532)	2, Babylonian-Persian	Flared, indeterminate, rectangular, slightly rounded rim. Paste is brown on exterior, dark grey interior, very few small white inclusions. Red-brown slip on exterior and inside lip, exterior burnishing, parallel brown stripes on neck (very faint)?
8	Juglet	Dump II x71	Dump	Unstratified	Shoulder fragment, similar vessel to R 366 I x36. Paste is light brown on exterior, light grey interior, few small to medium white inclusions. Exterior burnishing, six parallel red stripes on neck, shoulder, and body of vessel. Stripe on shoulder is thicker than the rest.
9	Juglet	no information marked on sherd, known to be from Tell en-Naṣbeh	?	?	Rim broken, similar vessel to R 366 I x36. Paste is salmon and brown on exterior, salmon interior, small white inclusions. Eight parallel red stripes on neck, shoulder, and body of vessel. Stripe just below shoulder is extremely broad.

Table 4.1. (continued).

No.	Object	Field #	Locus	Stratum	Description
10	Juglet	R 378 I x40	Room 378, Square T23 4-Room building (Zorn 1993a: 538–40, 1534)	2, Babylonian-Persian	Pointed base. Paste is salmon pink and grey on exterior, grey interior, few small to medium white inclusions. Three parallel red stripes on lower body.
11	Juglet	Dump AB17 I x2	Dump	Unstratified	Pointed base. Paste is grey on exterior and interior. Light brown wash, vertical burnishing, three parallel red stripes on lower body.
12	Juglet	AG19 I x17	Surface fill Square AG19	Unstratified	Pointed base. Paste is tan and grey on exterior, light grey interior, very few small white inclusions. Two parallel red stripes on lower body.
13	Sherd	Ci 176 I x10	Cistern 176, Square N17	3, Iron II	Body fragment. Paste is salmon on exterior, grey brown interior, with small to medium white inclusions. Cream colored slip, two parallel black lines. Likely fragment of krater AH20 x12.
14	Sherd	Ci 191 I x126	Cistern 191, Square AG25	3-2, ca. 625–500 BCE	Body fragment. Paste is dark brown on exterior, grey interior, with few small white inclusions. Burnished exterior, two parallel broad red stripes with broad white stripe painted between.
15	Sherd	Ci 216 x18	Cistern 216, square P17	3, Iron II	Body fragment. Paste is salmon on exterior, grey brown interior, with small to medium white inclusions. Cream colored slip and burnished, two parallel black lines. Likely fragment of krater AH20 x12.
16	Sherd	C 193 N x1	Cave 193, square AG28	3-2, ca. 700–400 BCE	Body fragment. Paste is salmon on exterior and interior, with few medium white inclusions. Wheel burnished exterior, two sets of two parallel black lines.
17	Sherd	Dump AD19 I x8	Dump	Unstratified	Body fragment. Paste is red on exterior, grey interior, with very few small to medium white inclusions. Light red slip and burnished exterior, three parallel black stripes.

Table 4.1. (continued).

Map of Tell en-Nasbeh: all phases

◨ = painted ware find, in context
◼ = black ware find, in context
☐ = painted ware find, by square
☐ = black ware find, by square

Fig. 4.9. Map of Tell en-Naṣbeh with distribution of stratified and unstratified Ammonite wares (Illustration by Aaron J. Brody).

The contexts of the stratified examples of Transjordanian ceramics are better understood once they are placed in their proper stratigraphic and architectural contexts. They are found in rooms and features from Stratum 3 and Stratum 2 at Tell en-Naṣbeh (Fig. 4.10), following the stratigraphic phasing of the site worked out by Zorn (1993a). The patterning of find spots between these two strata is quite opposite. The finds from Stratum 3 show a relatively even distribution throughout the majority of the excavated portions of the site, whose architecture is made up solely of agglutinated pillared houses. There are no significant concentrations of these Stratum 3 wares, nor any signs of the clustering of these imported ceramics in any particular building, compound, or specific area of the settlement.

No.	Object	Field #	Locus	Stratum	Description
1	Bowl	Si 295c II x32 = Museum #1809	Silo 295 Square V13	3, Iron IIC	Upright, simple rim; carinated body; depressed ring base. Paste is fired dark grey on exterior and interior, with numerous small white inclusions. Black slipped and burnished interior of vessel to top of rim (poorly preserved).
2	Bowl	AD21 I x8	Surface fill Square AD21	Unstratified	Direct, externally thickened oval rim; convex body. Paste is fired dark grey on exterior, light grey interior, with numerous small white inclusions. Black slipped interior and exterior, burnished on exterior from top of rim down to shoulder of vessel.
3	Bowl	R 371 I x5	Room 371 Square S22 4-Room building (Zorn 1993a: 505-506, 1533)	2, Babylonian-Persian	Upright, externally thickened, rounded rim, carinated body. Paste is fired dark grey on exterior, brown interior, with numerous small white inclusions. Black slip on rim and interior of vessel, with remnants of burnishing on top of rim.
4	Bowl	C 193 N x10	Cave 193, Square AG28	3-2, ca. 700–400 BCE	Flared, externally thickened, triangular rim; carinated body. Paste is fired dark grey on exterior, light grey interior, with numerous small white inclusions. Black streaked burnishing on rim and interior of vessel.
5	Bowl	AE19 I x13	Surface fill Square AE19	Surface fill	Flared, simple, triangular rim; recurved body. Past is fired dark grey on exterior, light grey interior, with numerous small white inclusions. Black slip and burnish on interior from the top of rim down.

Table 4.2. Ammonite Black Wares from Tell en-Naṣbeh Illustrated in Fig. 4.2 (continued on following pages).

No.	Object	Field #	Locus	Stratum	Description
6	Bowl	Ci 191 I x15	Cistern 191 Square AG25	3-2, ca. 625–500 BCE	Everted, simple rim; convex body. Paste is fired light grey on exterior and interior, with numerous small white inclusions. Black slipped interior and exterior, streaked burnishing on exterior, more solid burnishing with few streaks on interior from rim down.
7	Bowl	No information marked on sherd, known to be from Tell en-Naṣbeh	?	?	Flared, slightly thickened, oval rim; convex body. Paste is fired dark grey on exterior and interior, with numerous small white inclusions. Faint, infrequent, streaky burnish on exterior, rim, and interior.
8	Bowl	R 484 I x9	Room 484 Square Y17 4-Room building (Zorn 1993a: 584, 1560-61)	3, Iron II	Pendant, thickened, profiled rim. Paste is fired dark grey on exterior and interior, with numerous small white inclusions. No slip or burnish.
9	Bowl	R 648 I x12	Room 648 Square AA18 3-Room building (Zorn 1993a: 661–63, 1596)	3, Iron II	Incurved, externally thickened, profiled rim; convex body. Paste is fired dark grey on exterior and interior, with numerous small white inclusions. Black slipped and burnished on interior and exterior (not well preserved).
10	Bowl	AG18 I x32	Surface fill Square AG18	Unstratified	Incurved, simple, triangular rim; convex body; shallow ring base. Paste is fired dark grey on exterior, brown interior, with numerous small white inclusions. Black sipped and burnished on top of rim and interior.
11	Bowl	Dump AF17 Sub I x8	Dump	Unstratified	Ring base; convex body up to possible carination. Paste is fired dark grey on exterior, light grey interior with numerous small white inclusions. Black slip on exterior.

Table 4.2. (continued).

No.	Object	Field #	Locus	Stratum	Description
12	Bowl?	Q18 II x2	Surface fill Square Q18	Unstratified	Body fragment. Paste is fired dark grey on exterior, light grey interior, with numerous small white inclusions. Black slip and streaky burnish on interior.
13	Bowl?	Q18 II x6	Surface fill Square Q18	Unstratified	Body fragment. Paste is dark grey on exterior, light grey interior, with numerous small white inclusions. Black slip and burnish on interior.
14	Bowl, bar-handled	R 444 I x9, R 444 I x9, AF20 I x24 (joins), No information marked on sherd but joins with AF20 I x24	Room 444 Square AF20 3-Room building (Zorn 1993a: 774– 76, 1551)	3, Iron II	Direct, simple rim; convex body; bar handle. Paste is grey on exterior to tan interior, with numerous small white inclusions. Black slipped and burnished interior.
15	Bowl, bar-handled	No information marked on sherd, known to be from Tell en-Naṣbeh	?	?	Direct, simple, rounded rim; convex body; bar handle. Paste is fired dark grey on exterior to tan interior, with numerous small white inclusions. Black slipped and burnished interior to top of rim (poorly preserved).
16	Bowl, bar handled	R 562 I x24,	Room 562 Square AD20 3-Room building (Zorn 1993a: 790, 1577)	3, Iron II	Upright, simple, rounded rim; convex body; bar handle. Paste is fired dark grey exterior, grey interior, with numerous small white inclusions. Black slipped and streaky burnished interior, streaky burnished exterior.
17	Bowl, bar handled	Rock outcrop, peninsula (probable fit with R 562 I x24; interior burnishing streaks line-up)	Rock outcrop	Unstratified	Upright, simple, rounded rim; convex body; bar handle with two vertical piercings. Paste is fired dark grey exterior and interior, with numerous small white inclusions. Black slipped and streaky burnished interior, streaky burnished exterior.

Table 4.2. (continued).

No.	Object	Field #	Locus	Stratum	Description
18	Bowl, bar handled	R 484 I x8	Room 484 Square Y17 4-Room building (Zorn 1993a: 584, 1560-61)	3, Iron II	Direct, simple, rounded rim; convex body; bar handle. Paste is fired dark grey with grey interior, with numerous small white inclusions. Black slipped and burnished interior and exterior (poorly preserved).
19	Bowl, bar handled	R 438 I x23	Room 438 Square AF19 4-Room building (Zorn 1993a: 824, 1550)	3, Iron II	Incurving, internally thickened, oval rim; bar handle. Paste is fired dark grey on exterior, interior is red-brown, with occasional small white and grey inclusions. Black slipped and burnished on exterior and interior.
20	Bowl, footed or mortar	AB19 I x15	Surface fill Square AB19	Unstratified	Direct, simple, flanged rim; convex body; triangular foot. Paste is fired dark grey on exterior, brown interior, with numerous small white inclusions. Black slipped and burnished interior, black slipped exterior (poorly preserved
21	Large bowl or krater?	AG28 I x42, AG28 I x51	Surface fill Square AG28	Unstratified	Ring base. Paste is fired dark grey on exterior to light grey interior, with many small white inclusions. Black slipped and burnished on exterior and interior. Two fragments do not join, but clearly are from the same vessel.
22	Chalice	C 193 x5	Cave 193, Square AG28	3-2, ca. 700-400 BCE	Bottom of chalice bowl and top of pedestal base. Paste is fired grey exterior with light grey interior, with numerous small white inclusions. Black slipped and burnished interior of chalice bowl, black streaky burnished exterior of pedestal base. May be from same vessel as bowl C 193 N x10 detailed above, #4, since found in same locus and similar fabric but no direct mend.

Table 4.2. (continued).

No.	Object	Field #	Locus	Stratum	Description
23	Chalice	No information marked on sherd, known to be from Tell en-Naṣbeh	?	?	Stepped pedestal of chalice. Paste is fired grey on exterior to light grey interior, with numerous small white inclusions. Black slipped and burnished interior of bowl, black streaky burnish on exterior of pedestal.
24	Chalice	R 378 I x37	Room 378 Square T23 4-Room building (Zorn 1993a: 538-40, 1534)	2, Babylonian-Persian	Pedestal base. Paste is fired dark grey on exterior to light grey interior, with numerous small white inclusions. Black slipped and burnished exterior, black slipped interior of pedestal.
25	Lid	Tomb 29 x2	Tomb 29 West Cemetery	8th-7th centuries BCE, Iron IIB-C	Lid with nob handle, pierced through on four sides. Paste is fired dark grey on exterior to light grey interior, with numerous small white inclusions. Black slipped and burnished on exterior.

Table 4.2. (continued).

The patterning of a relatively even distribution of imported ceramics throughout a site has been singled out as the prime indicator of marketplace exchange in recent archaeological studies focused in the Americas (Hirth 2010; Feinman and Garraty 2010; Stark and Garraty 2010). In his research on pre-Hispanic Central Mexico, K. Hirth found that "foreign ceramics were readily available to, and evenly distributed throughout, all levels of Xochicalco society … (which) indicates that imported ceramics were readily available to all households," (Hirth 2000, 189). I see a similar patterning in the Ammonite wares in Stratum 3 at Naṣbeh, which can be explained best by this type of open access to goods provided by a marketplace.

This access to foreign, Ammonite ceramics in Stratum 3 is not necessarily a function of wealth. 57% (four out of seven) of Transjordanian wares found in architectural contexts were from three-room houses while 43% (three out of seven) were from larger four-room house structures. This interpretation is based on the assumption that wealthier families would have inhabited larger households. The fact that imported wares are not found in greater abundance in wealthier households is a further indication of market exchange, as this suggests that families of different economic means had access to, and bartered for, the same types of foreign goods.

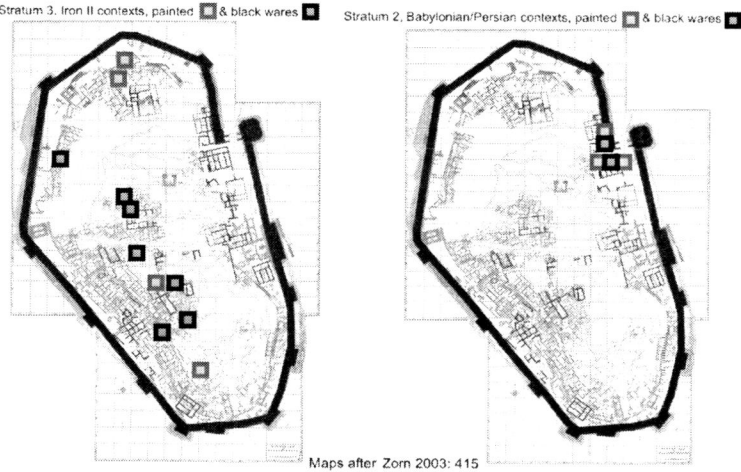

Fig. 4.10. Map of Tell en-Naṣbeh's Stratum 3 and Stratum 2 with find spots of stratified Ammonite wares by phase (Illustration by Aaron J. Brody).

This interpretation fits well with the scant textual evidence preserved in the Hebrew Bible that details several types of market places in regal centers and administrative cities (Master 2010; Nam 2012). To my knowledge, the patterning of Ammonite imports at Tell en-Naṣbeh is the first archaeological evidence presented that illustrates the utilization of market exchange in ancient Judah.

The Transjordanian ceramics from Stratum 2 at Naṣbeh tell a different story. They are clustered in two neighboring buildings located by the entrance to the site, the city gate. None of the other Stratum 2 buildings have any in situ finds of either painted wares or black wares. All five of the Stratum 2 Ammonite wares were found in four-room buildings. For this phase Zorn has reconstructed seven four-room houses and two three-room house structures (1993a). Larger, presumably wealthier, pillared houses dominate the site in the Babylonian–Persian phase at Naṣbeh, and the few imports

from Transjordan are found in more elite structures. This patterning is a clear indication of limited and restricted access to imported
Ammonite wares in the Babylonian–Persian periods.

While the numbers are quite limited, if we broaden our count
to include Transjordanian ceramics from features like silos, cisterns, or caves that are not found in three- or four-room buildings,
there are twelve examples phased to Stratum 3 and five phased to
Stratum 2. The remainder are either unstratified or come from
stratified contexts that could be dated to either phase. This 58%
reduction, twelve in Stratum 3 to five in Stratum 2, may signify a
decrease in interregional interactions with Transjordan in the Babylonian–Persian periods. By way of some comparison, Herr has noted a marked increase in the number of black-burnished wares at
Umayri in the Persian phases at the site compared with those in the
Iron IIC phases (2006: 540). This pattern of increase within Ammon over the span of the seventh–fifth centuries BCE, at least for
black-burnished wares at one Ammonite site, is the opposite of the
one at Naṣbeh, which shows decrease over the same periods.

It might be tempting to interpret the circumscribed configura-
tion of Ammonite ceramics in the Babylonian–Persian period at
Naṣbeh as a hallmark of redistributive exchange (Stark and Garraty
2010). However, the abundance of other imports, especially Greek
ceramics, are relatively evenly distributed throughout the settlement, suggesting that marketplace exchange was still taking place at
Naṣbeh in its Stratum 2 (McCown 1947: 204, fig. 50.B; von Bothmer 1947: 175–78, 304). Perhaps it simply signals a weakening of
commerce with Ammon, to the east of Tell en-Naṣbeh, and a
strengthening of trade to the west, since Greek pottery was exchanged through emporia on the southern Levantine coast of the
Mediterranean.

CONCLUSIONS

While this study has focused on the trade of Ammonite ceramic
vessels to Tell en-Naṣbeh, bronze bangles and Red Sea shells, including cowry and tridacna, are other material indicators of contacts to the east with Transjordan (McCown 1947: 248, pl. 48:22,
50:17, 90:22; Reese 1991; Brody and Friedman 2007; Friedman et
al. 2008). Certain semi-precious stones, traded to Naṣbeh in bead
form, have their sources in Arabia and Zorn has suggested that
Wedge and Circle Impressed pottery from Arabia and Transjordan

signifies an eastward connection to Naṣbeh's ceramic traditions of the same decorative pottery (2001). Interregional interactions to the west can be demonstrated through the presence of Phoenician, Cypriot, and Greek imports to the site (McCown 1947; Brody 2014). The overall numbers of these imports are quite low, suggesting the limited nature of interregional interaction to the overall economy at Tell en-Naṣbeh (Brody 2014). Yet it is intriguing that these foreign imports exist at all at a fortified village in Stratum 3, a third-tier settlement well below regal-ritual centers or regional administrative cities of the Judean settlement hierarchy; or in the Stratum 2 phase, which is diminutive but a top-tier site for the Babylonian–early Persian period. Naṣbeh's economy remained highly localized, and primarily agropastoral, focused around the survival of the extended families that inhabited the site (Brody 2009b; 2011).

What was exchanged for these wide-ranging goods is unclear at this time, but the most likely candidates are agricultural products or cloth. Judean ceramics have been identified by Groot in Iron IIC phases at Deir Alla (2007; 2011), and one would expect similar finds in contemporary sites on the Ammon plateau, hinting at the return trade of Judean products.

These data allow for a greater understanding of Judean economy and commercial relations with the kingdom of Ammon in the Iron II to Persian periods, historic periods when the political relations between these polities were typically hostile (Dion 2003; Tyson 2011: 148, 216). Tell en-Naṣbeh is usually identified as the biblical settlement of Mizpah in Benjamin in the time of the Divided Monarchy and Babylonian–Persian periods (Brody 2009a). Mizpah becomes the regional capital of the Babylonian province of Judah, and there are several incidents of political intrigue preserved in the Hebrew Bible that link Mizpah to the kingdom of Ammon (2 Kings 25:22–25; Jer. 40–41; Tyson 2011: 168).

Political enmity, however, does not preclude economic relations as commerce often continues between peoples despite antagonism among the ruling elite (for parallels from Mesoamerica see Smith 1990: 165; 1998: 122–27). Why was the fortified Stratum 3 village at Tell en-Naṣbeh a node of interregional contact, considering it was a third-tier site, ranked well below royal cities and regional administrative centers in the hierarchy of Judean settlements (Holladay 1995)? Why did the number of Ammonite ceramics decrease dramatically in the Stratum 2 settlement, an important site in

Babylonian–early Persian Judah, while Greek wares dominate the imports to the site? Who, and what, was carrying these goods in either of these periods? These, and further questions, await continued research, as does a program of material science testing to help verify or dismiss my visual attributions. The preliminary identification of Transjordanian ceramics at Tell en-Naṣbeh and the interpretation of their contextual patterning, however, provides refined understandings of interregional interactions and localized modes of economic exchange for the Iron II to the early Persian periods in northern Judah.

ACKNOWLEDGMENTS

This research was begun at the American Center of Oriental Research (ACOR) under a CAORC Senior Fellowship in the Spring of 2009, while on a sabbatical leave gratefully supported by my home institution, Pacific School of Religion. I would like to thank ACOR and CAORC for this grant, and especially thank Barbara Porter and Chris Tuttle, and all the staff at the institute. Heartfelt thanks goes to the late Fawwaz Al-Khraysheh, Katrina Hamarneh, Adeib Abu Shmais, Ayda Naghawy, Moawiyah Ibrahim, Mohammad Najjar, and Zeidan Kafafi for permissions, insights, access to collections, collegiality, and hospitality during my stay in Jordan. Thanks also to the Museum of Archaeology and Anthropology at the University of Pennsylvania for access to their Tall es-Saidiyeh collection and Hisban survey materials. And thanks to north American colleagues who excavate in Jordan for taking the time at the 2009 ASOR meeting in Boston to look over and comment on some of these ceramics from Tell en-Naṣbeh, as well as to Michèle Daviau who viewed and commented on the pottery while researching other aspects of the Naṣbeh materials in the collection at the Badè Museum of Biblical Archaeology at Pacific School of Religion.

REFERENCES

Abu Shmais, A.
2005   Khirbat Marbat Badran/Rujum abu Nusayr: Industrial and Agricultural Production Center Preliminary Study of the Excavations During 2003–2005. *Annual of the Department of Antiquities of Jordan* 49: 411–16.

Amiran, R.
1970   *Ancient Pottery of the Holy Land.* New Brunswick, NJ: Rutgers University Press.

Aznar, C. A.
2005   Exchange Networks in the Southern Levant During the Iron Age II: A Study of Pottery Origin and Distribution. Ph.D. dissertation, Harvard University.

Badè, W. F.
1934   *A Manual of Excavation in the Near East: Methods of Digging and Recording of the Tell en-Nasbeh Expedition in Palestine.* Berkeley, CA: University of California Press.

Bienkowski, P.
2001   The Iron Age and Persian Periods in Jordan. Pp. 265–74 in *Studies in the History and Archaeology of Jordan 7.* Amman: Department of Antiquities.

Bienkowski, P., and van der Steen, E.
2001   Tribes, Trade, and Towns: A New Framework for the Late Iron Age in Southern Jordan and the Negev. *Bulletin of the American Schools of Oriental Research* 323: 21–47.

Brody, A. J.
2009a   Mizpah, Mizpeh. Pp. 116–17 in *The New Interpreter's Dictionary of the Bible, Me–R,* Vol. 4, ed. K. D. Sakenfeld. Nashville, TN: Abingdon.
2009b   "Those who Add House to House": Household Archaeology and the Use of Domestic Space in an Iron II Residential Compound at Tell en-Naṣbeh. Pp. 45–56 in *Exploring the Longue Durée: Essays in Honor of Lawrence E. Stager,* ed. J. D. Schloen. Winona Lake, IN: Eisenbrauns.
2011   The Archaeology of the Extended Family: A Household Compound from Iron II Tell en-Naṣbeh. Pp. 237–54 in *Household Archaeology in Ancient Israel and Beyond,* ed. A. Yasur-Landau, J. R. Ebeling, and L. B. Mazow. Culture and History of the Ancient Near East 50. Leiden: Brill.
2014   Interregional Interaction in the Late Iron Age: Phoenician and Other Foreign Goods from Tell en-Naṣbeh. Pp. 55–69 in *Material Culture Matters: Essays on the Archaeology of the Southern Levant in Honor of Seymour Gitin,* ed. J. R. Spencer,

R. A. Mullins, and A. J. Brody. Winona Lake, IN: Eisenbrauns.

Brody, A. J., and Friedman, E.
2007   Bronze Bangles from Tell en Nasbeh: Cultural and Economic Observations on an Artifact Type from the Time of the Prophets. Pp. 97–114 in *To Break Every Yoke: Essays in Honor of Marvin L. Chaney*, ed. Robert B. Coote and N. K. Gottwald. The Social World of Biblical Antiquity, Second Series 3. Sheffield: Sheffield Phoenix Press.

Daviau, P. M. M.
2003   *Excavations at Tall Jawa, Jordan*, Vol. 1: *The Iron Age Town*. Culture and History of the Ancient Near East, Vol. 11.1. Leiden: Brill.

Daviau, P. M. M., and Chadwick, R.
2007   Shepherds and Weavers in a "Global Economy", Moab in the Late Iron II – Wadi ath-Thamad Project (Khirbat al-Mudayna). Pp. 309–314 in *Crossing Jordan: North American Contributions to the Archaeology of Jordan*, ed. T. E. Levy, P. M. M. Daviau, Randall W. Younker and M. Shaer. London: Equinox.

Daviau, P. M. M., and Dion, P.-E.
2002   Economy-Related Finds from Khirbat al-Mudayna (Wadi ath-Thamad, Jordan). *Bulletin of the American Schools of Oriental Research* 328: 31–48.
2007   Independent and Well-Connected: The Ammonites of Central Jordan. Pp. 301–307 in *Crossing Jordan: North American Contributions to the Archaeology of Jordan*, ed. T. E. Levy, P. M. M. Daviau, Randall W. Younker and M. Shaer. London: Equinox.

Daviau, P. M. M., and Graham, A. J.
2009   Black-Slipped and Burnished Pottery: A Special 7th-Century Technology in Jordan and Syria. *Levant* 41: 41–58.

Dion, P.-E.
2003   The Ammonites: A Historical Sketch. Pp. 481–518 in *Excavations at Tall Jawa, Jordan*, Vol. 1: *The Iron Age Town*, ed. P. M. M. Daviau. Culture and History of the Ancient Near East 11.1. Leiden: Brill.

Dornemann, R. H.
1983   *The Archaeology of the Transjordan in the Bronze and Iron Ages.*
        Milwaukee, WI: Milwaukee Public Museum.

Edens, C., and Bawden, G.
1989   History of Tayma' and Hejazi trade During the First Mil-
        lennium B.C. *Journal of the Economic and Social History of the
        Orient* 32: 48–103.

Faust, A., and Weiss, E.
2005   Judah, Philistia, and the Mediterranean World: Recon-
        structing the Economic System of the 7th Century B.C.E.
        Bulletin of the American Schools of Oriental Research 338: 71–92.

Feinman, G. M., and Garraty, C. P.
2010   Preindustrial Markets and Marketing: Archaeological Per-
        spectives. *Annual Review of Anthropology* 39: 167–191.

Franken, H. J.
1974   *In Search of the Jericho Potters: Ceramics from the Iron Age and
        from the Neolithicum.* North-Holland Ceramic Studies in Ar-
        chaeology 1. Amsterdam: North-Holland Publishing Com-
        pany.

Friedman, E. S.; Brody, A. J.; Young, M. L.; Almer, J. D.; Segre, C.
U.; and Mini, S. M.
2008   Synchrotron Radiation-Based X-ray Analysis of Bronze
        Artifacts from an Iron Age Site in the Judean Hills. *Journal
        of Archaeological Science* 35: 1951–60.

Groot, N. C. F.
2007   In Search of the Ceramic Traditions of Late Iron Age IIC
        Pottery Excavated at Tell Deir 'Alla in the Central Jordan
        Valley. *Leiden Journal of Pottery Studies* 23: 89–108.
2009   The Early Persian Period at Tell Deir 'Allā: a Ceramic Per-
        spective. Pp. 175–90 in *A Timeless Vale: Archaeology and Re-
        lated Essays on the Jordan Valley in Honour of Gerrit Van Der
        Kooij on the Occasion of His Sixty-Fifth Birthday*, ed. E. Kaptijn
        and L. P. Petit. Archaeological Studies of Leiden University
        19. Leiden: Leiden University Press.
2011   All the Work of Artisans. Reconstructing Society at Tell
        Deir 'Allā through the Study of Ceramic Traditions: Stud-
        ies of Late Bronze Age Faience Vessels and Iron IIc–III

Ceramics from Tell Deir 'Allā, Jordan. PhD dissertation, University of Leiden.

Herr, L. G.
1991   Pottery Typology and Chronology. Pp. 232–45 in *Madaba Plains Project: The 1987 Season at Tel el-'Umeiri and Vicinity and Subsequent Studies,* ed. L. G. Herr, L. T. Geraty, Ø. S. Labianca, and R. W. Younker. Madaba Plains Project 2. Berrien Springs, MI: Andrews University Press.
1999   The Ammonites in the Late Iron Age and Persian Period. Pp. 219–37 in *Ancient Ammon,* ed. B. MacDonald and R. W. Younker. Studies in the History and Culture of the Ancient Near East 17 Leiden: Brill.
2006   Black-Burnished Ammonite Bowls from Tall al-'Umayri and Tall Hisban in Jordan. Pp. 525–40 in *"I Will Speak the Riddles of Ancient Times:" Archaeological and historical Studies in honor of Amihai Mazar on the Occasion of his Sixtieth Birthday,* ed. A. M. Maeir and P. de Miroschedji. Winona Lake, IN: Eisenbrauns.

Herr, L. G., and Najjar, M.
2008   The Iron Age. Pp. 311–34 in *Jordan: An Archaeological Reader,* ed. R. B. Adams. London: Equinox.

Hirth, K.
2000   The Economics of Distribution: Marketplaces, Market Systems, and Long-Distance Trade. Pp. 182–209 in *Archaeological Research at Xochicalco,* Vol. 1: *Ancient Urbanism at Xochicalco: The Evolution and Organization of a Pre-Hispanic Society,* ed. K. Hirth. Salt Lake City, UT: University of Utah Press.

Holladay, J. S., Jr.
1995   The Kingdoms of Israel and Judah: Political and Economic Centralization in the Iron IIA–B (ca. 1000–750 BCE). Pp. 368–98 in *The Archaeology of Society in the Holy Land,* ed. T. E. Levy. New York: Facts on File.
2006   Hezekiah's Tribute, Long-Distance Trade, and the Wealth of Nations ca. 1,000–600 BC: A New Perspective. Pp. 309–31 in *Confronting the Past: Archaeological and Historical Essays on Ancient Israel in Honor of William G. Dever,* ed. S. Gitin, J. E. Wright, and J. P. Dessel. Winona Lake, IN: Eisenbrauns.

Hopkins, D. C.
1996   Bare Bones: Putting Flesh on the Economics of Ancient Israel. Pp. 121–39 in *The Origins of the Ancient Israelite States*, ed. V. Fritz and P. R. Davies. Journal for the Study of the Old Testament Supplement Series 228 Sheffield: Sheffield Academic Press.

Ji, C.-H. C.
1998   Archaeological Survey and Settlement Patterns in the Region of 'Iraq al-'Amir, 1996: A Preliminary Report. *Annual of the Department of Antiquities Jordan* 42: 587–608.
2001   'Iraq al-'Amir and the Hellenistic Settlements in Central and Northern Jordan. Pp. 379–89 in *Studies in the History and Archaeology of Jordan 7*. Amman: Department of Antiquities.

Katz, H.
2004   Commercial Activity in the Kingdoms of Judah and Israel. *Tel Aviv* 31: 268–77

Kenyon, K., and Holland, T. A.
1982   *Excavations at Jericho*, Vol. 4: *The Pottery Type Series and Other Finds*. London: British School of Archaeology in Jerusalem.

King, P. J., and Stager, L. E.
2001   *Life in Biblical Israel*. Louisville, TN: Westminster John Knox.

Kletter, R.
1998   *Economic Keystones: The Weight System of the Kingdom of Judah*. Journal for the Study of the Old Testament Supplement Series 276. Sheffield: Sheffield Academic Press.

Knauf-Belleri, E. A.
1995   Edom: The Social and Economic History. Pp. 93–118 in *You Shall Not Abhor an Edomite for He is Your Brother: Edom and Seir in History and Tradition*, ed. D. V. Edelman. Archaeology and Biblical Studies 3. Atlanta, GA: Scholars Press.

Levine, E.
2008   The Weight of the Evidence and the Evidence of the Weights: An Examination of the Interrelations of Econo-

mies in the Iron Age Levant. Ph.D. dissertation, Harvard University.

London, G.
1991   Aspects of Early Bronze and Late Iron Age Ceramic Technology at Tell el-ʿUmeiri. Pp. 383–419 in *Madaba Plains Project: The 1987 Season at Tel el-ʿUmeiri and Vicinity and Subsequent Studies*, ed. L. G. Herr, L. T. Geraty, Ø. S. Labianca, and R. W. Younker. Madaba Plains Project 2. Berrien Springs, MI: Andrews University Press.
1999   Central Jordanian Ceramic Traditions. Pp. 57–102 in *Ancient Ammon*, ed. B. MacDonald and R. W. Younker. Studies in the History and Culture of the Ancient Near East 17. Leiden: Brill.

London, G., Shuster, R. D., and Jacobs, L.
2007   Ceramic Technology of Selected Hellenistic and Iron Age Pottery Based on Re-firing Experiments. *Leiden Journal of Pottery Studies* 23: 77–88.

Lugenbeal, E. N., and Sauer, J. A.
1972   Seventh–Sixth Century B.C. Pottery from Area B at Heshbon. *Andrews University Seminary Studies* 10: 21–69.

Master, D. M.
2003   Trade and Politics: Ashkelon's Balancing Act in the Seventh Century B.C.E. *Bulletin of the American Schools of Oriental Research* 330: 47–64.
2010   Trade in I and II Kings. Pp. 501–16 in *The Books of Kings: Sources, Composition, Historiography and Reception*, ed. A. Lemaire and B. Halpern. Supplements to Vetus Testamentum 129. Leiden: Brill.

Mazar, A., and Panitz-Cohen, N.
2001   *Timnah (Tel Batash) II: The Finds from the First Millennium BCE, Text*. Qedem 42. Jerusalem: Institute for Archaeology.

McCown, C. C.
1947   *Tell en-Nasbeh*, Vol. 1: *Archaeological and Historical Results*. Berkeley, CA: The Palestine Institute of Pacific School of Religion.

Nam, R. S.
2012   *Portrayals of Economic Exchange in the Book of Kings.* Biblical Interpretation Series 112. Leiden: Brill.

Pritchard, J. B.
1985   *Tell es-Sa'idiyeh: Excavations on the Tell, 1964–1966.* University Museum Monograph 60. Philadelphia: The University Museum, University of Pennsylvania.

Reese, D. S.
1991   The Trade of Indo-Pacific Shells into the Mediterranean Basin and Europe. *Oxford Journal of Archaeology* 10: 159–96.

Sauer, J. A.
1994   The Pottery at Hesban and its Relationship to the History of Jordan: An Interim Hesban Pottery Report, 1993. Pp. 225–81 in *Hesban After 25 Years,* eds. D. Merling and L. T. Geraty. Berrien Springs, MI: Institute of Archaeology, Andrews University.

Sherratt, S., and Sherratt, A.
1993   The Growth of the Mediterranean Economy in the Early First Millennium BC. *World Archaeology* 24: 361–78.

Singer-Avitz, L.
1999   Beersheba – A Gateway Community in Southern Arabian Long-Distance Trade in the Eighth Century B.C.E. *Tel Aviv* 26: 3–74.
2007   On Pottery in Assyrian Style: A Rejoinder. *Tel Aviv* 34: 182–203.

Smith, M. E.
1990   Long-Distance Trade Under the Aztec Empire: The Archaeological Evidence. *Ancient Mesoamerica* 1: 153–69.
1998   Merchants, Markets, and Money. Pp. 114–33 in *The Aztecs.* Malden, MA: Blackwell.

Stark, B. L., and Garraty, C. P.
2010   Detecting Marketplace Exchange in Archaeology: A Methodological Review. Pp. 33–59 in *Archaeological Approaches to Market Exchange in Ancient Societies,* eds. C. P. Garraty and B. L. Stark. Boulder, CO: University Press of Colorado.

Steiner, M. L.
2001   I am Mesha, King of Moab, or: Economic Organization in
        Iron Age II. Pp. 327–29 in *Studies in the History and Archaeol-*
        ogy of Jordan 7. Amman: Department of Antiquities.
2002   Mesha versus Solomon: Two Models of Economic Organ-
        ization in Iron Age II. *Svensk Exegetisk Årsbok* 67: 37–45.

Stremlin, B.
2008   The Iron Age World-System. *History Compass* 6: 969–99.

Thompson, C. M.
2007   Silver in the Age of Iron and the Orientalizing Economies
        of Archaic Greece. Ph.D. dissertation, University of Cali-
        fornia, Los Angeles.

Tyson, C. W.
2011   Israel's Kin Across the Jordan: A Social History of the
        Ammonites in the Iron Age II (1000–500 BCE). Ph.D. dis-
        sertation, University of Michigan.

von Bothmer, D.
1947   Greek Pottery. Pp. 175–78, 304 in *Tell en-Nasbeh*, Vol. 1:
        Archaeological and Historical Results, ed. C. C. McCown.
        Berkeley, CA: The Palestine Institute of Pacific School of
        Religion.

Wampler, J. C.
1947   *Tell en-Nasbeh,* Vol. 2: *The Pottery.* Berkeley, CA: The Pales-
        tine Institute of Pacific School of Religion.

Zorn, J. R.
1993a   Tell en Nasbeh: A Re-evaluation of the Architecture and
        Stratigraphy of the Early Bronze Age, Iron Age and Later
        Periods. Ph.D. dissertation, University of California,
        Berkeley.
1993b   Nasbeh, Tell en-. Pp. 1098–1102 in *The New Encyclopedia of*
        Archaeological Excavations in the Holy Land, Vol. 3, ed. E.
        Stern. Jerusalem: Israel Exploration Society.
1997   An Inner and Outer Gate Complex at Tell en-Nasbeh.
        Bulletin of the American Schools of Oriental Research 307: 53–66.
2001   Wedge- and Circle-Impressed Pottery: an Arabian Connec-
        tion. Pp. 689–98 in *Studies in the Archaeology of Israel and*

Neighboring Lands in Memory of Douglas L. Esse, ed. S. R. Wolff. Chicago: Oriental Institute.

2003   Tell en-Naṣbeh and the Problem of the Material Culture of the Sixth Century. Pp. 413–47 in *Judah and the Judeans in the Neo-Babylonian Period*, ed. O. Lipschits and J. Blenkinsopp. Winona Lake, IN: Eisenbrauns.

Iron in the Iron Age: The Life-Cycle of Agricultural Implements from Tell en-Naṣbeh

Stephanie H. Brown
Department of Near Eastern Studies
University of California, Berkeley

Abstract

This paper examines iron agricultural implements from Tell en-Naṣbeh. Despite the fact that large, complete iron objects are not often found in great quantity from sites in the southern Levant, a number of iron agricultural implements were discovered at Tell en-Naṣbeh. This paper proposes a life-cycle for these iron artifacts that addresses their production, use, and abandonment on site. The life-cycle is constructed in reverse; it begins with the objects and then contextualizes them within their find spots on site. These find spots illustrate either the abandonment or the use phase of the objects. Once the abandonment and use phases have been discussed the paper moves to the production of the objects. The reconstruction of this life-cycle provides a window through which scholars can better understand iron production, the practice of agriculture, and the agency and actions of specific ancient actors at Tell en-Naṣbeh. The results of this study suggest two components related to the life-cycle of iron agricultural implements at Tell en-Naṣbeh. The first is that iron agricultural implements were relatively common, and so would have been accessible to most families living at the settlement. The second is that their distribution and individual contexts on site support the notion that agricultur-

al endeavors at Iron II Tell en-Naṣbeh were conducted within the realm of the family.

INTRODUCTION

Over the last decades several seminal works have addressed iron use in the Iron Age southern Levant. Prominent among these works are: Wertime and Muhly's, *The Coming of the Age of Iron* (1980), Waldbaum's, *From Bronze to Iron: The Transition from the Bronze Age to the Iron Age in the Eastern Mediterranean* (1978); and McNutt's, *The Forging of Israel: Iron Technology, Symbolism, and Tradition in Ancient Society* (1990). These works explore the emergence of iron technology and track the evolution of metallurgical practices into the Iron Age. However, because these works focus on the causes and effects that the introduction of iron had in various places, they do not go into any depth on iron production and use in later periods, specifically the late Iron II–Persian periods (ca. 1000–332 B.C.E.) in the southern Levant, when iron had been an important and widespread commodity for over half a millennium.[1] Furthermore, because these studies of iron attempt to cover a large geographic region there is little discussion of the interactions between specific iron objects and the people who made and used them on a small-scale, local level.

In recent years work at the southern Levantine iron production sites of Tell Hammeh (Veldhuijzen and van der Steen 1999) and Beth-Shemesh (Bunimovitz, and Lederman 2012) have begun to address this geographic and temporal gap. These studies have greatly furthered our knowledge of iron production in the Iron II southern Levant by examining the processes and products of both the primary and secondary iron production that occurred at these sites. The current study addresses similar issues of iron production and consumption during the Iron II–early Persian period (ca. 1000–425 BCE). However, the site under investigation in this

---

[1] The possible exception to this statement is McNutt's chapter entitled, "Biblical Symbols," which discusses portrayals of iron found in ancient texts from the Near East, mainly the Hebrew Bible, most of which was written during the Iron II–Persian periods.

study, Tell en-Naṣbeh, a settlement in the central highlands of Palestine, presents a special challenge. No actual evidence of iron production was excavated from the site; forcing the author to rely on other lines of evidence.

This study proposes the creation of a life-cycle for the iron agricultural implements from Tell en-Naṣbeh as a means of understanding their production, use, and abandonment. The life-cycle will be constructed in reverse; it will begin with the objects themselves and will then contextualize them within their find spots on site.[2] These find spots will illustrate various manifestations of either the abandonment or the use phase (depending on the context) of the objects. These manifestations may include storage, disposal, accidental loss, or a variety of other scenarios. Once the abandonment and use phases have been discussed the article will move to the production of the objects. The reconstruction of this life-cycle will provide a window through which scholars can understand iron production and aspects of the practice of agriculture at Tell en-Naṣbeh.[3]

This study ultimately addresses the issue of how to understand household agricultural practices at Tell en-Naṣbeh. By looking at the context of iron agricultural implements excavated from a rural site, dating to the Iron II–early Persian period, this study focuses on some of the issues that have been neglected in the previous studies of iron discussed above. By evaluating the procurement of raw materials, production processes, use, and abandonment of iron agricultural implements this article will show that such iron tools

---

[2] See below for details on the caveats associated with this approach at Tell en-Naṣbeh.

[3] While the approach implemented in this paper is my own, it was inspired by two approaches used by anthropologists and archaeologists to study "things" or "commodities." The first influence is I. Kopytoff's 1986 article in which he suggests approaching the study of commoditization by asking cultural questions of things, as one might in a more traditional ethnography of a person or group of people. The second influence is the well-known *chaîne-opératoire* approach to studying craft production and specialization. For a discussion of this approach see Dobres (1999); for an example of the approach's implementation as related to iron production see Bauvais and Fluzin (2009).

were relatively common and would have been accessible to most families living at Tell en-Naṣbeh. Second, the article will demonstrate that the distribution and context of the iron agricultural implements on site supports the inference that agricultural endeavors at Iron II–early Persian Tell en-Naṣbeh were conducted on a small-scale, household-based level.

IRON AT TELL EN-NAṢBEH

Tell en-Naṣbeh is located in the modern Palestinian West Bank, approximately 12 km north of Jerusalem; it is believed by many to be the ancient settlement of Mizpah of Benjamin (Zorn 2008). The site is a fortified town whose main occupation strata date to the Iron II–early Persian period (Strata 3–2). Aside from a monumental gate complex and fortification system, all of the excavated architecture at Tell en-Naṣbeh is domestic in nature, making the site an ideal place to investigate the daily practices associated with household contexts.

The site was excavated in five seasons between the years of 1926 and 1935 by William Frederic Badè. During these years Badè excavated approximately two thirds of the tell, an enormous portion by today's standards. Considering Badè's era, he conducted a highly scientific excavation. However, there are aspects of Badè's methodology that complicate any study of the site's associated materials. One such aspect is Badè's concept of stratigraphy and phasing. As was common in that era, rooms were excavated completely as one phase of occupation, from the tops of walls to floor levels, if such could be estimated from thresholds and the like, or to the base of the walls. Subtle changes in wall orientation or construction material that could indicate a change in phase or occupation were not often noted. Moreover, the precise find spots for specific objects within such room deposits were usually not recorded. On only rare occasions do the excavation notes or publications provide some details about the find spots of specific objects; for the most part it is impossible to completely understand the objects' relationships to each other, or to the surrounding architecture. For example, an object that was recorded as coming from Room X might have been found in situ on a surface in the room, but it also may have been found in a fill layer a meter (or more) above the surface. These methods of recovery and recording present the greatest challenge when one attempts to look at the objects associated with a specific architectural feature. Nonetheless, because Badè excavated such a large portion of the site we have a much more comprehensive sample of artifact types, which helps to balance the rapidity of excavation and early understanding of stratigraphy and deposition. Furthermore, the large amount of exposed architecture facilitates contextual studies of the excavated materials, painting a more complete picture of the distribution of a specific material or class of objects across the entirety of the site.

Ideally, when attempting an analysis based on context, one should have access to more information regarding the precise provenience of the objects under study. However, as noted above, this is not the case for the great majority of the excavated materials from Tell en-Naṣbeh. Despite the short-comings of the recorded information, Badè's published excavation manual does indicate that he excavated stratigraphically and that he differentiated between types of occupation layers.[4] Additionally, the manual indicates that he understood the basic concepts of taphonomy and primary refuse deposition.[5] Though this does not allow one to assume that any of the iron artifacts discussed in this study were found in contexts of primary deposition (save one example, discussed below), it does suggest that Badè's association of artifacts with specific architectural features might actually reflect either a primary or a secondary use context. It is equally possible that finds belonged to an up-

---

[4] "There is a widespread popular delusion, fostered by writers who have had little or no experience in the field, that the débris which an excavator undertakes to remove from the sites of Near East cities overlies them in even horizontal strata which can be peeled off like the layers of an onion. Since the sites are rarely level...the excavator has to account of complexities which arise out of this fact. There is stratification, but it is not of the simple kind imagined," (Badè 1934: 60).

[5] "The former type of deposit [occupational] accumulated slowly under foot while the inhabitants of a city were pursuing their customary peaceful activities. The breakage of pottery in such strata generally consists of small sherds, the discard of broken water-jars and other common ceramic utensils of daily life, trodden into the soil. The accumulation of occupational rubbish may still be observed in modern cities...The catastrophic [deposit] type is different, for it has resulted from sudden, not gradual, accumulation." (Badè 1934: 60–61).

per story of a building, or were part of a leveling fill. Considering these artifacts critically as parts of larger assemblages associated with a particular context is where we must begin, given the methods of excavation and recording we have inherited.

The iron from Tell en-Naṣbeh is one such class of material. When research on the current project began, well over a hundred iron objects were documented in Tell en-Naṣbeh's final report (McCown 1947: 255; pl. 96) and housed in the object storage room in Berkeley, though a total of 366 iron artifacts were recorded on the excavations millimeter cards from various contexts.[6] The artifacts used in this study were restricted to agricultural implements for three reasons: first, because there is a more manageable number of these artifacts ($n=22$); second, because these types of artifacts are relatively easy to recognize and have functions about which scholars are reasonably certain; third, because these objects fit appropriately into the context of daily life. The corpus was then further restricted to objects that were associated with architectural features, excluding tombs, which date to roughly the Iron II–early Persian period.[7] Lastly, it should be noted that this article deals only with the agricultural implements that could be physically located, either at the Badè Museum at Pacific School of Religion in Berkeley or at the Semitic Museum at Harvard University in Cambridge. There were a small number of instances where the excavation report mentions a sickle or plow point that could not be found in the museum storeroom and was therefore omitted from this study.[8]

The agricultural implements can be divided into two types of objects: plow points and sickles/blades. The plow points (Fig. 5.1) ($n=5$) would have been attached to a wooden shaft, part of a larger

---

[6] Many of these objects were whole or fragmented projectile points that likely served some kind of military function. Additionally, there was a small amount of iron jewelry, though most jewelry from the site was made of bronze.

[7] The architecture of Tell en-Naṣbeh was reinterpreted in a 1993 UC Berkeley dissertation by Jeffrey R. Zorn. The Iron II–early Persian periods correspond to Zorn's Strata 3 and 2.

[8] All of the iron pieces in this study have experienced varying degrees of corrosion. Additionally, because of the small sample size, statistical conclusions should be regarded as tenuous.

wooden plow framework, and used to gouge narrow furrows into the earth of a field prior to planting. The plow points from Tell en-Naṣbeh are relatively easy to identity. The objects range slightly in size, but appear to have a rather standardized form.

Fig. 5.1. Iron plow points from Tell en-Naṣbeh (Photograph by Stephanie Brown).

The five plow points range in length from 16.4 cm to 34.2 cm, with an average length of 21.3 cm and a median length of 19.0 cm. The width and depth of these objects reflect similar indications of standardization. The width and the depth of the plow points were measured at the areas at which the object appeared to be the widest and the deepest. For all five objects that was where a wooden shaft would have been inserted into the plow point. The width of the objects ranged from 2.5 cm to 6.9 cm with an average of 4.0 cm and a median width of 3.7 cm. The depth of the objects range from 2.4 cm to 7.0 cm with an average of 4.0 cm and a median depth of

3.7 cm. Another indication of proportional standardization is found in the width of each of the four objects, which is within a tenth of a centimeter from its respective depth, meaning that the spaces within which wooden shafts were inserted were almost perfect circles, except for the largest example for which the space formed an almost perfect square.

#	Object Type	New Object Number	Feature	Length (cm)	Width (cm)	Depth (cm)	Weight (g)
1	Plow point	N/A	Room 625A	34.2	6.9	7.0	1950
2	Plow point	B2011.1.161	Room 625A	17.9	3.7	3.7	218.1
3	Plow point	B2011.1.181	Room 625A	19.1	3.8	3.7	243.8
4	Plow point	B2011.1.182	Room 407	19.0	2.5	2.4	196.8
5	Plow point	B2011.1.162	Room 587	16.4	3.2	3.1	207.3

Table 5.1. Iron Plow Points from Tell en-Naṣbeh

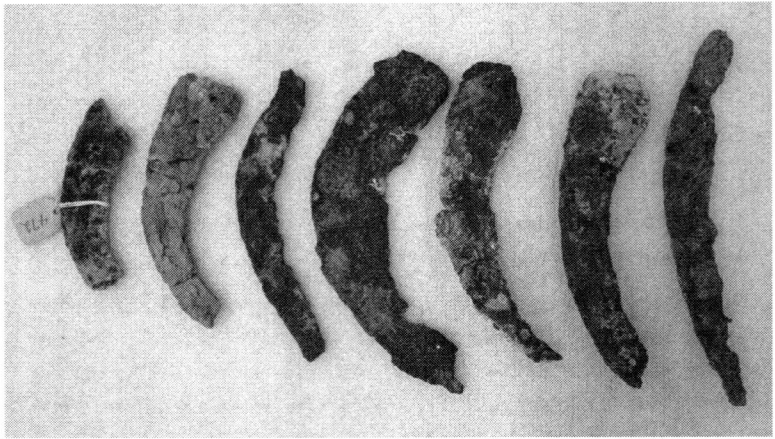

Fig. 5.2. Iron sickles from Tell en-Naṣbeh (Photograph by Stephanie Brown).

The sickles/blades were harder to identify. Some of the artifacts take a crescent shape (Fig. 5.2), which is traditionally associated with sickles, while other objects are a straighter shape (Fig. 5.3), and are usually identified as blades or on rare occasions daggers. The sickles and blades are grouped together for two reasons: first, because some of the objects are so fragmentary or corroded that their original shape is hard to determine; second, because both groups could have functioned as cutting or reaping implements. The sickle/blades make up the majority of the corpus ($n=14$).

Fig. 5.3. Iron blades from Tell en-Naṣbeh (Photograph by Stephanie Brown).

The crescent-shaped sickles ($n=9$) were almost certainly used as reaping implements, because similarly shaped metal objects are attested as reaping tools even to the present day. The sickles are not quite as standardized as the plow points, though they still seem to fall within a relatively consistent range.

At first glance, the sickles appear to be quite varied, aside from their crescent shape. For example the length of the sickles ranges from 8.6 cm to 23.5 cm. However, it must be noted that this discrepancy in size is due to the fact that some of the examples are not completely preserved. When considering the average and median measurements of both complete and fragmentary sickles a much greater degree of standardization is observable. The sickles from

Tell en-Naṣbeh have an average length of 16.2 cm and a median length of 16.4 cm. The width of the objects ranges from 2.0 cm to 4.1 cm with an average width of 3.1 cm and a median width of 3.1 cm. The closeness of the average measurement and the median measurement of these tools argues for a standard size of the Tell en-Naṣbeh sickles.

#	Object Type	New Object Number	Feature	Length (cm)	Width (cm)	Depth (cm)	Weight (g)
6	Sickle	B2011.1.183	Room 386	18.6	4.1	0.4	105.5
7	Sickle	B2011.1.170	Room 625A	16.4	3.6	0.9	68.1
8	Sickle	B2011.1.159	Sub-Room 430	16.1	2.4	0.3	40.9
9	Sickle	B2011.1.152	Room 297	20.1	2.5	0.6	48.5
10	Sickle	B2011.1.157	Room 467	13.9	3.5	1.0	104.6
11	Sickle	B2011.1.165	Room 625A	8.6	2.9	0.8	22.9
12	Sickle	B2011.1.166	Room 436	17.1	3.7	0.4	51.3
13	Sickle	B2011.1.172	Room 97	23.5	2.0	0.7	69.9
14	Sickle	B2011.1.173	Cistern 159	11.1	3.1	0.7	36.2

Table 5.2. Sickles from Tell en-Naṣbeh

The blades ($n=5$) are the least standardized of the three studied types of agricultural implements. Furthermore, it is difficult to determine the function of these blades. The blades could have been used as reaping or cutting implements in agricultural work, but they also could have served other functions, such as tools for food preparation, or as weapons. It is also likely that the shape of the blades would have varied related to the purpose(s) for which they were created. An analysis of these functional distinctions is beyond the scope of this project, so the author will simply refer to all of the blades in this study as agricultural implements. The blades range from 8.0 to 17.2 with an average length of 12.2 and a median length of 14.5. The width of the blades ranges from 1.5 to 2.3, with an average of 1.9 and a median width of 2.0. The numbers here might suggest standardization, because the shortest blade examples are not fragments of larger pieces (as was the case with the crescent-shaped sickles), but are complete objects. Therefore the large range of the blades' lengths is, in this case, a better representation of the corpus, than is the average or median length.

#	Object Type	New Object Number	Feature	Length (cm)	Width (cm)	Depth (cm)	Weight (g)
15	Blade	B2011.1.156	Room 328	8.6	2.0	0.8	24.3
16	Blade	B2011.1.158	Room 515	17.2	1.8	0.8	30.6
17	Blade	B2011.1.164	Room 363	14.5	2.0	0.5	34.6
18	Blade	B2011.1.175	Room 443	12.7	2.3	0.9	28.7
19	Blade	B2011.1.176	Room 463	8.0	1.5	1.1	10.5

Table 5.3. Blades from Tell en-Naṣbeh

#	Object Type	New Object Number	Feature	Length (cm)	Width (cm)	Depth (cm)	Weight (g)
20	Mattock	N/A	Room 476	17.6	4.5	4.0	650
21	Misc. Object	B2011.1.168	Cistern 176	14.3	4.0	2.1	86.0
22	Misc. Object	B2011.1.179	Room 409	11.3	3.6	1.4	75.2

Table 5.4. Miscellaneous Iron Objects from Tell en-Naṣbeh

Also included in this study are three miscellaneous objects that are thought to have served an agricultural purpose but which do not seem to be either plow points or sickle/blades (Fig. 5.4).

One of these objects appears to be a mattock or a pick axe that could have been used for either digging or chopping. The other two objects, #21 and #22, seem to be tools used for chiseling and scraping, respectively. Object #22 (Fig. 5.5) is very fragmentary, and its function is highly speculative, but it does have a sharp, curved edge. Object #21, perhaps an adze, has a sharp, slightly triangular end that could have been ideal for chiseling, but may have also served a scraping function.

Fig. 5.4. Photo of iron agricultural implements from McCown 1947: pl. 96. Objects 11 and 17 in this photo correspond to this study's Objects 21 and 20 respectively (Courtesy of Badè Museum of Biblical Archaeology, Pacific School of Religion).

Fig. 5.5. Object 22 (Photograph by Stephanie Brown).

THE MEANS OF PRODUCTION: CONTEXT AND SIGNIFICANCE

The agricultural implements are found across the site of Tell en-Naṣbeh in both Stratum 2 and 3. Though two of the artifacts were found in cisterns, most of them came from room contexts associated with domestic complexes (Fig. 5.6). Also, in all cases but one there is only one agricultural implement associated with each architectural feature.

The majority of the iron agricultural objects were found in the southwest quadrant of Tell en-Naṣbeh, where Iron Age remains were the most well-preserved and which was excavated in the 1935 season, when excavation and recording methods were most developed (McCown 1947: fig. 1; Fig. 5.7).[9]

---

[9] Zorn (1993) assigned the rooms to specific buildings and attempted to interpret the function of each architectural feature. Zorn's work reaffirmed the suggestion of the original excavators that Tell en-Naṣbeh lacked monumental architecture, and was made up primarily of domestic buildings. The buildings and architectural elements referenced henceforth in this article come from Zorn's reinterpretation of the site.

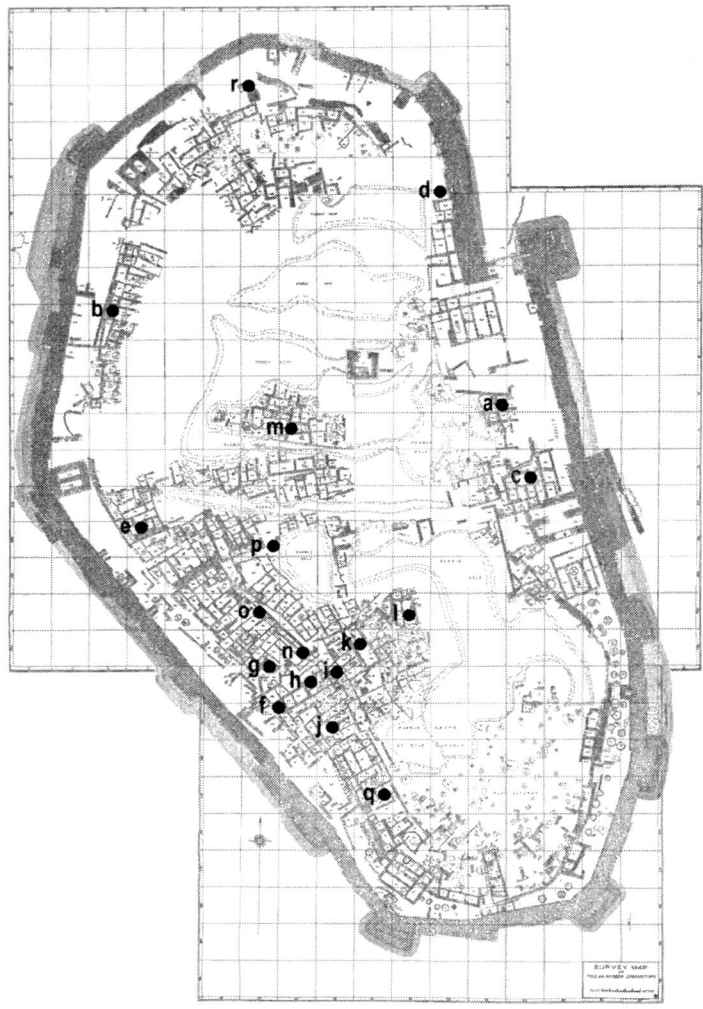

Fig. 5.6. Map of Tell en-Naṣbeh with iron agricultural implement find spots indicated: a = Rm 97, b = Rm 297, c = Rm
328, d = Rm 363, e = Rm 386, f = Rm 407, g = Rm 409, h =
Rm 430, i = Rm 436, j = Rm 443, k = Rm 463, l = Rm 467, m
= Rm 476, n = Rm 515, o = Rm 587, p = Rm 625A, q = Ci
159, r = Ci 176. Adapted from the 1:400 Tell en-Naṣbeh site
plan (Courtesy of Badè Museum of Biblical Archaeology, Pacific School of Religion).

Architectural Feature (Square Number) Code in Figs. 5.6–7	Stratum (Revised Dating)	Date (Original Dating)	Iron Agricultural Implements
Room 97 (X23) a	2 (586–425)	530–330	1 sickle
Room 297 (V13) b	3C–2 (1000–425)	600–450	1 sickle
Room 328 (Z24) c	1 (280–70 CE)	600–450	1 blade
Room 363 (R22) d	2 (586–425)	900–330?	1 blade
Room 386 (AB14) e	3C–3A? (1000–586?)	900–330	1 sickle
Room 407 (AG17) f	2?–1? (586?–70 CE?)	600–450	1 plow point
Room 409 (AE17) g	2?–1? (586?–70 CE?)	600–450	1 misc. object
Sub Room 430 (AF18) h	Below 3C–3A? (1000–586)	700–586	1 sickle
Room 436 (AF19) i	3C–3A (1000–586)	900–330	1 sickle
Room 443 (AG19) j	3C–3A (1000–586)	900–330	1 blade
Room 463 (AE20) k	2 (586–425)	600–450	1 blade
Room 467 (AD21) l	1 (280–70 CE)	699–500	1 sickle
Room 476 (Y18) m	2?–1? 586?–70 CE?	600–450?	1 mattock
Room 515 (AE18) n	3A–? (850–70 CE?)	900–330	1 blade
Room 587 (AD17) o	3C–2? (1000–425?)	650–550	1 plow point
Room 625A (AB17) p	3C–2? (1000–425?)	700–586	3 plow points and 2 sickles
Cistern 159 (AJ20) q	3C–2? (1000–425?)	750–586	1 sickle
Cistern 176 (N17) r	3B–3A? (900–586?)	750–650	1 misc. object

Stratum (Revised Dating) is from Zorn 1993: 1410–1645.
Date (Original Dating) is from McCown 1947: 2 and Wampler 1947: 120–125.
Dates are BCE unless otherwise noted.

Table 5.5. Architectural Features Associated with Iron Agricultural Implements

This area of the site has received a great deal of scholarly attention aimed at understanding the architecture, domestic life, and urban organization at Tell en-Naṣbeh (for example, McClellan 1984: 53–69; also Zorn's chapter on water use in this volume). The following contextual analysis of Tell en-Naṣbeh's iron agricultural implements will deal almost exclusively with material found in this area of the site.

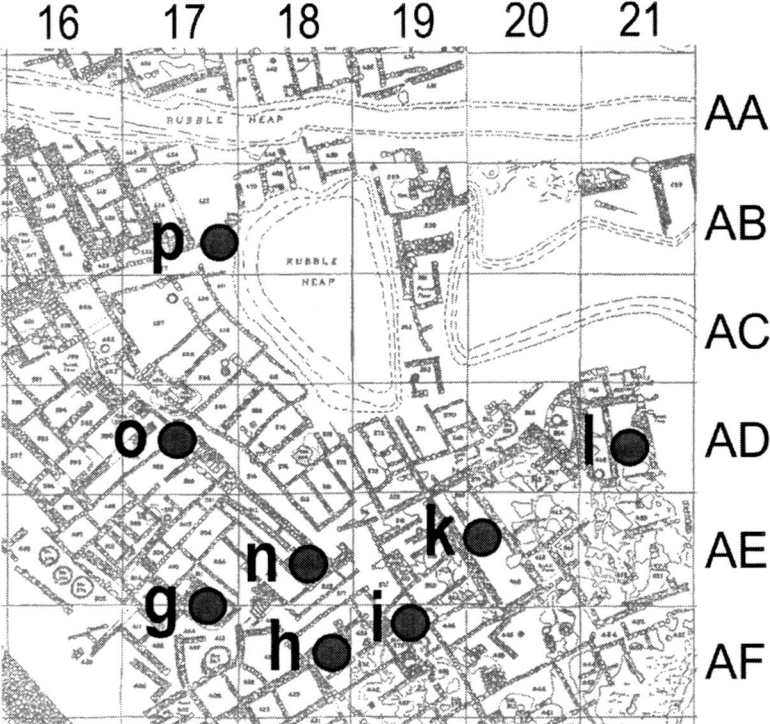

Fig. 5.7. View of southwest portion of Tell en-Naṣbeh: g = Rm 409, h = Rm 430, i = Rm 436, k = Rm 463, l = Rm 467, n = Rm 515, o = Rm 587, p = Rm 625A,. Adapted from the 1:400 Tell en-Naṣbeh site plan (Courtesy of Badè Museum of Biblical Archaeology, Pacific School of Religion).

The implements were found in diverse contexts. Most objects were found inside domestic buildings (of both the three- and four-room type) in rooms whose specific function is unknown, though one object was found in a long-room that was thought to have been used as a storage space (Zorn 1993: 788). Other objects were found outside of the buildings, in courtyards and in one instance in a road or alleyway. Since Tell en-Naṣbeh Stratum 3 was peacefully abandoned and the reason for the end of Stratum 2 is unclear, though given the handful of associated in situ deposits it seems to have involved some violence, it is difficult to determine which objects were found in the use phase of their life (since the objects would have technically been used off site in the fields, perhaps this phase would best indicate storage) and which were found in the abandonment phase.

Additionally, there appears to be no pattern to the other objects found along with the agricultural implements. Some of these objects include: various ceramic forms (including: typical table wear, incised handles, storage jars, lamps, and an incense burner), figurine fragments, basalt grinding stones and bowls, lithics and flint chips, bone spatulas, shells, beads, and small metal implements (including several iron spearheads). Despite the variety of finds, these objects do not argue for any specific function associated with most of the rooms. However, among all of the objects found at the site there was nothing that would argue for the interpretation of the contexts as anything other than domestic.

An exception is one specific room, Room 625A, part of Building 142.06, where a cache of five agricultural implements was found (Fig. 5.8; Zorn 1993: 659–61). This closet-like room is just off the southern end of large courtyard Room 625 and protrudes slightly into cross-road 627; it is adjacent to storage Bin 366. The rear of the building, where Room 654 is located, probably consisted of two small chambers. The building was east of four-room Building 142.05 and west of fragmentary three-room Building 142.07, with which it may have shared a doorway (Fig. 5.8; Zorn 1993: 656–59, 661–63, 1045). The building is similar in plan to Building 142.02 to the south which also has a large courtyard (Room 607) and rear chamber (Room 609; Fig. 5.7; Zorn 1993: 649–51). Two olive presses were found nearby in reuse in Stratum 2 walls that blocked the road system of Stratum 3. Possibly one of the presses was in use in Room 625 while the other was in use in Room 607. This may be additional evidence, in addition to the iron agricultural tools, that Building 142.06 had a role in agricultural processing.

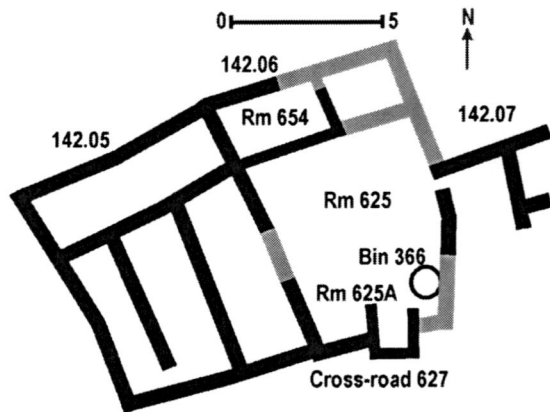

Fig. 5.8. Four-room house Building 142.05 and adjoining courtyard Building 142.06; Room 625a is where the cache of iron tools was found (Image courtesy of Jeffrey R. Zorn; adapted from the 1:100 Tell en-Naṣbeh site plan. Used with the permission of the Badè Museum of Biblical Archaeology, Pacific School of Religion).

The relatively large number of complete iron agricultural implements concentrated in this small room suggests that the implements were stored in this space in antiquity. Because these objects seem to be in situ this example may adequately represent the storage aspect of the use phase in the biography of these objects. This discovery should be seen in contrast to the objects found at the bottom of cisterns that would clearly seem to illustrate the disposal or abandonment phase of those objects.

In general, there are several assumptions that can be made about the use or consumption of the iron agricultural implements from Tell en-Naṣbeh. First, because these objects were found within the fortifications of the site we can assume that these objects held some degree of value for the inhabitants of Tell en-Naṣbeh. As agricultural implements these objects, especially the plow points and sickles, would have been used outside of the city walls where agricultural activities would have taken place. The fact that after the reaping or plowing was finished the items were brought back to the settlement, implies that the owners of these implements valued them enough to want to store them in a way that would preserve them for reuse in the future.

An additional conclusion can be drawn from the fact that the iron objects were sometimes found associated with stone tools that functioned as agricultural implements, such as flint blades. Because these objects are found intermingled it seems reasonable to assume that families were using both iron and stone technology. Though it is possible that some of these blades were in redeposition from the Early Bronze I levels at Tell en-Naṣbeh, the use of flint blades in the Iron Age is fairly common. Though earlier scholars assumed that the introduction of iron caused flint and copper tools and weapons to become obsolete (McCown 1947: 62), more recent studies have shown that stone tools were used in the Levant well into the Ottoman period (Rosen 1997: 13).

The excavation report from Tell en-Naṣbeh also discusses, albeit briefly, the stone assemblages from the site, reporting that, "In many regards Hebrew Palestine was still in the stone age ... the vast number of stone implements is astonishing until one remembers that stone was the one material of which there was an unlimited abundance and that it required little skill, though great patience, to manufacture such articles as are found," (McCown 1947: 249). Though McCown may have been oversimplifying the issue, he does bring up the valid point that the creation of a stone tool requires only suitable stone and the knowledge and experience of the craftsperson. This should be seen in marked contrast to the amount of materials and labor needed to produce a metal tool (see below).

Lastly, the distribution of the implements throughout the site of Tell en-Naṣbeh may support the notion that agricultural endeavors at Iron II–early Persian Tell en-Naṣbeh were conducted on a household-based level. In the large area excavated there are no monumental architectural features, such as a large granary, that would suggest large-scale, state-sponsored agricultural activities were taking place at the site. That such agricultural products were, however, collected for the benefit of the state is attested by the eighty-six examples of the much discussed *lmlk* jars found in Stratum 3 at the site of Tell en-Naṣbeh, the fifth largest collection of these inscriptions from any site in Judah (Vaughn 1999: 190). Though their precise function is debated, these large, standardized storage jars that bore the *lmlk* ("to/of the king") inscription do seem to link some stored agricultural products at the site with the Judean state. The stone-lined storage bins in the southern intramural zone may be another indicator of the state's interest in the agricultural products of Tell en-Naṣbeh (Zorn 1993: 251–57).

As mentioned earlier, the iron agricultural implements were found across the site, and with the exception of the small hoard in Room 625A they were typically found as solitary examples within a context. Because the agricultural implements were found scattered across the site in both three- and four-room domestic dwellings, these implements do not seem to be an indication of their owners' socio-economic status. Therefore the contextual evidence seems to indicate that the iron objects were themselves common enough that individual families could possess them to aid in their agricultural enterprises.

Was the Production of Iron a Specialized Craft?

When considering the biography of a particular corpus of objects it is important to address these objects' production in order to understand the variety of decisions made by the producers that would have affected the consumption of the objects. Each step in the *chaîne-opératoire* ultimately influences the final product, in this case the iron agricultural implements from Tell en-Naṣbeh. Therefore, the sourcing of raw materials and the degree of specialization required to produce the finished product are directly related to the distribution, availability, and affordability of these objects.

Cathy Costin defines specialization as "differential participation in specific economic activities," and explains several methods in which craft specialization can manifest itself in the archaeological record (1991: 43). Several of these methods involve evidence of production on site, but she suggests that specialization can also be observed by examining the products of specialized production systems. She claims that these objects will exhibit one or more of the following features: standardization, efficiency, skill, or regional variation (1991: 44).

When thinking about the production of iron one must first consider what natural sources are available for the extraction of iron ore. Iron is the fourth most abundant element in the earth's crust, and deposits of iron ore exist widely across the Near East, especially in Anatolia and North Syria. The southern Levant however, is relatively poor in rich iron ore, despite the claim made by the biblical author who describes the southern Levant as, "a land whose stones are iron, and out of whose hills you can dig copper," (Deut. 8:9). The only recognized major iron ore deposit in the southern Levant is in the Ajlun hills north of Amman in modern Jordan, where large heaps of iron slag have been reported (McNutt 1990: 115). Poorer quality ores are more prolific in the southern Levant and have been reported at places such as the Wadi es-Sabrah, south of Petra, southwest of the Dead Sea, around the Galilee, along the Wadi Araba, and in other small deposits in Jordan and Lebanon (Waldbaum 1978: 59).

Aside from these larger sources of iron ore, iron is also often found on the earth's surface. Surface iron may have been more accessible because it does not necessarily require mining. Finding evidence of iron exploitation of any type, however, is a difficult task for two primary reasons. First, the mining of iron sources over a long period of time obscures, if not destroys earlier evidence; second, the exploitation of iron sources on the earth's surface is simply difficult to identify (McNutt 1990: 116). McNutt interestingly suggests that the quote from Deut. 8:9 might suggest that the ancient inhabitants of the southern Levant used surface sources of iron. She suggests that the reference to Palestine's "stones of iron" should be seen in contrast to the "hills from which copper can be dug," because digging copper from hills requires an extensive mining operation while the exploitation of iron may have only required the utilization of the surface deposits (McNutt 1990: 116).

Based on the reported sources of iron ore it seems that iron would have been relatively accessible to the Iron Age inhabitants of the southern Levant. However, it is the act of separating the iron from the ore in the smelting process that presents perhaps the greatest challenge in iron manufacturing. The first difficulty in the process is the procurement of enough charcoal to fuel the smelting process. The heat needed to produce a workable iron substance is 1150–1350 degrees Celsius, compared to the temperature at which copper melts, 1083 degrees Celsius. If the temperature of the furnace does not reach the necessary temperature, the result is a mass that cannot be forged into an object. The second challenge in iron smelting is that the high temperature, 1150–1350 degrees Celsius, must be maintained so that the smelter simultaneously permits enough air to pass through the smelting area, while enough carbon monoxide is produced to achieve the reduction of iron ore to iron (McNutt 1990: 112).

Because the melting point of iron is about 1537 degrees Celsius (a temperature that could not be achieved during the Iron Age) iron objects could not be melted and cast, like bronze, copper, silver, or gold. However, when the reduction of iron from the iron ores occurred at a high enough temperature, the result was a spongy mass, called a bloom, which could then be hammered and forged into wrought iron. The bloom itself was not made up of pure iron, but was rather mixed with impurities, such as slag and charcoal. The bloom would therefore have to be broken apart in order to extract the iron desired for the production of iron objects (McNutt 1990: 112–13).

Lastly, there is the skill required to craft the iron into the finished product, in this case, plow points, sickles, and blades. This process involves reheating the iron, and working it into its final form, and then quenching it in cold water. There are two main properties involved with working iron that are unique from working other metals, such as bronze or silver. The first is that iron can be reheated and reworked at any point during its use life. For example, any piece of iron can be heated and hammered to another piece and the two will weld together. This property was advantageous since it made recycling the material relatively easy, as long as someone skilled in the above-described iron manufacturing processes was available to do the work (Bauvais and Fluzin 2009: 172). The second property is that, as mentioned above, iron could not be melted and cast in antiquity. Therefore, molds could not be used to produce iron objects, and so each piece had to be forged individually.

By the late Iron II period iron was the preferred metal for the manufacture of agricultural implements because it had the potential to be superior to bronze in its strength and toughness, forgeability, hardness, and hardenability (Moorey 1999: 283). However, these attributes are only achieved when the iron object is worked under the right conditions. For example, if the iron is allowed to cool normally after forging, rather than being quenched in cold water, the worked iron is no stronger than work-hardened bronze.

The manufacturing of iron objects required a great amount of skill and knowledge, and as described above every detail of the production process had a direct influence on the finished product, and whether or not that product would be capable of performing the task for which it was fashioned. By considering the skill required to produce the iron objects found at Tell en-Naṣbeh, as well as their relative standardization, it can therefore be surmised that the production of iron was indeed a specialized craft.

PRODUCTION OF THE IRON OBJECTS FROM TELL EN-NAṢBEH

There is little that can be said definitively about the production of the iron agricultural implements found at Tell en-Naṣbeh. In terms of the source(s) of the iron ore used to make the agricultural implements, it seems likely that the individuals who collected the iron ore for the Tell en-Naṣbeh's implements would have exploited regional sources of iron, rather than importing the ore from Anatolia or North Syria. Unfortunately, since iron is a metal on which source testing is not very effective or reliable, this suggestion remains speculative. It is also possible, as mentioned above, that iron was often recycled. The reusability of iron would likely decrease the amount of raw materials that would need to be imported in order to fabricate new products. Using local ore, and manufacturing the finished iron products somewhere in the region around the site, would have most likely made the iron agricultural implements less expensive, and therefore more accessible to the inhabitants of Tell en-Naṣbeh. This hypothesis seems to be supported by the distribution and contexts of these somewhat common iron agricultural implements across the site, which indicates that they were available to both large and small households. This distribution pattern is the classic hallmark of a marketing economy (Brody, this volume).

Tell en-Naṣbeh's excavation report states that although three ceramic kilns were found at Tell en-Naṣbeh no evidence of smelting, such as a furnace or slag, was found on site (McCown 1947: 62, 258). That may not be surprising when one considers the potential hazards inherent in the smelting process. It is possible that if the actual working of iron ore did occur at Tell en-Naṣbeh, it would have taken place outside the city walls, where the fires necessary to reach the extreme temperatures for smelting would pose less risk to Tell en-Naṣbeh's homes and inhabitants. However, it is also possible that the smelting process occurred closer to the location of the raw iron ore. Such was certainly the case with the contemporary copper smelting well-known from the Faynan region of southern Jordan (Ben-Yosef et al. 2010). In such a scenario, the iron could have been separated from the ore, prior to its transport to a secondary processing, or smithing, facility, reducing the resources necessary to transport the iron.

With regard to the actual forging of the iron agricultural implements, this was likely conducted either at the site, or at a nearby site. Since the natural resources were likely available in the southern Levant there would have been no need to import finished objects from far distances; this would have kept the objects affordable. It does seem, however, that if there had been a metal workshop on-site it would have been obvious to the excavators, who would have at least made note of the unusual amount of finished and unfinished metal objects coming from one, specific area. It is again possible that the working of the metal objects, like the smelting, may have taken place just off of the tell. However, the evidence of a ninth century iron workshop from Tell Beth-Shemesh, suggests that secondary working, or smithing, of iron artifacts did occur within city walls (Bunimovitz and Lederman 2012: 103–12).

The possible role that Jerusalem may have played in the production and distribution of Tell en-Naṣbeh's iron agricultural implements should certainly be considered. As mentioned above, Tell en-Naṣbeh was located only twelve kilometers from Jerusalem, which was an important cultural center during the Iron Age II and early Persian periods. Various biblical passages attest to their authors'/editors' familiarity with aspects of metal working (Isa. 44:12; Jer. 6: 28–30, 28:13; Ezek. 22:17–22; Prov. 27:21); since these authors were likely associated with Jerusalem this may be additional evidence for Jerusalem as a metal working center. It is perhaps likely then that Tell en-Naṣbeh's iron agricultural implements were finished in Jerusalem and then distributed to neighboring sites. The lack of evidence for production at Tell en-Naṣbeh seems to support this scenario.

Considering the relative standardization in shape and size of the plow points and the sickles it seems likely that these objects were being produced by a person, or group of people, who at the very least shared the same set of ideas about what made a proper sickle or plow point. There was certainly a demand for the objects at Tell en-Naṣbeh, but whether these objects were produced at the site or were imported from other sites is unknowable from these data. A future study of the iron agricultural implements from neighboring or even regional sites might prove a better way to address this question.

CONCLUSION

The number and distribution of iron agricultural implements at Tell en-Naṣbeh examined in this study suggest two things. The first is that these were reasonably common objects that would have been accessible to individual farmers or families; the second is that there was a real demand for such agricultural implements.[10] In addition, the technique and knowledge necessary to work the iron objects, along with their relative standardization, establish that the production of the iron agricultural implements found at Tell en-Naṣbeh was a specialized craft. Lastly, the common nature, relative standardization, availability and affordability of these objects imply that the objects were produced relatively near the site perhaps from local sources of iron ore, and not imported from far distances such as Anatolia or North Syria.

Additionally, the numerous domestic contexts in which these objects were found suggest that agricultural practices in the Iron II–early Persian periods at Tell en-Naṣbeh happened at the household level. Even though the primary context of many of the objects could not be determined from the available data, the lack of a palace or other monumental architecture at Tell en-Naṣbeh supports the claims that it was the average inhabitants of Tell en-Naṣbeh who kept the tools necessary to work the land, and therefore likely worked the land themselves. While other forms of craft, for example bone tool manufacture (Maeir et al. 2009: 57) and even the iron working that created the agricultural implements examined in this study, show evidence of centralization and specialization in the southern Levant during the Iron II–early Persian period, agricultural work seemed to remain the work of the household.

---

[10] This is further supported by the large number of iron objects (over 360 total) found scattered across the site that could not be studied here.

REFERENCES

Badè, W. F.
1934 *A Manual of Excavation in the Near East: Methods of Digging and Recording of the Tell en-Nasbeh Expedition in Palestine.* Berkeley, CA: University of California.

Bauvais, S., and Fluzin, P.
2009 Archaeological and Archaeometrical Approaches of the *chaîne-opératoire* in Iron and Steelmaking: Methodology for a Regional Evolutionary Study. Pp. 159–80 in *Techniques and People: Anthropological Perspectives on Technology in the Archaeology of the Proto-Historic and Early Historic Periods in the Southern Levant*, ed. S. A. Rosen and V. Roux. Mémoires et Travaux du Centre de Recherche Français à Jérusalem, Archéologie et Sciences de l'Antiquité et du Moyen Âge 9. Paris: De Boccard.

Ben-Yosef, E.; Levy, T. E.; Higham, T.; Najjar, M.; and Tauxe, L.
2010 The Beginning of Iron Age Copper Production in the Southern Levant: New Evidence from Khirbat al-Jariya, Faynan, Jordan. *Antiquity* 84 (325): 724–46.

Bunimovitz, S., and Lederman, Z.
2012 Iron Age Iron: From Invention to Innovation. Pp. 103–12 in *Studies in Mediterranean Archaeology: Fifty Years On*, ed. J. M. Webb and D. Frankel. Studies in Mediterranean Archaeology 137. Uppsala: Åströms Förlag.

Costin, C. L.
1991 Craft Specialization: Issues in Defining, Documenting, and Explaining the Organization of Production. *Archaeological Method and Theory* 3: 1–56.

Dobres, M. A.
1999 Technology's Links and *Chaînes:* The Processual Unfolding of Technique and Technician. Pp. 124–46 in *The Social Dynamics of Technology: Practice, Politics, and World Views*, ed. M. A. Dobres and C. R. Hoffman. Washington, D.C.: Smithsonian Institute.

Kopytoff, I.
1986   The Cultural Biography of Things: Commoditization as Process. Pp. 64–91 in *The Social Life of Things: Commodities in Cultural Perspective*, ed. A. Appadurai. Cambridge: Cambridge University.

Maeir, A. M.; Greenfield, H. J.; Lev-Tov, J.; and Horwitz, L. K.
2009   Macro- and Microscopic Aspects of Bone Tool Manufacture and Technology in the Levantine Iron Age: A 9th Century BCE Workshop from Tell es-Safi/Gath, Israel. Pp. 41–68 in *Techniques and People: Anthropological Perspectives on Technology in the Archaeology of the Proto-Historic and Early Historic Periods in the Southern Levant*, ed. S. A. Rosen and V. Roux. Mémoires et Travaux du Centre de Recherche Français à Jérusalem, Archéologie et Sciences de l'Antiquité et du Moyen Âge 9. Paris: De Boccard.

McClellan, T. L.
1984   Town Planning at Tell en-Naṣbeh. *Zeitschrift des Deutschen Palästina-Vereins* 100: 53–69.

McCown, C. C.
1947   *Tell en-Naṣbeh*, Vol. 1: *Archaeological and Historical Results*. Berkeley, CA: Palestine Institute of Pacific School of Religion.

McNutt, P. M.
1990   *The Forging of Israel: Iron Technology, Symbolism and Tradition in Ancient Society*. The Social World of Biblical Antiquity Series 8. Journal for the Study of the Old Testament: Supplement Series 108. Sheffield: Almond.

Moorey, P. R. S.
1999   *Ancient Mesopotamian Materials and Industries: The Archaeological Evidence*. Winona Lake, IN: Eisenbrauns.

Rosen, S. A.
1997   *Lithics After the Stone Age: A Handbook of Stone Tools from the Levant*. Walnut Creek, CA: AltaMira.

Vaughn, A. G.
1999   *Theology, History, and Archaeology in the Chronicler's Account of Hezekiah.* Archaeology and Biblical Studies 4. Atlanta, GA: Scholars.

Veldhuijzen, X., and van der Steen, E.
1999   Iron Production Center Found in the Jordan Valley. *Near Eastern Archaeology* 62: 195–99.

Waldbaum, J. C.
1978   *From Bronze to Iron: The Transition from the Bronze Age to the Iron Age in the Eastern Mediterranean.* Studies in Mediterranean Archaeology 54. Göteborg: Paul Åströms Förlag.

Wampler, J. C.
1947   *Tell en-Naṣbeh,* Vol. 2: *The Pottery.* Berkeley, CA: Palestine Institute of Pacific School of Religion.

Wertime, T. A., and Muhly, J. D. ed.
1980   *The Coming of the Age of Iron.* New Haven: Yale University.

Zorn, J. R.
1993   Tell en Naṣbeh: A Re-evaluation of the Architecture and Stratigraphy of the Early Bronze Age, Iron Age and Later Periods. Ph.D. dissertation, University of California, Berkeley.
2008   "Mizpah, Mizpah Wherefore Art Thou Mizpah?" Tell en–Naṣbeh, Nebi Samwil and the Identification of a Biblical Site, *BAR Web Extra.* http://www.bib-arch.org/bar/extra .asp?ArticleID=12&ParentArticleID=3.

CURATING BADÈ'S LEGACY: MANAGEMENT OF THE TELL EN-NAṢBEH COLLECTION

CATHERINE P. FOSTER
ANCIENT MIDDLE EAST EDUCATION AND RESEARCH INSTITUTE

ABSTRACT

Documentation, care, and study of the archaeological objects, excavation records, and photographic archive from Tell en-Naṣbeh have been primary goals of the Badè Museum of Biblical Archaeology since its establishment at Pacific School of Religion in 1928 (originally the Palestine Institute). This chapter details more recent initiatives by museum staff to ensure the continued preservation and use of this important collection. The results provide an example of economical solutions to management of small- to mid-sized collections while also increasing outreach to the academic community and interested public, and, perhaps most importantly, continuing the preservation of the Tell en-Naṣbeh artifacts and excavation records for future generations.

FROM FIELD TO MUSEUM

This volume is a perfect example of the breadth and depth of research that is still possible for an archaeological collection formed over 85 years ago. It is testament not only to the resilience of the archaeological objects themselves, but also to Dr. William Frederic Badè and his team, whose care and precision in the excavating, recording, and initial curating of this material has allowed for continuing research, often employing the most modern scientific tech-

123

niques, to generate complex studies of the caliber contained in these pages. Badè's enduring legacy is the continuing capacity of Tell en-Naṣbeh to stimulate and excite both scholars and the public through the Badè Museum of Biblical Archaeology ("Badè Museum") on the campus of Pacific School of Religion in Berkeley, California.[1]

Other contributors to this volume have offered studies on water systems, human diet in Iron Age Judah, burial practices in the Roman Period, and more, based on reevaluations of materials from the site. In this chapter I instead relate a different story—a twenty-first century CE story—about the management of the Tell en-Naṣbeh collection, which includes excavated objects, artifact drawings, site plans, photographic prints and negatives, slides, film reels, field books and other documentation. This important collection of artifacts from ancient Israel is one of only a few in North America—the University of Chicago, Harvard University, and the University of Pennsylvania are other examples—and stands as the largest collection of this type west of the Mississippi River. Recent initiatives by museum staff to ensure the continued preservation and use of this unique collection include preventive conservation in the object and archive storage, formal accessioning and cataloging in a digital inventory system, and dissemination of the digitized collection via an open access database. The significance of these efforts is three-fold: 1) increased outreach to the academic community and interested public, 2) use as an example of economical solutions to the management of small- to mid-sized collections and 3) perhaps most important, preservation of the Tell en-Naṣbeh artifacts and excavation records for future generations.

The journey of the Tell en-Naṣbeh collection from field to museum is steeped in the historical narrative of the earliest formal archaeological explorations in Southwest Asia following World War I. During the early years of the twentieth century the British Mandatory government enacted several laws regarding cultural heritage in Palestine, including the 1918 Antiquities Proclamation that es-

---

[1] Formerly the Palestine Institute (established in 1928) and later Badè Institute of Biblical Archaeology. For a thorough treatment of the history of the Institute and Dr. Badè, see Zorn 1988a and 1988b.

tablished a Department of Antiquities ("DOA"), and the 1920 Antiquities Ordinance that vested ownership of moveable and immovable cultural heritage in the Civil Government of Palestine (Garstang 1922; Kersel 2008, 2010). The DOA and its archaeological advisory board were responsible for the protection and preservation of cultural heritage in Palestine, and the issuance of permits for archaeological excavations and licenses for the trade in antiquities. It was in the context of this system that Dr. Badè obtained a license from the DOA that allowed him to excavate at Tell en-Naṣbeh between 1926 and 1935. As a common practice in the region at the time, and as stipulated by law,[2] the antiquities discovered in the course of each year's excavation season were divided between the project director and the DOA. Dr. Badè was then granted a license to export his share of finds, along with his meticulous records, back to the Port of Oakland, and then on to Pacific School of Religion.[3]

Larger objects were shipped in wooden packing crates filled with straw to cushion against the bumps of transport (Fig. 6.1). Smaller items like jewelry, bronze pins, and Roman glass juglets, were nested in soft cotton batting or thin tissue paper and then stored in smaller brown cardboard boxes. Like today's excavators, Dr. Badè and his team were quite resourceful and often used whatever materials were on hand. The prevalent empty cigarette boxes left over from his workmen served as prime repositories for tiny stone beads and gold earrings. These boxes and crates (with the addition of a few others garnered on an ad-hoc basis) would protect the artifacts from Tell en-Naṣbeh for the next 75 years, until

---

[2] Previously mentioned legislation as well as Antiquities Ordinance No. 51 of 1929, § 3, art. 8(c).

[3] As was also common practice for the time, portions of the excavator's share would be given to any sponsoring organizations. For its financial support of the Tell en-Naṣbeh expeditions, the Nelson-Atkins Museum of Art (formerly William Rockhill Nelson Gallery of Art) in Kansas City, MO received 327 objects. Other institutional donors who did not receive objects include the City Commons Club (Berkeley, CA) and First Congregational Church (Winchester, MA).

museum staff undertook a preventive conservation project to re-house the collection.

Fig. 6.1. Outside the excavation house local workmen pack ar-tifacts into crates for shipment to Berkeley, CA. Badè Museum photograph #108 (Courtesy of Badè Museum of Biblical Ar-chaeology, Pacific School of Religion).

When Dr. Badè's share of the finds from the Tell en-Naṣbeh exca-vations reached Berkeley, they were stored temporarily in the attic of the main building (Holbrook Hall) of Pacific School of Religion. In 1941, with funding from Badè's widow Elizabeth and friends, a wing was added to the west side of Holbrook Hall to accommodate the newly acquired collection.[4] With the museum came display cas-es and an exhibit gallery, along with offices, laboratory space, and collections storage for most of the objects (Fig. 6.2). It was not until the 1980s, however, that the entire collection totaling nearly

---

[4] Sadly Dr. Badè died in 1936 and was unable to see the completion of this wing or the formal establishment of the Institute that bears his name.

6,000 objects was finally centralized in its current secure location in the east wing of Holbrook Hall in the seminary's former library.

Fig. 6.2. Interior view of the Badè Museum in its original location on the northwest side of Holbrook Hall, circa 1940's. Badè Museum photograph #1561 (Courtesy of Badè Museum of Biblical Archaeology, Pacific School of Religion).

MANAGING THE COLLECTION

Between 2003 and 2006, an incremental preventive conservation program was undertaken in the primary storage area with the result that objects from Tell en-Naṣbeh now represent a modern categorized and stored collection (Caple 2011). Due to budgetary constraints—namely a smaller than $3000 a year operating budget—a massive one-time renovation was not possible. Thus after a preliminary assessment (Avrami et al. 1999; Wolf Green 1990), the goal instead was to utilize extant assets and gradually create discrete microenvironments to ensure the continued preservation of the collection. The storage area already benefitted from its basement location where a single, small, north-facing window is both secured with bars and lets in little to no light. The double-sided sliding metal shelving and open metal cupboards—remnants of the former library—are ideal for object storage as metal, unlike wood or plastics, does not outgas. The mild northern California climate also ensures the dark storage room maintains a stable relative humidity throughout the year, though the occasional water seepage causes problems that can be alleviated with the use of the installed dehumidifier.

Fig. 6.3. Preventive conservation interventions in the storage area include upgraded drawer liners and inert foam and shaped paper object supports (Courtesy of Badè Museum of Biblical Archaeology, Pacific School of Religion).

To begin, the old padded shelf liners comprised of cotton batting, which was attractive to pests, especially rodents, were replaced with white quarter-inch-thick closed cell polyethylene foam sheets (Ethafoam) that serve as an inert, padded barrier between the metal shelves and the objects (Fig. 6.3). Artifacts are further protected with new shaped supports using both inert foam and tissue paper that prevent tipping of larger ceramics, or damage to fragile items, that could result from vibrations of the sliding shelves. The entire collection was lifted above the floor surface to avoid the risk of flood damage, and all shelving units were covered with plastic sheeting to protect the objects from water and dust. Objects that had remained in temporary or overflow storage areas throughout the museum were also moved to fully consolidate the Tell en-Naṣbeh collection in the primary storage area. Finally, objects of similar type were arranged to be stored together in numbered and labeled locations (room, row, shelf).

The boxes originally used to house artifacts at the excavation—artifacts now in their own right[5]—were replaced with short lid boxes made of acid-free and lignin-free boxboard with reinforced corners. Boxing objects, instead of simply storing them on open shelving, accomplishes three goals. It reduces handling of and physical damage to the objects; reduces the accessibility to the objects by pests; and insulates the objects against temperature or humidity changes. In essence, the practice increases environmental protection by building barriers or "envelopes" between the object and the outside conditions, whether in the exhibition hall (cases), storage area (boxes), or shipping crate (padding) (Cassar 1995).

Preventive conservation was not reserved for the archaeological objects alone. The photographic archive received the same treatment with fresh archival sleeves and acid-free paper separating print from negative. Two reels of silent excavation footage filmed by George Hedley and James Philmore Collins during the 1926 and 1935 seasons also received digital preservation. While the physical reels remain to be conserved, early conversion by museum staff of the film into video home system (VHS) cassette format allowed the further conversion into digital video formats like DVD and mp4. A compilation of the two films is now available on display in the gallery, on the museum website, and on the video sharing website Vimeo.[6]

Another large part of curating the Tell en-Naṣbeh collection involves creating an accurate catalog integrated within a digital in-

---

[5] These boxes were marked with labels and notes representing yet another type of field record. They were also imbued with their own history and offered a window into the British Mandate Period. The 2005 Badè Museum exhibit *Artifacts Holding Artifacts* explored the development of Palestinian tobacco production and entrepreneurship after the fall of the Ottoman Empire through the cigarette and match boxes used to hold small excavated objects from Tell en-Naṣbeh.

[6] http://vimeo.com/7745103 (Accessed June 9, 2013).

ventory system. The collections management software PastPerfect is affordable, and provides a robust and flexible relational database. The structure of the digital inventory within this database is built on a hierarchical classification system. The top tier consists of material classes followed by sub–categories of object types in that material class, then object names that adhere to an established naming convention. For example: ceramic (material), vessel (object type), jug (object name). This naming convention is based on the Getty Research Institute's Art and Architecture Thesaurus ("AAT")—an internationally recognized and authoritative tool—to ensure data value standards are in place for uniform organization and reliable retrieval of information by staff, and by outside researchers and the general public through the museum's Web initiatives. A standardized lexicon that adheres to archaeological conventions—for example, ceramic typologies and attributes—is also used throughout the inventory to ensure accuracy and consistency across database users. Other aspects of the content management system, like preset menus for condition assessments and maintenance schedules, are also useful in reaching the museum's goal of a robust and comprehensive catalog.

This goal is further realized through a modern numbering system. Two distinct object numbering systems using museum numbers and/or provenience information (e.g. the artifact designated "Tomb 32 x245" also has the museum number 2150) had been originally applied to all excavated objects. As part of the current digital inventorying initiative, a modern uniform system was implemented using a standard three-part registration number that stipulates an accession year, accession number, and object number (e.g., B2009.1.9). Modern registry of objects not only helps to better organize the collection, it also provides an inventory in case of theft or damage, and facilitates consistent and periodic condition assessments and tracking of objects.

From a practical research and documentation perspective, a comprehensive digital catalog also enables the centralization of information about Tell en-Naṣbeh drawn from a myriad of separate sources. Until now the excavation final reports (McCown 1947, Wampler 1947) and subsequent studies (McClellan 1984, Zorn 1993) served as the primary means of accessing comprehensive, though synthesized, archaeological evidence from Tell en-Naṣbeh. The final reports, however, are neither widely circulated nor user-friendly. [7] For example, a researcher would be unable to compile a list of all the objects found in a single context, or list all the find spots for a ceramic type from the reports alone. The final publications also necessarily lack primary documentary evidence from the excavation itself. The digital catalog remedies this situation by including all information related to objects in the collection drawn from field notes, the handwritten object ledger, object registry cards on millimeter paper, as well as the final publications and extensive preliminary and thematic reports. To these metadata are added new digital photographs of objects and high resolution scans of original object registries and photographic prints, the products of which can be easily stored in the digital catalog and cross-referenced. The result is a relational, searchable database capable of linking all materials in the collection including artifacts, photographs, and archival notes that together constitute the socio-cultural history of the excavation project as well as ancient Mizpah.

To accomplish the wider dissemination of the catalog, the museum has teamed with the Alexandria Archive Institute, the creator and manager of the Open Context system, a free open access digital resource for the Web publication of archaeological research data, to include the Tell en-Naṣbeh collection as one of its 29 hosted projects (Fig. 6.4; Brody 2010, Kansa and Kansa 2007, 2011). Currently there are 188 items/objects in the online catalog that have been viewed a total of nearly 25,000 times between 2010 and 2013; 500 additional items are expected to be added soon with the ultimate goal of having the entire collection on Open Context. Faceted browsing by date, context, or object type makes exploring the collection easy for researchers and casual users alike. A project editorial review system and stable web uniform resource identifier (URI) for each individual item also guarantees a robust dataset that scholars can be confident using and citing. All accompanying metadata and high resolution images are licensed under a Creative

---

[7] With the exception of Jeffrey R. Zorn's work, which is openly accessible through his research website: http://www.arts.cornell.edu/jrz3 (Accessed June 1, 2013).

Commons Attribution 3.0 license,[8] which means anyone is free to share or adapt the work, provided proper attribution is given.

One example of such sharing is the reuse of Tell en-Naṣbeh object images on Wikimedia Commons, a media file repository making available public domain and freely-licensed educational media content. Also with the use of data value standards for cataloging through the AAT, the collection can be cross-referenced with other digital datasets.

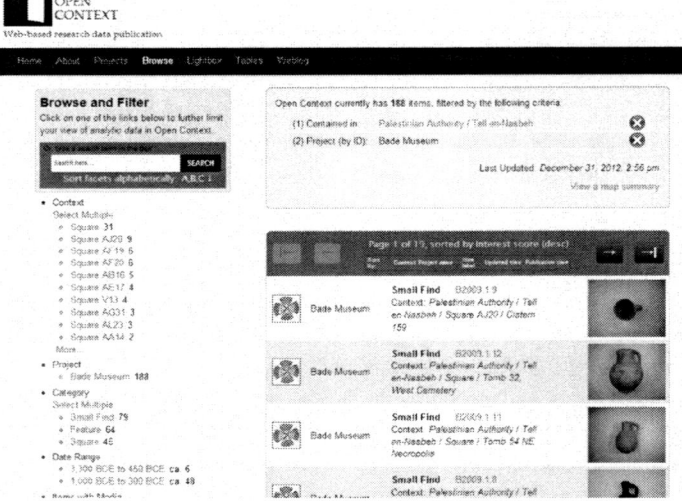

Fig. 6.4. The Tell en-Naṣbeh digital catalog on Open Context.

Along with Open Context, the museum also partnered with the Cuneiform Digital Library Initiative ("CDLI") at the University of California, Los Angeles to make more widely accessible one of the more distinct artifacts in the Tell en-Naṣbeh collection: a bronze circlet inscribed with an Akkadian dedication that attests to a Neo-Babylonian presence at Mizpah sometime between the eighth and sixth centuries BCE (Vanderhooft and Horowitz 2002). Through CDLI's online database, high-resolution images of the circlet, along

---

[8] http://creativecommons.org/licenses/by/3.0 (Accessed June 1, 2013).

with other inscribed objects from the Badè Museum collection, are readily available to scholars for study and to budding Assyriologists for practice reading.[9] The broader goals of access and transparency for the Tell en-Naṣbeh collection are thus being realized through these digital initiatives while at the same time making a significant contribution of archaeological data to a "semantic web."[10]

EDUCATION, OUTREACH, AND CURRENT RESEARCH

Professor Badè always had the intention that the results of his work be used as an educational device (Kay Schellhase, personal communication). This was most certainly true in his published manual (Badè 1934), which outlined, in the most instructive way, the methods and techniques for modern archaeological excavations in the early twentieth century.[11] His goal was to elevate the practice and perception of archaeology in the public mind above its antiquarianism past by reinforcing the application of rigorous scientific methodology. The manual also served as a record of Badè's field collection, allowing "the educated reader of the preliminary as well as the prospective final reports...the opportunity to see how the evidence [was] gathered and to form his own opinion of the historical verdict" (Badè 1934: vii). In this and many other respects, Badè was a progressive archaeologist both among his peers and even future generations of scholars who, in the summation of synthetic reports, often exclude the inclusion of excavation and sampling

---

[9] http://www.cdli.ucla.edu; CDLI #P405502 (Accessed January 21, 2014).

[10] The Semantic Web provides a common framework that allows data to be shared and reused across application, enterprise, and community boundaries. See the World Wide Web Consortium: http://www.w3.org/2001/sw (Accessed June 1, 2013).

[11] The book is one of the earliest explicit excavation manuals. Anyone intimately familiar with the Tell en-Naṣbeh collection will also know that the manual is a key cipher for understanding what are relatively obscure final reports (McCown 1947; Wampler 1947). The manual is conveniently located on the Museum website: http://bade.psr.edu/content/other-media.

methods that necessarily affect the evidence on which interpretations are based.

This focus on education continues today as the Tell en-Naṣbeh collection and Badè Museum enjoy a wide variety of uses thanks in part to increased outreach to the academic community and interested public. Museum curators and docents continue to provide tours of the permanent exhibitions that chronicle the tools and techniques of archaeological excavation in the early twentieth century, and provide a glimpse into the many interesting facets of ancient Mizpah including fortifications, burial practices, and everyday life some three thousand years ago. Beyond general tours for public and private groups, the museum and adjoining Doug Adams Gallery play an integral role in the university curricula of several neighboring institutions including the Graduate Theological Union (of which Pacific School of Religion is part), the University of California Berkeley, and Mills College. Courses in the art and archaeology of the ancient Near East, Hebrew Bible/Old Testament studies, and household archaeology have benefited from the exhibits and "behind the scenes" storage tours. Even students from such varied subjects as theological anthropology and "Visual Arts in Worship" have used the museum displays to explore aspects of aesthetics and visual culture as a storytelling medium.

Education has also gone beyond the museum gallery directly into the classroom. For decades the museum has administered a traveling exhibit program as part of its outreach efforts. Informal object loans during the early days of the institute developed into a fully-fledged exhibit under the supervision of Margaret Harrison in the 1940s (Kay Schellhase, personal communication). By the mid-1970s, the program was circulating approximately 15 boxes comprising two exhibits among churches and schools across the United States.

Today this self-sustaining program implements a single exhibit model (*Daily Life in an Ancient Judean Town*) with real and replicated objects from a cross section of the Tell en-Naṣbeh collection including lamps, oil juglets, sling stones, and ceramic pitchers (Fig. 6.5). The accompanying labels and display panels can be adapted for use in elementary school curricula up through college and post–graduate teaching. Each exhibit is supplemented by a DVD (*Digging Up a Buried Town: The Excavations of Tell en-Naṣbeh*) that features images from hand colored slides created at the time of the excavations and later images from the museum visual archive. The DVD describes excavation techniques and the types of interpretations researchers can gain from archaeological remains. For younger users of the exhibit, an eight-page illustrated storybook is also available. *The Secret of a Tell*, authored by Jeffrey R. Zorn, explores how *tells* are created over the centuries and how they are excavated by archaeologists to tell the story of ancient Mizpah. These educational resources, along with several others, are also available free of charge on the museum's website, [12] allowing for greater access and use by teachers and parents.

Fig. 6.5. One panel from the travel exhibit *Daily Life in an Ancient Judean Town* with bronze needle and stone loom weight mounted inside plexiglass boxes (Courtesy of Badè Museum of Biblical Archaeology, Pacific School of Religion).

The traveling exhibit program is important in four ways. First, for those not able to visit the museum in Berkeley, the traveling exhibit "brings the museum to them" in a more concrete and tactile way

---

[12] http://bade.psr.edu (Accessed June 9, 2013).

than virtual exhibits and digital gallery walkthroughs. Second, the exhibit has travelled from California throughout the US, and been shown at such varied venues as churches, middle schools, universities, colleges, seminaries, retirement homes, private foundations, educational institutes, and, of course, museums. The program thus elevates the Tell en-Naṣbeh collection from the local to the national level as part of broader efforts by archaeologists and educators to bring awareness of, and education about, ancient history, particularly that of the southern Levant, to the public through lectures, field schools, and museum exhibits. Third, the inclusion of clean gloves and detailed instructions for how to properly handle and secure objects teaches exhibit borrowers not only about archaeology and daily life at ancient Mizpah but how to appreciate and be good stewards of the products of archaeological research.[13] Fourth, the temporary circulation of objects has the potential to bring history alive in the classroom and spark interest in both archaeology and the ancient world at a young age. My own fascination with archaeology began with the visit of a traveling exhibit to my middle school history class. The power of objects, and the story they can tell, cannot be overstated.

Beyond education and outreach, this edited volume is also testament to the breadth and depth of research questions archaeologists and biblical scholars continue to ask of the Tell en-Naṣbeh collection. Was there a Babylonian occupation at Mizpah? A reconsideration of the excavated strata at Tell en-Naṣbeh shows that, indeed, the fortified town was occupied during the Neo-Babylonian period (6th century BCE) in which an urban renewal rendered it an administrative center for the region (Zorn 1993, 1997, 2003). What was the nature of town planning in ancient Judah? House design at Mizpah was strikingly uniform, being influenced largely by the street system, massive casemate town wall, and water drainage patterns that necessitated efficient use of the available space (McClellan 1984). Were the pillared-houses at Mizpah the residences of nuclear or extended families? Household archaeological approaches

---

[13] The smallest and most fragile objects in the exhibit—jewelry, fibula, spindle whorls—are mounted and secured in lightweight plexiglass boxes for added protection.

have revealed that in at least one five-building housing compound at the site resources were pooled among a single extended family (a small *beit 'av*), comprised of three nuclear families and their dependents linked both physically and by the bonds of kinship (Brody 2009, 2011). Other projects position Mizpah within the broader contexts of interregional interaction and ethnicity in the Iron IIB-IIC southern Levant (Brody 2014), and in Persian Period regional economic developments as reflected in the use, distribution, and context of *yehud* stamp impressions (Lipschits and Vanderhooft 2011).

Yet there are also other communities that bring questions and interpretations to the Tell en-Naṣbeh material. In particular the museum has enjoyed a burgeoning relationship with local contemporary artists through interactions with the Doug Adams Gallery ("DAG"), part of the Center for Arts, Religion, and Education at the Graduate Theological Union and, conveniently, physically located inside the Badè Museum main gallery. Since 2010, the DAG Artist-in-Residence program has encouraged artists to mine the museum collections to create a body of work inspired by, or in reaction to, the archaeological objects.[14] As part of this program, artists gain full access to the Tell en-Naṣbeh collection, collaborate with museum curators and staff, and conduct research related to their individual projects. The result is a joint exhibition each summer that explores themes of the artists' choosing with accompanying programming between the Badè Museum and DAG.

The great strength of the Artist-in-Residence program is its ability to facilitate cross-disciplinary dialog whereby artists are exposed to new art sources, and artifacts from ancient Mizpah are recontextualized within a contemporary framework. Artists and archaeologists are also enabled to explore common theoretical

---

[14] The program was inspired in part by the influential work of Fred Wilson, in particular his *Mining the Museum* exhibition at the Maryland Historical Society in 1992–1993, in which he used satirical techniques to recontextualize the society's collection in light of the hitherto unexplored history of the African-American experience in eighteenth and nineteenth century Maryland (Garfield 1993). For a synopsis of Wilson's work, see Corrin 2004.

themes between their respective fields such as materiality, the constitution of "art objects" in past and contemporary societies, and how concepts like religion, power structures, and human emotions are physically manifested. In particular the 2010 dual exhibition of *An Archaeology of the Senses* (curated by Carin Jacobs) and *Lived Experience in Ancient Judah* (curated by the author) together explored aspects of physicality, embodiment, and human interactions with the material world. The resident artist Pamela Blotner highlighted the sensual nature of art through fully interactive pieces that engaged the senses. Visitors were encouraged to smell, touch, and listen to the exhibitions while contemplating how ancient peoples experienced their worlds and the role of contemporary art in archaeological interpretations (Foster 2013).

Later shows continued this reinterpretation of ancient history and the archaeological record through artistic eyes. In *The Meaning of the Bone Room*, artist Julia Nelson-Gal explored the life story of artifacts in the museum's collection storage ("Bone Room") and how these objects are physical reminders of what we, as humans, leave behind "when the soft flesh of life is gone" (Nelson-Gal 2011). The artwork of Cathy Richardson in *Dimensions of Dark* reflects upon the role of light and darkness in the spiritual beliefs of Mizpah residents, along with questioning if our brightly lit modern towns "have fragmented our connection to supernatural elements of the Universe" (Richardson 2012). With a focus on experimental archeology and an interest in sculptural work in *Site/Structure*, David Sleeth used lithic tools, iron implements, ceramic vessels, and photographs from the Tell en-Naṣbeh excavations to create a related series of pen and ink drawings that "opened up the context of the archaeology through artistic articulation" and to see the "artifacts of the everyday as 'ready-mades' awaiting further visual interpretation" (Sleeth 2013). Finally, a precursor to the Artist-in-Residence program was the 2009 exhibit *Ancient Tell, Modern Art* in which faculty, staff, and students of the Graduate Theological Union were invited to simply react to the Tell en-Naṣbeh collection on display in the gallery. The result was a variety of mediums and expressions, from unbaked clay sculpture to mixed media encaustic that explored themes of light and its symbolism, the female divine form, and collective memory.

Collaboration with the DAG and modern-day artists has enabled curators at the Badè Museum to re-conceptualize the role of contemporary art in archaeological interpretations. Art can represent in physical form the more ephemeral aspects of the archaeological past, giving shape to the unknown, conveying emotions, and acting as "the expression in the material world of a concept" (Renfrew 2003: 99). Art also helps to visualize the theoretical link archaeologists make between objects and ideas, and it can even push us into new realms of interpretation and understanding. These possibilities are what make the connection between art and archaeology at the Badè Museum a unique aspect of the continued use and reuse of the Tell en-Naṣbeh collection.

THE FUTURE OF BADÈ'S LEGACY

The story of the Tell en-Naṣbeh collection continues to be written. Digital cataloging of the objects will carry on for many years to come and expand to include digital archiving of the site plans, field notes, and extensive corpus of photographic prints. In Open Context the database will continue to grow in an effort to lend more transparency to the collection and encourage increased use of the Tell en-Naṣbeh assemblage by researchers and the public alike. The museum has often been called a "hidden gem" that would benefit from increased public outreach and programming that highlight the multifaceted aspects of the larger collection and museum story. Improvements to the main gallery, including upgraded lighting and environmental conditions inside and outside the displays, have yet to be realized. And finally, it is my hope that the relationship between the Badè Museum and the Doug Adams Gallery—between archaeology and contemporary art—continues to flourish through increased collaboration. Today the two galleries share a single space but remain distinct. Perhaps the future will see a fuller integration of exhibitions and mission.

Unfortunately it is with sadness that I acknowledge one of the great supporters of the museum—Professor William G. Badè Jr., who died in 2012 at the age of 88—will not be able to see these future goals come to fruition. It was his belief, and that of his mother Elizabeth (Marston) Badè, sister Betsy (Badè) Bacon, and wife Eleanor (Barry) Badè, that the Badè Museum will continue to serve as a resource for those fascinated by the people and places of the ancient Near East, and will also stand as a focal point for lifelong learning. So long as the museum is able to fulfill this mission, Badè's legacy is in good hands.

ACKNOWLEDGMENTS

I wish to thank Jeffrey R. Zorn and Aaron Brody for inviting me to participate in the conference session honoring William F. Badè, and for their dedication in organizing and editing this volume. I am especially grateful to Rebecca Hisiger, Kiersten Neumann, Kay Schellhase, Eleanor Badè, Andrea Creel, Carin Jacobs, Christina Vander Vos, and Aaron Brody for their commitment to the Tell en-Naṣbeh collection during my seven years as curator at the Badè Museum. This chapter has also benefitted from the editorial comments of Brian A. Brown and Kiersten Neumann. Finally, I would like to thank all past and present museum staff and volunteers for preserving and sharing the story of William F. Badè and the Tell en-Naṣbeh collection with future generations.

REFERENCES

Avrami, E.; Dardes, K.; de la Torre, M.; Harris, S. Y.; Henry, M.; and Jessup, W.C.
1999   *The Conservation Assessment: A Proposed Model for Evaluating Museum Environmental Management Needs.* Los Angeles: Getty Conservation Institute. http://www.getty.edu/conservation /publications_resources/pdf_publications/evaluating_mus eum_environmental_mngmnt.html.

Badè, W. F.
1934   *A Manual of Excavation in the Near East: Methods of Digging and Recording of the Tell en-Naṣbeh Expedition in Palestine.* Berkeley, CA: University of California Press.

Brody, A. J.
2009   "Those Who Add House to House," Household Archaeology and the Use of Domestic Space in an Iron II Residential Compound at Tell en-Naṣbeh. Pp. 45–56 in *Exploring the Longue Durée: Essays in Honor of Lawrence E. Stager*, ed. J. D. Schloen. Winona Lake: Eisenbrauns.
2010   "Badè Museum: (Overview)" Open Context. http://open context.org/projects/B4345F6A-F926-4062-144E-3FBC1 75CC7B6 (accessed 1 June 2013).
2011   The Archaeology of the Extended Family: A Household Compound from Iron II Tell en-Naṣbeh. Pp. 237–54 in *Household Archaeology in Ancient Israel and Beyond*, ed. A.

Yasur-Landau, J. R. Ebeling, and L. B. Mazow. Culture and History of the Ancient Near East 50. Leiden: Brill.

2014   Interregional Interaction in the Late Iron Age: Phoenician and Other Foreign Goods from Tell en-Nasbeh. Pp. 55–69 in *Material Culture Matters: Essays on the Archaeology of the Southern Levant in Honor of Seymour Gitin*, ed. J. R. Spencer; R. A. Mullins; and A. J. Brody. Winona Lake, IN: Eisenbrauns.

Caple, C.
2011   Conservation Skills: Preventive Conservation - Storage. Pp. 79–84 in *Preventive Conservation in Museums*, ed. C. Caple. Leicester Readers in Museum Studies. London: Routledge.

Cassar, M.
1995   *Environmental Management: Guidelines for Museums and Galleries*. London: Routledge.

Corrin, L. G.
2004   Mining the Museum: Artists Look at Museums, Museums Look at Themselves. Pp. 381–402 in *Museum Studies: An Anthology of Contexts*, ed. B. M. Carbonell. Malden, MA: Blackwell.

Foster, C. P.
2009   *Digging Up a Buried Town: The Excavations of Tell en-Nasbeh*. DVD. Berkeley: Badè Museum of Biblical Archaeology.
2013   Beyond the Display Case: Creating a Multisensory Museum Experience. Pp. 371–89 in *Making Senses of the Past: Toward a Sensory Archaeology*, ed. J. Day. Center for Archaeological Investigations Occasional Paper 40. Carbondale, IL: Southern Illinois University.

Garfield, D.
1993   Making the Museum Mine: An Interview with Fred Wilson. *Museum News* 72.3 (May–June): 46–49, 90.

Garstang, J.
1922   Eighteen Months' Work of the Department of Antiquities for Palestine, July 1920–December 1921. *Palestine Exploration Fund Quarterly Statement*: 57–62.

Kansa, E. C., and Kansa, S. W.
2007   Open Context: Collaborative Data Publication to Bridge
Field Research and Museum Collections. In *International
Cultural Heritage Informatics Meeting (ICHIM07): Proceedings*,
ed. J. Trant and D. Bearman. Toronto: Archives & Museum Informatics. Accessed June 1, 2013.
www.archimuse.com/ichim07/papers/kansa/kansa.html
2011   Towards a Do-It-Yourself Cyberinfrastructure: Open Data, Incentives, and Reducing Costs and Complexities of
Data Sharing. Pp. 57–91 in *Archaeology 2.0: New Approaches
to Communication and Collaboration*, ed. E. C. Kansa, S. W.
Kansa, and E. Watrall. Cotsen Digital Archaeology Series
1. Los Angeles: Cotsen Institute of Archaeology.

Kersel, M. M.
2008   The Trade in Palestinian Antiquities. *Jerusalem Quarterly* 33:
21–38.
2010   The Changing Legal Landscape for Middle Eastern Archeology in the Colonial Era, 1800–1930. Pp. 85–90 in *Pioneers
to the Past: American Archaeologists in the Middle East, 1919–
1920*, ed. G. Emberling. Oriental Institute Museum Publications 30. Chicago: Oriental Institute of the University of
Chicago. http://oi.uchicago.edu/pdf/oimp30.pdf.

Lipschits, O., and Vanderhooft, D. S.
2011   *The Yehud Stamp Impressions: A Corpus of Inscribed Stamp Impressions from the Persian and Hellenistic Periods in Judah*.
Winona Lake, IN: Eisenbrauns.

McClellan, T. L.
1984   Town Planning at Tell en-Naṣbeh. *Zeitschrift des Deutschen
Palästina-Vereins* 100: 53–69.

McCown, C. C.
1947   *Tell en-Naṣbeh*, Vol. 1: *Archaeological and Historical Results*.
Berkeley, CA: Palestine Institute of Pacific School of Religion.

Nelson-Gal, J.
2011   Artist's Statement. *Mining the Collection: The Meaning of the
Bone Room Featuring Artist-in-Residence Julia Nelson-Gal*, curated by C. Jacobs. Berkeley: Doug Adams Gallery.

http://care-gtu.org/MiningCollection2011/TheMeaningof
theBone_R.doc

Renfrew, C.
2003   *Figuring It Out: What Are We? Where Do We Come From? The
        Parallel Vision of Artists and Archaeologists.* New York:
        Thames and Hudson.

Richardson, C.
2012   Artist's Statement. *Mining the Collection: Dimensions of Dark
        Featuring the Work of Cathy Richardson,* curated by C. Jacobs.
        Berkeley: Doug   Adams   Gallery.   http://care-
        gtu.org/past_exhibitions.php.

Sleeth, D.
2013   Artist's Statement. *Mining The Collection: Site/Structure Featur-
        ing David Sleeth,* curated by C. Jacobs. Berkeley: Doug Ad-
        ams Gallery. http://care-gtu.org/past_exhibitions.php

Vanderhooft, D., and Horowitz, W.
2002   The Cuneiform Inscription from Tell en-Naṣbeh: The
        Demise of an Unknown King. *Tel Aviv* 29: 318–27.

Wampler, J. C.
1947   *Tell en-Naṣbeh,* Vol. 2: *The Pottery.* Berkeley, CA: Palestine
        Institute of Pacific School of Religion.

Wolf Green, S (ed.)
1990   *The Conservation Assessment: A Tool for Planning, Implementing,
        and Fundraising.* Washington, DC: National Institute for the
        Conservation of Cultural Property and the Getty Conser-
        vation Institute.

Zorn, J. R.
1988a   William Frederic Badè. *Biblical Archaeologist* 51: 28–35.
1988b   The Museum Trail: The Badè Museum of Biblical Archae-
        ology. *Biblical Archaeologist* 51: 36–45.
1993   Tell en-Naṣbeh: A Re-evaluation of the Architecture and
        Stratigraphy of the Early Bronze Age, Iron Age and Later
        Periods. Ph.D. dissertation, University of California Berke-
        ley.
1997   Mizpah: Newly Discovered Stratum Reveals Judah's Other
        Capital. *Biblical Archaeology Review* 23: 28–38.

2003   Tell en-Nasbeh and the Problem of the Material Culture of the 6th Century. Pp. 413–47 in *Judah and the Judeans in the Neo-Babylonian Period*, ed. O. Lipschits and J. Blenkinsopp. Winona Lake, IN: Eisenbrauns.

"LET ME EAT SOME OF THAT RED STUFF, FOR I AM FAMISHED!" (GEN. 25:30): PRELIMINARY INSIGHTS INTO IRON AGE COOKING PRACTICES AT TELL EN-NAṢBEH RESULTING FROM GAS CHROMATOGRAPHY/MASS SPECTROMETRY ANALYSES

MARY LARKUM
DEPARTMENT OF ANTHROPOLOGY,
UNIVERSITY OF MASSACHUSETTS

ABSTRACT

This chapter presents preliminary results of gas chromatographic analysis of Tell en-Naṣbeh cooking pottery dating to the Iron Age I–IIA (ca. 1200–840 BCE) and Iron IIB–C (ca. 840–586 BCE). Clay pot cookery was a common food preparation method in ancient homes. Research has shown that unglazed, fired ceramics, such as cooking pottery, absorb substantial quantities of lipids (fats and oils) from foodstuffs during the cooking process. Gas chromatography/mass spectrometry is a tried and tested laboratory method used to identify chemical compounds in complex lipid mixtures. Initial findings indicate a range of potential foodstuffs preserved in Tell en-Naṣbeh cooking vessels. These results support textual evidence regarding Judean domestic cooking during the Iron Age.

145

INTRODUCTION

Ceramics are among the most ubiquitous of remains encountered during archaeological excavation, and their durability in the archaeological record provides analysts with abundant material for the study of vessel use (Heron and Evershed 1993: 247). The most commonly encountered ceramics are probably those associated with the storage, preparation and consumption of food. The study of food use has been a source of valuable archaeological data on ancient populations because food is not only nourishment for the body, but also "food for thought" about social relations (Haaland 2007: 165). Food preparation and consumption have been characterized as socially mediated activities invested with cultural significance that can shed light on social relations within communities and, more narrowly, within households (Goody 1982; Mintz 1996). Cooking within the home has been characterized as conservative by nature because the symbolism invested in foods gives them a kind of "cultural inertia", so food habits usually change gradually and incrementally, facilitating traceability (Hesse and Wapnish 1998: 124; Mintz 1996: 7).

The Israelite diet, as attested by the biblical text, was based on the Mediterranean triad of grains, primarily wheat and barley, grapes and olives (Mic. 6:15; Deut. 11:13–15; Job 24:10–11; Ps. 104:14–15). These basics could be supplemented by various fruits (e.g. figs, dates, pomegranates; Joel 1:12), nuts (e.g. pistachios and almonds; Gen. 43:11), vegetables (e.g. lentils and garlic; Ezek. 4:9; Num. 11:5) and meat for special occasions (Isa. 22:13). Many of these food products are also attested in the archaeological record. For example, at the Phoenician town of Tel Dor one room containing layers of grasses, including wheat, was identified and another structure contained a room in which lentils and chickpeas were found; as with many other sites, animal bones were the most common class of find after pottery (Gilboa and Sharon 2008: 155; Raban-Gerstel et al. 2008). These food products could be processed and consumed in a variety of ways. For example, grain could be baked into bread, parched, and eaten raw (Lev. 23:14), grapes could be turned into wine (Isa. 48:33b) and olives were crushed for their oil (Job 24:11).

One of the most common ways of preparing and consuming food, both for meat and grains/vegetables, was in the form of a stew or porridge cooked in a pot (Gen. 25:29–30, 34; Exod. 29:31;

1 Sam. 2:12–15; 2 Kings 4:38–40; Ezek. 24:3–5; Hag. 2:12). Such stews could also incorporate milk (Deut. 14:21b). Given the evidence of ancient diet available from the texts and in archaeological deposits, it is therefore worth investigating how ancient cooking pots themselves can also contribute to our knowledge of Israelite diet and food preparation practices. The study of cooking vessels from Tell en-Naṣbeh has the potential to contribute to the discourse regarding food use in Judean households because of the site's overwhelmingly domestic context. According to Brody (2009: 45) the extended family was the foundation of Judean society and the vantage point of the family offers an opportunity to view Judean society from the bottom up, rather than depending on the royal or elite view typically preserved in the Hebrew Bible for the period of the United and Divided Monarchies. It also serves to correct the archaeological bias toward elite contexts found in numerous Iron Age archaeological excavations, which have focused primarily on monumental structures and large urban centers. The following preliminary study investigates absorbed food residues extracted from cooking pottery dating typologically to the Iron Age I–II periods excavated from Tell en-Naṣbeh.

LIPIDS

Research has shown that unglazed, fired ceramic vessels such as cooking pottery absorb substantial quantities of lipids (fats and oils) from the foodstuffs stored and processed in them (Evershed et al. 1991; 2001). Cooking processes, such as boiling or roasting, alter the organic chemical compounds in food, liberating or mobilizing them, thereby facilitating the absorption of constituent lipids into the fabric of the vessel wall (Heron and Evershed 1993: 251). Moreover, fired but unglazed clay functions as a "trap" to preserve lipids during burial over many millennia (Evershed et al. 2001: 332).

Lipids are a broad group of chemically diverse compounds that are soluble in solvents (not in water, this hydrophobicity enhances their preservation), and food lipids are normally referred to as fats (solid) and oils (liquid) indicating their physical state at ambient temperatures (McClements and Decker 2007: 156). Fatty acids are major components of lipids. A fatty acid typically contains an aliphatic chain with a carboxylic acid terminal group (Fig. 7.1). Most fatty acids feature an even number of carbons in an unbranched and straight chain. This is due to the biological process of fatty acid elongation where two carbons are added at a time (McClements and Decker 2007: 157). Most natural fatty acid chains range from fourteen to twenty-four carbons in length and, while some chains contain less than fourteen carbons, significant levels of these short chain fatty acids are usually found only in tropical oils and dairy fats. Fatty acids are mainly classified as saturated (no double bonds) or unsaturated (double bonds) (McClements and Decker 2007: 157). Both saturated and unsaturated fatty acids are subject to degradation by oxidation and hydrolysis, however the double bonds in unsaturated fatty acids can be particularly suscep-tible to degradation even under anaerobic conditions (Evershed et al. 1991: 202).

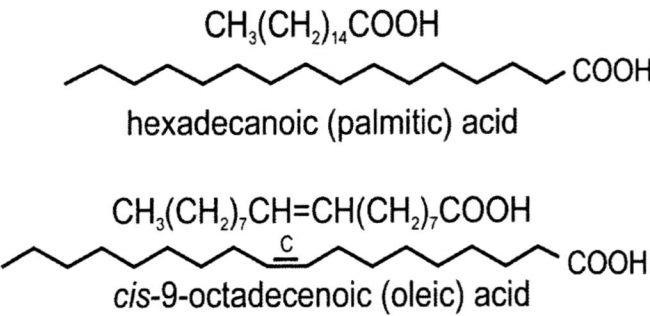

Fig. 7.1. Examples of saturated (C16:0) and unsaturated (C18:1) fatty acids (Christie 2011).

SAMPLING

A total of ten sherds from cooking vessels typologically attributed to two main phases of the Iron Age, the Iron Age I–IIA (ca. 1200–840 BCE; six sherds) and Iron IIB–C (840–586 BCE; four sherds), were chosen for this study to investigate cooking during this time period (Table 7.1; Fig. 7.2). The ceramic samples used in this study were collected from vessels stored in the Badè Museum of Biblical Archaeology at Pacific School of Religion during January 2010. The sampled sherds all come from undifferentiated fills of the designat-ed spaces (a common recording practice at the time of Badè's ex-cavations). In the 1947 site report any space bounded by at least three walls was designated a "Room." However, not all architectur-al features so identified were actual rooms. For example, Room 521 is part of the town's ring-road and Room 507 is an amorphous space in the intramural zone. Moreover, for the most part there is no way to know if the sherds originated from an in situ deposit on top of a living surface, or from redeposited debris from around the tops of the surrounding walls, or from somewhere else within the room debris. Most of the samples likely derive from Stratum 3 of Iron Age II, the best preserved stratum at the site. Two sherds, however, were reported as coming from below floors of buildings assigned by Zorn to Stratum 3, the main Iron Age II period at the site, and so might belong to fills of Stratum 4 of the Iron I (sherds from sub Room 414 and 521; Zorn 1993: 792, 820–21, 1544, 1568). Because of their problematic stratigraphic contexts the sherds discussed here are assigned to archaeological periods based on their typological forms.

Provenience	Tell en-Naṣbeh Type Number and Period (after Amiran 1970)	Badè Museum Registration Number
Room 243 x2	Type not recorded: Iron I–IIA	B2010.1.27
Room 346 I x4	1003: Iron IIB–C	B2010.1.23
Room 414 sub I x7	984: Iron I–IIA	B2010.1.33
Room 432 I x24	1023: Iron IIB–C	B2010.1.21
Room 507 I x6	982: Iron I–IIA	B2010.1.26
Room 513 I x33	1005: Iron IIB–C	B2010.1.35
Room 516 I x16	982: Iron I–IIA	B2010.1.32
Room 521 sub I x12	985: Iron I–IIA	B2010.1.37
Room 549 x7	985: Iron I–IIA	B2010.1.31
Room 575 I x13	1004: Iron IIB–C	B2010.1.18

Table 7.1. List of Ceramic Samples

All samples were taken from the top third of each vessel, avoiding body sherds, for two reasons. First, vessel rims are important typological indicators. They aid in distinguishing vessels of differing time periods and forms. Second, studies have shown that the abundance of absorbed lipids is greater in the top third of cooking vessels. The concentration of lipids in pottery rim sherds may be ten times higher than in body sherds, and thirty times higher than the concentration of lipids in vessel base sherds (Charters et al. 1997: 1–7). This makes sense given the structural characteristics of lipids—their hydrophobicity and density. It is generally assumed that residues in cooking pots were likely formed by boiling, i.e., cooking foods in water at a temperature of at least 100°C. Lipids, being less dense than water, normally rise and form a separate layer at the surface. Therefore, the greatest concentration of lipids would naturally occur at the surface of a liquid in the cooking pot. Malainey notes that cooking pots may not always be filled to the rim, and evaporative water loss during boiling may reduce a pot's liquid level (2011: 203). So the neck and shoulder of cooking pottery, the top third of the vessel, should be the best candidates for sampling.

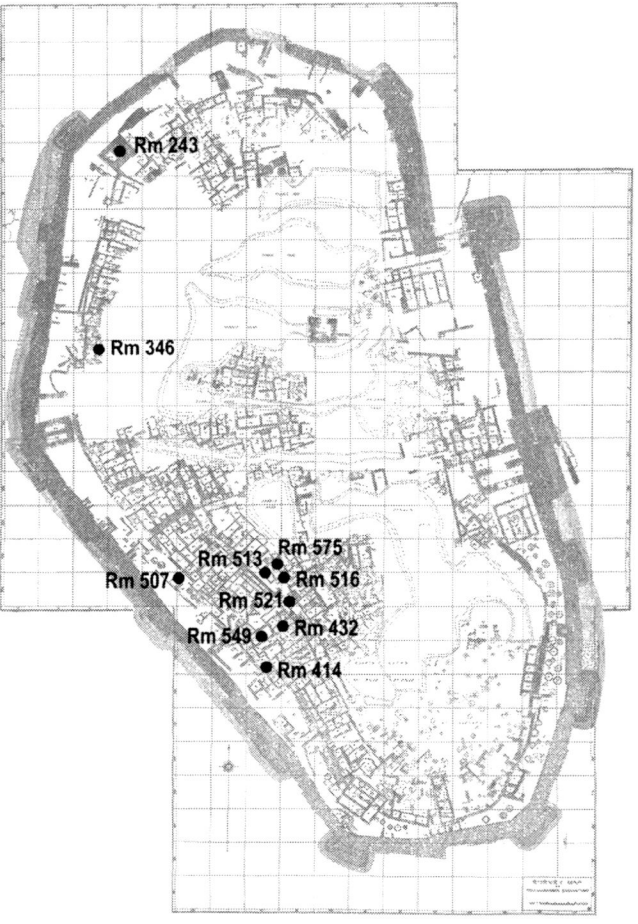

Fig. 7.2. Map showing room locations of ceramic samples.

LABORATORY PROCESSING

All samples were processed in the University of Massachusetts Geosciences Biogeochemistry Laboratory. The outer surface of each sample was cleaned using a modeling drill to remove exogenous lipids potentially deposited through past handling. The remaining pottery was ground to a fine powder using a mortar and pestle. Approximately 1.57 grams of ground ceramic was weighed for each sample and twenty microliters (μL) of 1.065 mg/mL C_{36} n-alkane (n-hexatriacontane) in toluene was added as an internal standard. An Accelerated Solvent Extractor (ASE) was used to separate lipids from the ground pottery using a 9:1 v/v mixture of dichloromethane/methanol (Dionex Corporation 1999). Following extraction, the solvent was evaporated under nitrogen to obtain a total lipid extract (TLE). Total lipid extracts were derivatized using N,O-bis(trimethylsilyl)trifluoroacetamide trimethylchlorosilane (BSTFA/TMCS) in hexane (20 μL, 60°C, 30 min.) to create silylated TMS esters.

Samples were analyzed by a Hewlett Packard 6890 gas chromatograph. They were injected splitless onto a DB-5 column using a temperature program of 50(2)/5/300(3). Analysis of raw data derived from the GC/MS processing of lipid extracts eluted from potsherds was performed according to well-established procedures. The identification of peaks displayed in a total ion current (TIC) chromatogram (see appendix below) relies on an assessment of the recorded mass spectra and GC elution orders (Evershed et al. 1991: 193). Mass spectra of the individual components of the lipid mixtures are commonly interpreted either manually, on the basis of known fragmentations of organic compounds, or automatically, by computer searching of mass spectral databases. Mass spectral interpretations for this study were interpreted manually, based on known fragmentation times of organic compounds, and also compared with search results generated by a Wiley 275 mass spectral library (National Institute of Standards and Technology).

FATTY ACIDS TMS ESTERS

All ten Tell en-Naṣbeh ceramic samples eluted a restricted range of primarily saturated fatty acid TMS esters (Table 7.2).

Shorthand Designation	Systematic Name	Common Name
C10:0	Decanoic acid	Capric acid
C12:0	Dodecanoic acid	Lauric acid
C14:0	Tetradecanoic acid	Myristic acid
C16:0	Hexadecanoic acid	Palmitic acid
C17:0	Heptadecanoic acid	Margaric acid
C18:1 cis-9	Cis-9-octadecenoic acid	Oleic acid
C18:0	Octadecanoic acid	Stearic acid
C20:0	Icosanoic acid	Eicosanoic acid
C22:0	Docosanoic acid	Behenic acid
C24:0	Tetracosanoic acid	Lignoceric acid
C_{28}	Octacosan-1-ol	Octacosyl alcohol
C_{36}	Hexatriacontane*	n-Hexatriacontane*
* = Internal Standard (= IS in spectra charts in Appendix below)		

Table 7.2. Fatty Acids in the GC/MS Spectra.

Medium-chain fatty acids, such as decanoic (10:0) and dodecanoic (12:0), are found in esterified form as minor components of most milk fats, including those of non-ruminants, but not at significant amounts elsewhere in animal tissues (Christie 2011). According to Evershed et al. dairy product residues are readily recognizable by the presence of short-chain fatty acids with *less* than twelve carbons (1991: 203; see also Rottländer and Schlichtherle 1979). Decanoic acid (C10:0) is the most significant fatty acid in the milk from both sheep and goat, and both genera share the same range of fatty acids in their dairy products (Gunstone and Herslöf 1992: 49). Short chain fatty acids are absent from most vegetable fats (Christie 2011). However they occur in seed fats such as coconut oil and palm oils (Gunstone and Herslöf 1992: 49). Coconut was unknown in the southern Levant during the Iron Age. Palm oil is derived from the kernel of *Elaeis guineensis*, which is native to West Africa and, while its history of use can be dated back to 3000 B.C.E. in Africa (Berger and Martin 2000: 397), it was probably not used for cooking in a modest Iron Age II period south Levantine town such as Tell en-Naṣbeh.

Tetradecanoic acid (14:0) is a ubiquitous component of lipids in most living organisms, but usually at levels of 1–2% only. For example, C12:0 and C14:0 feature as minor components in animal fats, particularly in the adipose tissues of ruminants (Gunstone and Herslöf 1994: 156). Both C12:0 and C14:0 are also found in chicken fat (Beare-Rogers et al. 2001: 737). Tetradecanoic acid is more abundant in cow's milk fat, some fish oils and in seed oils enriched in medium-chain fatty acids (e.g. coconut and palm kernel). It is also found in *Pisum sativum* oil (Villalobos Solis et al. 2013). The pea is one of the oldest cultivated legumes. It is descended from the wild genus *Pisum* L., which is indigenous to the Mediterranean Basin and the Near East. Remains of *Pisum* species have been found in Near Eastern archaeological deposits dating as far back as the Pre-Pottery Neolithic B period (Zohary and Hopf 2000: 101, 105).

Hexadecanoic acid (16:0) is usually considered the most abundant saturated fatty acid in nature, and it is found in appreciable amounts in the lipids of animals, plants and lower organisms such as bacteria. It comprises 20–30% of the lipids in animal tissues (for example, lard and tallow) and is present in amounts that vary from 10–40% in seed oils such as palm kernel oil (Beare-Rogers et al. 2001: 715).

Octadecanoic acid (18:0) is the second most abundant saturated fatty acid in nature and, again, it is found in the lipids of most living organisms. It occurs in the highest concentrations in ruminant fats (milk fat and tallow) and in vegetable oils (Christie 2011).

Oleic acid (C18:1), an unsaturated fatty acid, is the most widely distributed of all natural fatty acids. It is present in practically all animal and plant fats (Gunstone and Herslöf 1994: 49). Animal and plant fats rich in oleic acid include seeds such as sesame, nuts such as pistachio and almond, lard, beef tallow and mutton fat. It makes up 71.1 weight percent of total fatty acids in the olive and its oil (McClements, and Decker 2008: 161). Lipids derived from ruminant animals, especially, can include isomers of oleic acid while the fat of monogastric animals, such as pigs, contains only oleic acid (cis-9-octadecenoic acid) (Evershed et al. 2002: 664).

Odd-chain fatty acids, such as heptadecanoic acid (C17:0), are found in esterified form in the lipids of many bacterial species, and they can be detected at trace levels in most animal tissues, presumably having been taken up as part of the food chain and/or formed by "bacterial activity in the digestive tract of ruminant animals" (Colombini and Modugno 2009: 197). In particular, they occur in appreciable amounts (5% or more) in the tissues of ruminant animals. Adipose tissues, such as lard from pigs, tallow from cows and mutton/goat fat, all contain heptadecanoic acid (Gunstone and Herslöf 1994: 157).

Eicosanoic acid (20:0) can be detected at low levels in most lipids derived from animals, and often in those of plants and microorganisms (Christie 2011).

Very-long-chain saturated fatty acids (23:0 to 32:0) are not usually considered to be common constituents of lipids. However, they do occur in many plant waxes, which by some estimates are the most abundant lipids on earth, and also in some animal waxes such as wool wax (Christie 2011).

DISCUSSION

Ceramic samples from Tell en-Naṣbeh eluted a restricted range of fatty acid TMS (trimethylsilyl) esters. Six samples are Iron Age I–IIA in form. The remaining four belong typologically to the Iron Age IIB–C. Fatty acid content is similar across all samples regardless of vessel form and period. However, samples from the 500 series of rooms contain a greater range of fatty acids, specifically long chain fatty acids (C20:0, C22:0, C24:0) typically associated with plant oils and waxes, for example as found in oil from the legume *Pisum sativum* (Solis et al. 2013: 989.) The most common esters recorded across all ten GC/MS spectra are tetradecanoic acid TMS (C14:0), commonly called myristic acid; hexadecanoic acid TMS (C16:0) commonly called palmitic acid; and octadecanoic acid TMS (C18:0), also known as stearic acid.

Results of gas chromatographic analysis indicate three general ratios of hexadecanoic acid (C16:0) to octadecanoic acid (C18:0) in the Tell en-Naṣbeh data set (fig. 3):

1. Elevated levels of C18:0 compared with C16:0.
2. Elevated levels of C16:0 when compared with C18:0.
3. Approximately equal levels of both C16:0 and C18:0.

Although hexadecanoic and octadecanoic fatty acids derive from both plant and animal fats, a greater abundance of octadecanoic acid (C18:0) in any ratio of C16:0 to C18:0 is generally interpreted as indicating an animal fat while a greater abundance of C16:0 is primarily associated with dairy and plant lipids (Deal and Silk 1988). Fatty acids in fresh dairy products feature greater percentages per weight of C16:0 compared with C18:0. For example, cow dairy fat has 27% C16:0 to 12% C18:0, goat dairy fat has 25% C16:0 to 12% C18:0. However, decay of original organic matter occurs during burial so potsherd extracts rarely match those of contemporary foodstuffs (Evershed et al. 1991: 206). The significance of the approximately equal C16:0 and C18:0 ratio in the sample from room 521 is currently unknown.

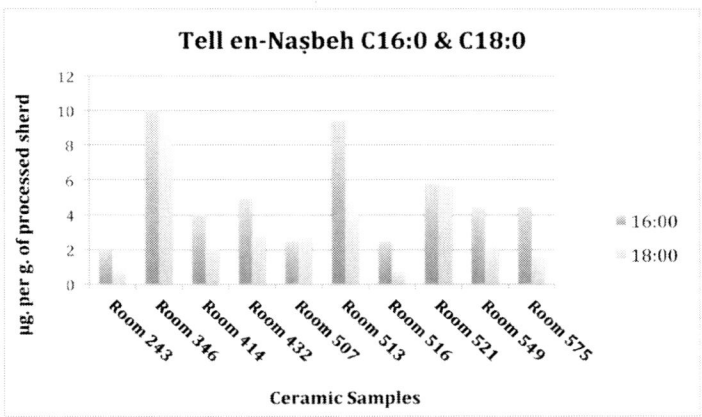

Fig. 7.3. Comparative C16:0 and C18:0.

Only one sample features oleic acid (Table 7.3). Moreover, no other unsaturated fatty acids eluted from the studied samples. Poor preservation of oleic acid indicates lipid degradation by oxidation and/or hydrolysis (Skibo 1992). Six out of ten samples contain only the TMS esters of short to medium chain saturated fatty acids C10:0, C12:0, C14:0, C16:0 and C18:0. Samples 513 and 521 eluted long-chain fatty acid esters (C22:0, C24:0) associated with plant waxes. Nine out of ten samples feature heptadecanoic acid TMS (C17:0) derived primarily from bacterial species associated with ruminant milk and/or meat but also found in lard and tallow (see above). This fatty acid is missing from sample 516.

The mass spectrum from the Room 513 sample (Fig. 7.9) exhibits the greatest range of fatty acids within the Tell en-Naṣbeh dataset showing peaks from saturated fatty acids ranging from C10:0 to C24:0, and unsaturated oleic acid (C18:1). In addition, it eluted a 28-carbon fatty alcohol, 1-octacosanol, found in the epicuticular waxes of cereal grains and legume genera such as *Pisum* sp. (Baker 1982:152).

Fatty Acids	Room 243	Room 346	Room 414	Room 432	Room 507
10:0	0.76	1.82	1.55	0.76	0.64
12:0	0.37	1.47	1.12	0.64	0.66
14:0	1.56	3.62	2.67	2.36	1.52
16:0	2.05	10.03	4.07	4.94	2.52
17:0	0.26	1.82	1.09	0.77	0.74
18:0	0.97	8.59	2.06	2.77	1.38
20:0					
22:0					
24:0					
18:1					
Total μg.	5.98	27.35	12.56	12.24	8.85

Table 7.3. Fatty acid abundance, μg. per g. of processed sherd (rounded to two decimal places). (Table is continued on following page.)

CONCLUSION

The study of lipids from archaeological samples can be an analytical challenge because of the range of molecules that may be present and because of the damage affecting lipid products through the degrading action of time (Evershed et al. 1991; Skibo 1992). This is compounded by the fact that gas chromatographic methods cannot distinguish between cooking events, so cooking residues preserved in pottery must be interpreted as representing a vessel's use life—a palimpsest of everything cooked in a pot.

The use life of an Iron Age cooking vessel is undeterminable. However, ethnoarchaeological studies provide analogies to predict the length of time ancient, utilitarian ceramics were typically used prior to breakage and discard (DeBoer 1974; Foster 1960; Nelson 1991). For example, the Kalinga Ethnoarchaeology Project conducted fieldwork to track the use life of utilitarian ceramics among the Kalinga society of the Philippines between 1975 and 1988 (Tani and Longacre 1999). Using ethnographic interviews, inventories and documentation of vessel breakage, researchers tracked a total of 1,160 cooking pots, calculating a mean vessel use life of 2.2 years. This mean is similar to results from comparable ethnographic case studies recorded cross-culturally (see Nelson 1991, Table 8.3). So the accumulation of fatty acids within the fabric of a cooking vessel potentially occurred over a period of approximately two

Fatty Acids	Room 513	Room 516	Room 521	Room 549	Room 575
10:0	2.26	1.10	0.62	1.06	0.92
12:0	1.50	0.80	0.83	1.16	1.15
14:0	3.30	1.68	2.23	2.98	2.27
16:0	9.38	2.46	5.77	4.46	4.47
17:0	1.50	0.0000	2.05	1.39	1.10
18:0	4.71	0.72	5.67	2.18	1.53
20:0	1.81		0.92	1.15	2.28
22:0	1.50		0.66		
24:0	0.88				
18:1	1.70				
Total µg.	**28.55**	**6.76**	**18.75**	**14.38**	**13.73**

Table 7.3. (continued).

years. However, whether fatty acid accumulation actually represents the initial use of a pot—a vessel's "seasoning," represents numerous cooking episodes over time, or represents the final use of a vessel before breakage and discard, is unknown.

Fatty acid distributions are complicated by factors such as non-specific usage, another reason why lipid profiles will represent contributions from a variety of foodstuffs. The use of a range of ingredients in recipes will also yield complex lipid profiles. Interpretation of GC/MS spectra is also hampered by the redundancy of many fatty acids, "multiple sources of mixtures, and the variations in the way fatty acids are damaged (e.g., unsaturated fatty acids, such as C18:1, are damaged much more quickly than saturated ones, such as C16:0)" (Evershed et al. 1991: 206).

It would also be unrealistic to broadly interpret cooking and diet at Tell en-Naṣbeh based on a small number of samples—ten in total—and by studying only one cooking method. There were many cooking methods employed by ancient south Levantine populations that are potentially more difficult, if not impossible, to trace in the archaeological record—e.g., baking, grilling, roasting, drying, and parching; moreover, food was also eaten raw. However, with these caveats in mind, this initial study does offer preliminary information about clay pot cookery during the Iron Age I–IIA and IIB–C periods. First, samples show that dietary data can be extracted using the analytical methods employed for this study. Secondly, GC/MS results suggest that the examined pottery was used to prepare foods containing fat not inconsistent with fats found in meat, dairy products, and edible plants such as vegetables, grain and legumes. The suite of fatty acids found across all ten pottery samples, combined with C16:0 to C18:0 ratios favoring C16:0, which eluted from eight out of ten samples support an interpretation that vegetal foods and dairy products were common ingredients cooked in the examined vessel types, which are all shallow and open in form. Additionally, long chain fatty acids found in samples 513, 521, 549 and 575 suggest the inclusion of grains and/or legumes. Gas chromatographic results to date support textual evidence for the domestic preparation of meals such as stews and porridges made with vegetables, grain or legumes, and milk as noted in the introduction above. Finally, the current preliminary data set shows no difference in the nature of Israelite food consumption between the early formative years of the Israelite people (Iron I–IIA) and the later mature period of the Judean monarchy (Iron IIB–C).

This study is a component of a doctoral dissertation project restricted in scope to the examination of early forms of cooking pottery. Postdoctoral study of a greater number of Judean cooking ceramics, including late, tall, closed vessels, in comparison with shallow open forms, has the potential to expand on results of this initial study and contribute more data pertinent to Iron Age II cooking in Judah.

ACKNOWLEDGMENTS

The author would like to acknowledge and thank Dr. Kiersten Neumann for the professional quality pottery photographs, Dr. Aaron J. Brody and family for kindly opening their home to facilitate project sampling, Dr. Jeffrey R. Zorn, the Badè Museum of Biblical Archeology, Dr. Steven Petsch of the UMass Geosciences Department, Dr. Michael Sugerman of the UMass Anthropology Department, the American Schools of Oriental Research, National Science Foundation Doctoral Dissertation Research Improvement Grant 1038273, and the UMass Amherst Biogeochemistry Laboratory.

REFERENCES

Amiran, R.
1970   *Ancient Pottery of the Holy Land.* New Brunswick, NJ: Rutgers University.

Baker, E. A.
1982   Chemistry and Morphology of Plant Epicuticular Waxes.
         Pp.139–65 in *The Plant Cuticle: Papers Presented at an Interna-
         tional Symposium Organized by the Linnean Society of London,
         Held at Burlington House, London, 8–11 September 1980*, ed. D.
         F. Cutler, K. L. Alvin and C. E. Price. Linnean Society
         Symposium Series 10. London: Academic Press.

Beare-Rogers, J.; Dieffenbacher, A.; and Holm, J. V.
2001   Lexicon of Lipid Nutrition (IUPAC Technical Report).
         Pure and Applied Chemistry 73: 685–744.

Berger, K. G., and Martin, S. M.
2000   Palm Oil. Pp. 397–410 in *The Cambridge World History of
         Food*, Vol. 1, ed. K. F. Kiple and K. C. Ornelas. Cambridge:
         Cambridge University.

Brody, A. J.
2009   "Those Who Add House To House": Household Archae-
         ology and the Use of Domestic Space in an Iron II Resi-
         dential Compound at Tell en-Naṣbeh. Pp. 45–56 in *Explor-
         ing the Longue Durée, Essays in Honor of Lawrence E. Stager*, ed.
         J. D. Schloen. Winona Lake, IN: Eisenbrauns.

Charters, S.; Evershed, R. P.; Quye, A.; Blinkhorn, P. W.; and
Reeves, V.
1997   Simulation Experiments for Determining the Use of An-
         cient Pottery Vessels: The Behaviour of Epicuticular Leaf
         Wax During Boiling of a Leafy Vegetable. *Journal of Archae-
         ological Science* 24: 1–7.

Colombini, M. P., and Modugno, F.
2009   *Organic Mass Spectrometry in Art and Archaeology*. Chicester:
         Wiley.

Christie, W. W.
2011   A Lipid Primer: Fatty Acids and Eicosanoids. *The AOCS
         Lipid Library*. Online: http://lipidlibrary.aocs.org/Lipids/
         fa_eic.html (accessed May 2014).

Deal, M., and Silk, P.
1988   Absorption Residues and Vessel Function: A Case Study
         from the Maine-Maritimes Region. Pp. 105–25 in *A Pot for*

All Reasons: Ceramic Ecology Revisited, ed. C. C. Kolb and L. M. Lackey. Philadelphia: Laboratory of Anthropology, Temple University.

DeBoer, W. R.
1974   Ceramic Longevity and Archaeological Interpretation: An Example from the Upper Ucayali, Peru. *American Antiquity* 39: 335–43.

Dionex Corporation
1999   *ASE® 200 Accelerated Solvent Extractor Operator's Manual.* Document No. 031149, Revision 04.

Evershed, R. P.; Dudd, S. N.; Copley, M. S.; Berstan, R.; Stott, A. W.; Mottram, H.; Buckley, S. A.; and Crossman, Z.
2002   Chemistry of Archaeological Animal Fats. *Accounts of Chemical Research* 35: 660–68.

Evershed, R. P.; Dudd, S. N.; Lockheart, M. J.; and Jim, S.
2001   Lipids in Archaeology. Pp. 331–49 in *Handbook of Archaeological Sciences*, ed. D. R. Brothwell and A. M. Pollard. Chichester: Wiley.

Evershed, R. P.; Heron, C.; Charters, S.; and Goad, L. J.
1991   The Survival of Food Residues: New Methods of Analysis, Interpretation and Application. Pp.187–208 in *New Developments in Archaeological Science*, ed. A. M. Pollard. Proceedings of the British Academy 77. Oxford: Oxford University Press.

Foster, G. M.
1960   Life-Expectancy of Utilitarian Pottery in Tzintzuntzan, Michoacan, Mexico. *American Antiquity* 25: 606–09.

Gilboa, A., and Sharon, I.
2008   Between the Carmel and the Sea: Tel Dor's Iron Age Reconsidered. *Near Eastern Archaeology* 71: 146–70.

Goody, J.
1982   *Cooking, Cuisine and Class: A Study in Comparative Sociology.* Cambridge: Cambridge University.

Gunstone, F. D., and Herslöf, B. G.
1992   *A Lipid Glossary.* Oily Press Lipid Library 3. Ayr: The Oily Press.

Haaland, R.

2007   Porridge and Pot, Bread and Oven: Food Ways and Symbolism in Africa and the Near East from the Neolithic to the Present. *Cambridge Archaeological Journal* 17.2: 165–82.

Heron, C., and Evershed, R. P.

1993   The Analysis of Organic Residues and the Study of Pottery Use. *Archaeological Method and Theory* 5: 247–84.

Hesse, B., and Wapnish, P.

1998   Pig Use and Abuse in the Ancient Levant: Ethnoreligious Boundary-Building with Swine. Pp 123–35 in *Ancestors for the Pigs: Pigs in Prehistory*, ed. S. M. Nelson. MASCA Research Papers in Science and Archaeology 15. Philadelphia: University of Pennsylvania Museum of Archaeology and Anthropology.

Malainey, M. E.

2011   *A Consumer's Guide to Archaeological Science: Analytical Techniques*. Manuals in Archaeological Method, Theory and Technique. New York: Springer.

McClements, D. J., and Decker, E. A.

2007   Lipids. Pp. 155–216 in *Fennema's Food Chemistry*, ed. S. Damodaran, K. L. Parkin, and O. R. Fennema. 4th ed. Food Science and Technology. Boca Raton, FL: CRC Press.

Mintz, S. W.

1996   *Tasting Food, Tasting Freedom: Excursions into Eating, Culture and the Past*. Boston: Beacon.

National Institute of Standards and Technology

2011   NIST/EPA/NIH Mass Spectral Library 2011. New York: Wiley. DVD.

Nelson, B. A.

1991   Ceramic Frequency and Use-Life: A Highland Mayan Case in Cross-Cultural Perspective. Pp. 162–81 in *Ceramic Ethnoarchaeology*, ed. W. A. Longacre. Tucson: University of Arizona.

Raban-Gerstel, N.; Bar-Oz, G.; Zohar, I.; Sharon, I.; and Gilboa, A.
2008   Early Iron Age Dor (Israel): A Faunal Perspective. *Bulletin of the American Schools of Oriental Research* 349: 25–59.

Rottländer, R. C. A., and Schlichtherle, H.
1979   Food Identification of Samples from Archaeological Sites. Pp. 260–67 in *Proceedings of the 18th International Symposium on Archaeometry and Archaeological Prospection, Bonn, 14–17 March 1978.* Archaeo-Physika 10. Köln: Rheinland-Verlag.

Skibo, J. M.
1992   *Pottery Function: A Use Alteration Perspective.* Interdisciplinary Contributions to Archaeology. New York: Plenum Press.

Solis, M. I. V.; Patel, A.; Orsat, V.; Singh, J.; and Lefsrud, M.
2013   Fatty Acid Profiling of the Seed Oils of Some Varieties of Field Peas (*Pisum Sativum*) by RP-LC/ESI MS/MS: Towards the Development of an Oilseed Pea. *Food Chemistry* 139: 986–93.

Tani, M., and Longacre, W. A.
1999   On Methods of Measuring Ceramic Uselife: A Revision of the Uselife Estimates of Cooking Vessels among the Kalinga, Philippines. *American Antiquity* 64: 299–308.

Zohary, D., and Hopf, M.
2000   *Domestication of Plants in the Old World: The Origin and Spread of Cultivated Plants in West Asia, Europe, and the Nile Valley.* 3rd ed. Oxford: Oxford University.

Zorn, J. R.
1993   Tell en-Nasbeh: A Re-evaluation of the Architecture and Stratigraphy of the Early Bronze Age, Iron Age and Later Periods. Ph.D. dissertation, University of California at Berkeley.

APPENDIX

The following appendix catalogues the data on which this chapter is based. Each sample was processed using gas chromatography/mass spectrometry, which generates a mass spectrum. A mass spectrum is a graph illustrating the retention time (or time of flight –TOF) of molecules within a sample. A programed amount of a derivatized sample (see laboratory processing, above) is automatically injected into the chromatograph and transferred from the injector port to a coated capillary column. Molecules within the sample have greater or lesser affinity, according to their molecular weight, with the column's coating (polysiloxane in this instance) and come off it at differing rates. This is the retention time or time of flight. Increasing molecular weight generally corresponds with increasing retention times. This difference in retention time allows the mass spectrometer component of the GC/MS to capture molecules and bombard them with electrons, fragmenting them and detecting the ionized molecular fragments separately. The mass spectrometer detects these fragments using their mass-to-charge ratio (m/z—where m equals the molecular mass and z equals the ion charge). The result is a mass spectrum where each fragment is illustrated by a peak corresponding with the retention time. Peak abundance is calculated in comparison to an internal standard (IS) that is injected into the sample during processing. Each mass spectrum below is accompanied by a photograph of the sherd sample, a vessel profile, ware description, and vessel diameter—where this information is available—as well as a typological parallel (Amiran 1970: 75–76).

Fig. 7.4. Room 243 x2 (B2010.1.27)

Wampler Type Unknown
Amiran pl. 76.1 = Iron I: 1200–1000 BCE
Diameter: Unknown
Ware: Unknown

Drawing: Not Available

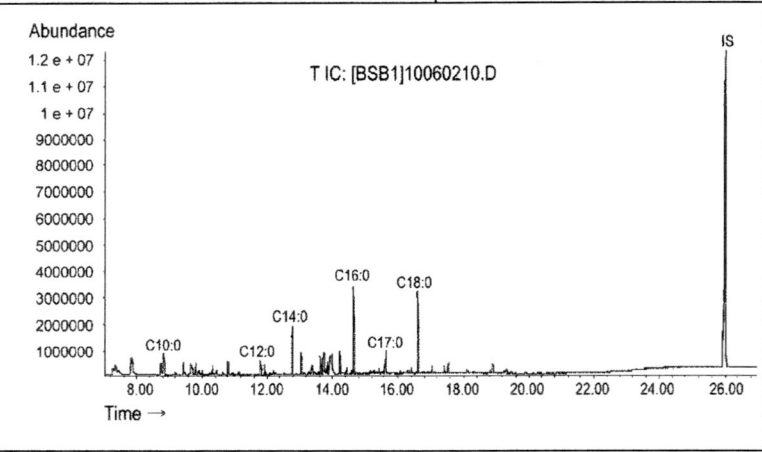

Fig. 7.5. Room 346 I x4 (B2010.1.23)

Wampler Type 1003 = Iron II: 1000–586 BCE
Amiran pl. 76.13 = Iron IIC: 1000–586 BCE
Ca. 170 mm diameter
Ware: fairly hard. Surfaces: dull red brown, fine, white grits; fire-blackened.

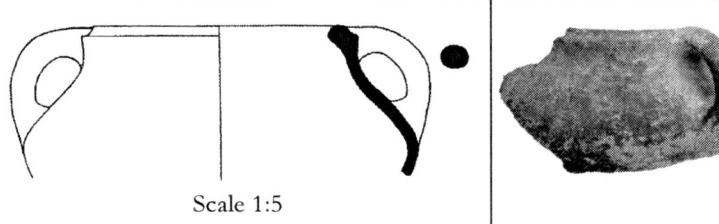

Scale 1:5

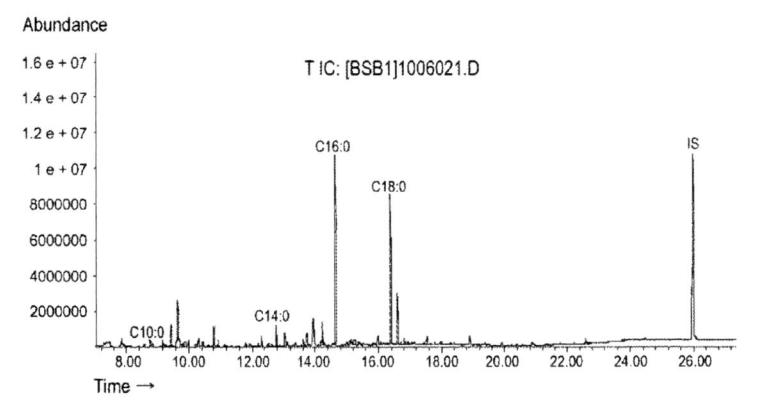

Fig. 7.6. Room 414 sub I x7 (B2010.1.33)

Wampler Type 984 = Iron I: 1200–1000 BCE
Amiran pl. 76.1 = Iron I: 1200–1000 BCE
Ca. 320 mm diameter
Ware: medium hard. Surface: medium red brown and core of dark grey
drab containing many small white grits and occasional scintillating
particles. Finish: wet-smoothed; outer surface smoke blackened.

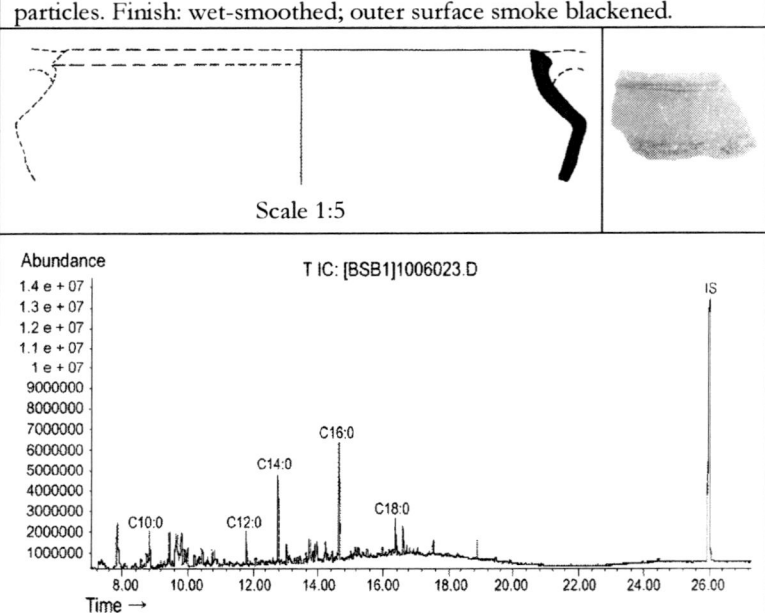

Scale 1:5

Fig. 7.7. Room 432 I x24 (B2010.1.21)

Wampler Type 1023 = Iron II: 1000–500 BCE
Amiran pl. 76.13 = Iron IIC: 800–586 BCE
Ca. 230 mm diameter
Ware: medium hard; Surfaces: dark reddish brown with core containing many scintillating particles. Finish: wet-smoothed, handle smoke blackened.

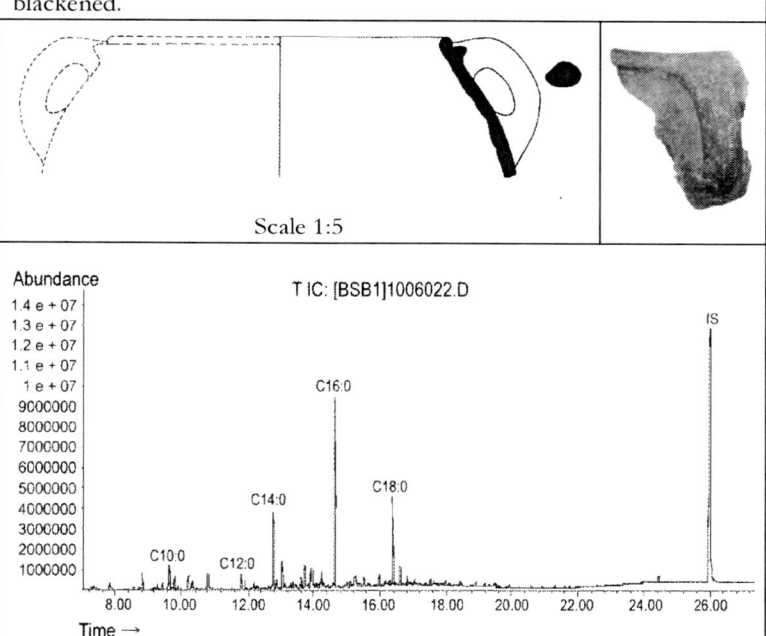

Scale 1:5

Fig. 7.8. Room 507 I x6 (B2010.1.26)

Wampler Type 982 = LB/Iron I: 1300–1100? BCE
Amiran pl. 76.1 = Iron I: 1200–1000 BCE
Ca. 280 mm diameter
Ware: hard. Surfaces: dark red brown over core of black containing many white grits of various sizes and some very fine scintillating particles. Finish: wet-smoothed; outer surface smoke blackened.

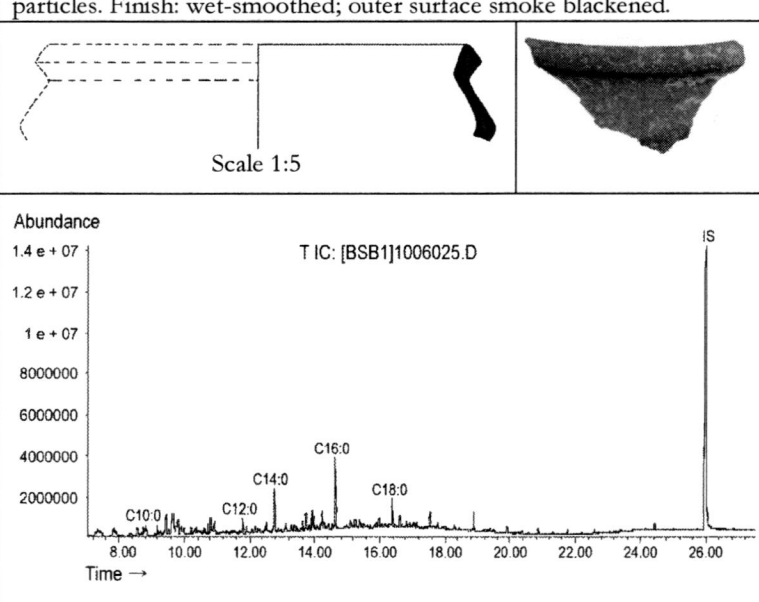

Scale 1:5

Fig. 7.9. Room 513 I x33 (B2010.1.35)

Wampler Type 1005 = Iron II: 1000–586 BCE
Amiran pl. 76.13 = Iron IIC 800–586 BCE
Ca. 155 mm diameter
Ware: hard. Surface: medium red brown over core of light to dark grey drab containing some very fine and occasional small white grits. Finish: wet-smoothed; outer surface smoke blackened.

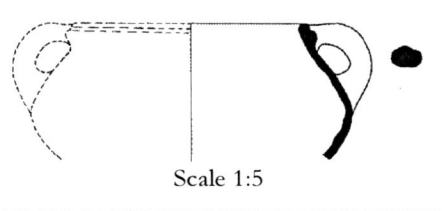 

Scale 1:5

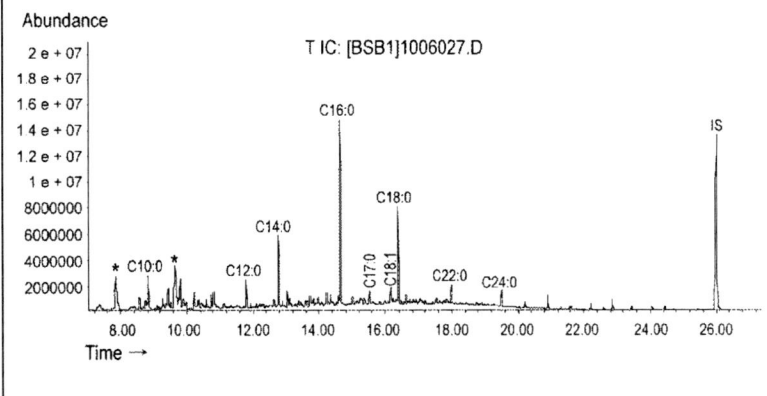

Abundance

T IC: [BSB1]1006027.D

Fig. 7.10. Room 516 I x16 (B2010.1.32)

Wampler Type 982 = LB/Iron I: 1300–1100? BCE
Amiran pl. 76.1 = Iron I: 1200–1000 BCE
Diameter: Unknown
Ware: Ware: medium hard. Outer Surface: medium red. Inner Surface:
medium red orange over core of medium brown containing some
white grits of various sizes. Finish: wet-smoothed; outer surface slightly
smoke blackened

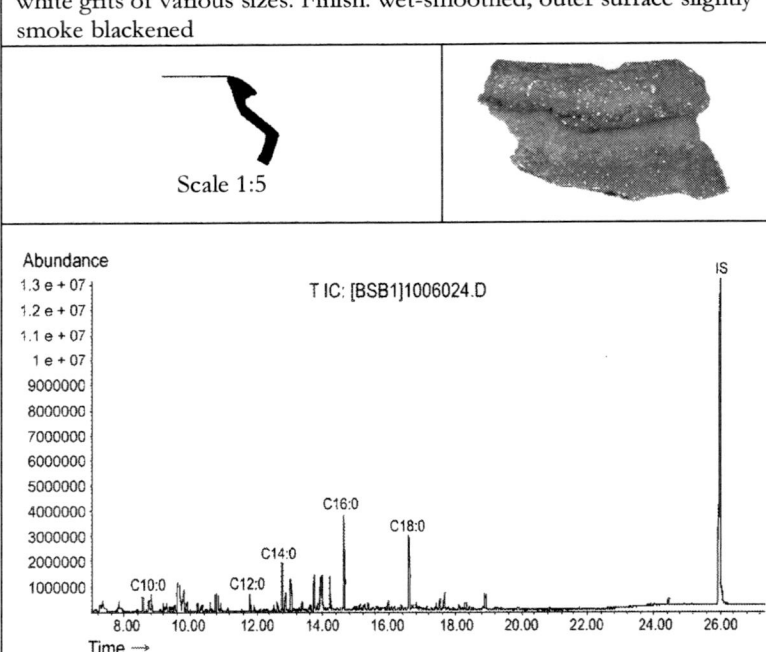

Scale 1:5

Fig. 7.11. Room 521 sub I x12 (B2010.1.37)

Wampler Type 985 = Iron II: 1000–586 BCE
Amiran pl. 76.1 = Iron I: 1200–1000 BCE
Diameter: Unknown
Ware: medium hard. Surfaces: medium red brown over core of black containing white grits and scintillating particles of various sizes. Finish: wet-smoothed; outer surface smoke blackened.

Scale 1:5

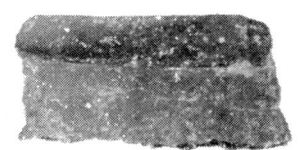

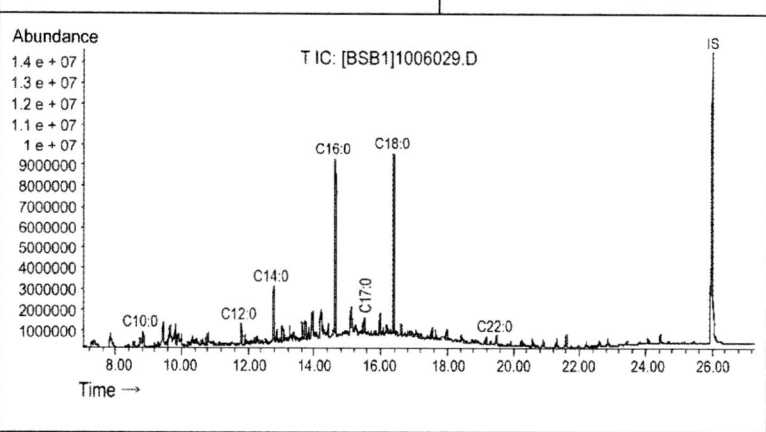

Fig. 7.12. Room 549 x7 (B2010.1.31)

Wampler Type 985 = Iron II: 1000-586 BCE
Amiran pl. 76.1 = Iron I: 1200-1000 BCE or 76.8 Iron IIA—B: 1000—800 BCE
Ca. 280 mm diameter
Ware: medium hard. Surfaces: medium red brown over core of dark grey brown containing some white grit of various sizes and a few very scintillating particles. Finish: wet-smoothed; inner surface smoke blackened.

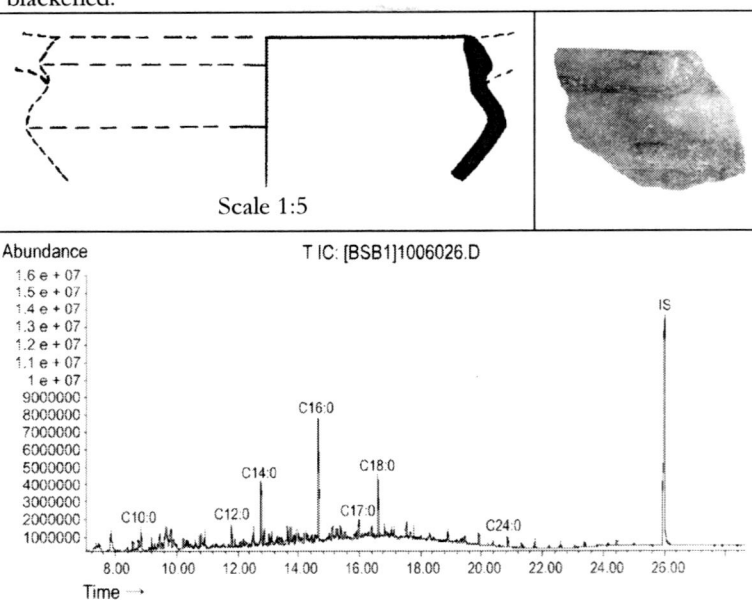

Scale 1:5

Abundance   T IC: [BSB1]1006026.D

Fig. 7.13. Room 575 I x13 (B2010.1.18)

Wampler Type 1004   –586 BCE

Ca. 160mm diameter.
Ware: medium hard. Surfaces: light red brown over core of light grey brown containing very fine white grit. Finish: wet-smoothed; outer surface smoke blackened

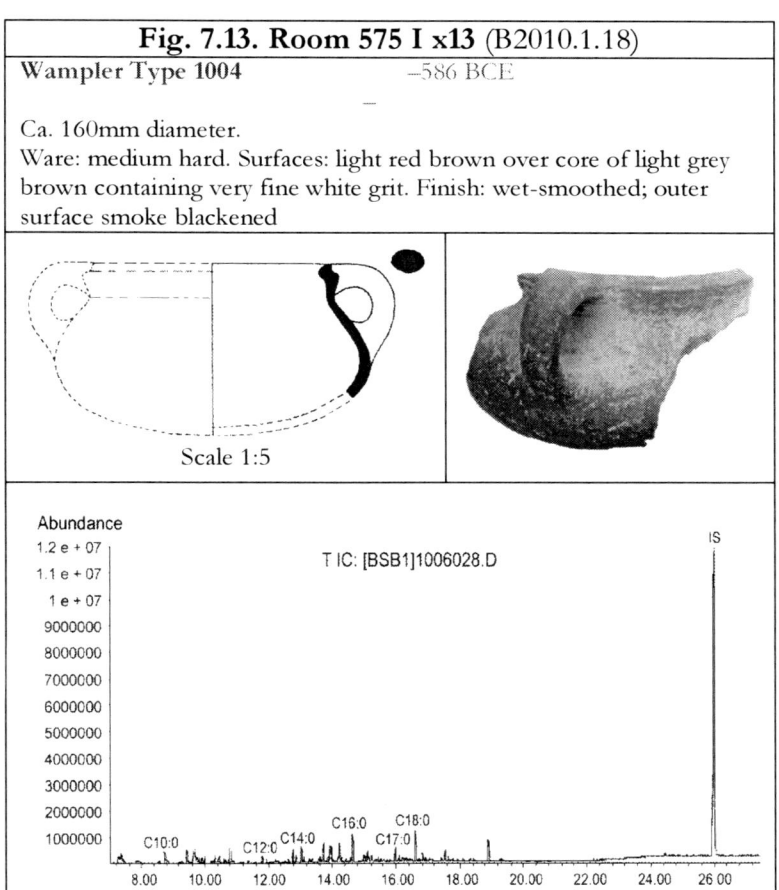

Scale 1:5

Observations Regarding an Oil Lamp of the Late Roman–Byzantine Period from Tell en-Naṣbeh

Varda Sussman
Bar Ilan University

Abstract

A recent analysis of the square shape pedestals supporting an arcade depicted on a multiple-wick-hole lamp from Tomb 33 at Tell en-Naṣbeh allows the following observations to be made. First, such pedestals on which twisted columns stand are typical of Beit Nattif type lamps. Second, such pedestals are rare in Israel; the origin for such pedestals is found in Syria. Third, the capital of the left column of the Tell en-Naṣbeh is decorated similarly to a multiple-wick-hole lamp discovered at Shiloh, and also to the left capital on a terracotta shrine from Beit Nattif; such decorated capitals also have parallels in Syria. Fourth, the decorations on the five pedestals are hard to decipher, but they portray the arches of a basilica. The clearest is the second pedestal from the right which bears a tree with rounded fruits and two flanking human figures. Trees are very rare on local mosaic pavements (Roglit, Shiloh) from the fifth century CE that could be a source for the imagery on the Tell en-Naṣbeh. However, trees accompanied by human figures are abundant on mosaics in Jordan of the sixth century CE. The above observations suggest a possible artistic connection with the artists working at Shiloh and in Jordan. Sixth, a date in the fifth century CE and a Christian association for the Tell en-Naṣbeh lamp seem likely.

INTRODUCTION

The discovery that the pedestals on a Late Roman–Byzantine lamp found in a tomb at Tell en-Naṣbeh (Mizpah; north-west of Jerusalem) were covered with decorations in relief was exciting and surprising. This discovery has inspired the author to discuss this phenomenon, to suggest an elucidation of the hard-to-identify patterns on the pedestals, and to place the lamp in its cultural and chronological context.

Fig. 8.1. On the left: the base of the lamp from Tell en-Naṣbeh Tomb 33. Palestine Archaeological Museum 32.2256. On the right: the upper part of the lamp decorated with an arcade (Courtesy of the Israel Antiquities Authority).

This multiple-nozzle oil lamp of the Beit Nattif type (Fig. 8.1) was found as an offering or a lighting device in Tomb 33 in the west cemetery of Tell en-Naṣbeh (McCown 1947: fig. 19.2, pl. 23:4–6). It was first published in 1947 by McCown (pl. 42:19; Palestine Archaeological Museum 32.2556). It was studied again by Goodenough (1953: 263), followed later by many others, including this author (Sussman 1985–86: fig. 32). Three additional lamps with multiple-wick-holes were found in the same tomb associated with burials C, E and F, among them an oil lamp (Fig. 8.2) belonging to the same Beit Nattif type (McCown 1947: fig. 23:10–11). These lamps were only obliquely mentioned in the excavation report: "In the collapsed kok [sic] in a Byzantine tomb which produced the expedition's finest glass vases and terra cotta lamps," which was followed by this general evaluation of the lamps: "all these oil lamps were unusually ambitious in design," (McCown 1947: 112–16). Because this lamp stands among the masterpieces of decorated oil lamps attributed to the Late Roman–Byzantine period, scholars have long enjoyed and admired its fine artistic achievement.

DESCRIPTION

Both the base and the upper part of the lamp were carefully molded. The base (Fig. 8.1 left) was decorated with a multiple ring-base from which seven elongated tongues, equal to the number of wick-holes, ran towards the top. This treatment is similar to that on other elaborately decorated lamps belonging to this type (including single-nozzle lamps).

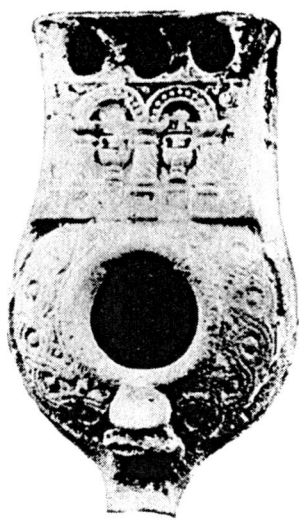

Fig. 8.2. Multiple-nozzle lamp decorated with an arcade and two large amphorae-shaped lamps(?) (McCown 1947: pl. 42:18, fig. 23:10; courtesy of the Badè Museum of Biblical Archaeology, Pacific School of Religion).

The upper part (Fig. 8.1 right) has a wide front. The *discus* features a wide filling-hole surrounded by a flange decorated with *ovuli*. The molded shoulders of the lamp, which were left undecorated, and the flange around the filling-hole, decorated with a necklace of *ovu-li*, resemble an architrave (cornice) of the *cyma recta* type. The loop handle at the rear is missing; it was probably secured by a disc that covered the point of attachment—now the gap between the handle and the rim of the *discus*/filling-hole—as on the handles of the lamps in Figs. 8.2–3. The lamp is painted with a red-brown slip and bears heavy traces of burning. Its measurements are: width 9.2 cm and length 14.0 cm.

Fig. 8.3. Multiple-nozzle lamps depicting hanging lamps from 1936 Hizme excavation (Palestine Archaeological Museum 43.156; courtesy of the Israel Antiquities Authority).

THE DECORATION

Our main interest, however, is the decoration appearing on the wide, flattened-nozzle—a scene in high relief depicting an almost three-dimensional arcade. The arcade consists of five high pedestals supporting twisted/screw-type columns. These stand on low, drum-shaped bases and have widening capitals supporting four arches. Each arch is decorated with a string of dots. Within the space created by each arch there is a circle with a high dome-shaped center. Five of the same high-centered circles occur under the wick-holes, between the arches, and in the spaces at the ends of the arches, which are surrounded by three symmetrically arranged dots.

The spaces on both sides of the central column are filled by images of fish depicted in linear relief. Each fish faces upwards, towards the circle within the arch, as if hanging from it. The author has previously suggested (Sussman 2001: 58) that the fish be identified as a pair of oil lamps in the shape of fish, known from the Byzantine period (Figs. 8.4–5; see also Schloessinger 1950–51: pl. 21: B–C).

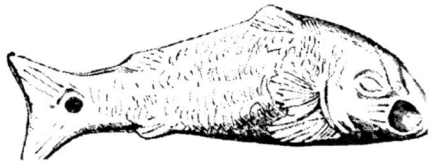

Fig. 8.4. Metal lamp made in the shape of a fish (Lowrie 1947: pl. 149c.)

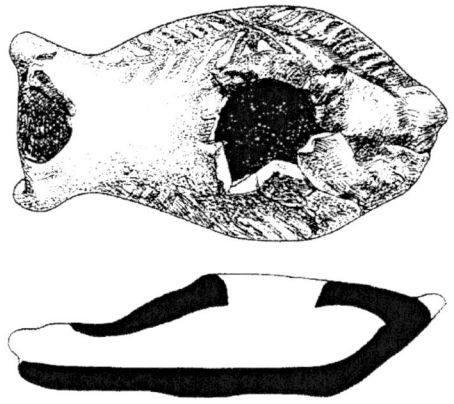

Fig. 8.5. Clay lamp in the shape of a fish; said to be found in the Samaria region near Shechem (Nablus).

In the spaces between the pairs of outer columns "hang" chains composed of three geometric patterns. These consist of a central circle with a high, dome-shaped center flanked by rhomboids which frame a raised central device identical to the design on the lamp in Fig. 8.6. The pattern of the hanging chain may represent a curtain leading to a holy place, as on a shrine depicted on a single-nozzle lamp typical of the Beit Nattif type with a filling hole surrounded by a heavy rim (Sussman 1985–86: type 3; Fig. 8.6). The pattern of rhomboids between circles with high centers is common on the shoulders of lamps of the Beit Nattif type. It was probably inspired by, or adapted from, jewelry. Such jewelry is known from hems of the clothing worn by sculptured figures on limestone burial chests from Palmyra (Mackay 1949: figs. 5, 5a).

Fig. 8.6. A single-nozzle lamp of unknown provenance decorated with a shrine containing a curtain decorated with geometric patterns.

While describing the decoration of the multiple-nozzle lamp from Tell en-Naṣbeh for a catalogue of lamps of the Byzantine period (in preparation), I was surprised to observe previously unnoticed details. Despite its pleasing artistic appearance, the execution itself is not entirely perfect and symmetric, perhaps intentionally so. The columns grow slightly taller and wider from left to right, as if shown in perspective. I suggest that the left capital is decorated with pointed leafs, as in the left capital which supports the vault in which a goddess stands in the terracotta from Cistern I found in the workshop at Beit Nattif (Fig. 8.7). In addition, the high, framed pedestals on which the columns stand differ from one another in size and shape. One is square, the other is rectangular, and the central one ends in a curved top. The most interesting feature, however, is that the framed pedestals not only differ in shape, but they are also decorated in relief, each with a different scene.

Fig. 8.7. Terracotta of a Syrian city goddess standing within a shrine; from Cistern I at Beit Nattif (Baramki 1936: pl. II:3).

The artist's first step in laying out his design was probably to outline the frame in which he intended to depict his tableau. He did so by drawing a ground line, still visible under the pedestals, and another line at the top, below the wick-holes. On the lower line he built the pedestals and columns, so as to "stabilize" the structure. The upper line ends the scene below the wick-holes so that the wick-holes do not interrupt the design. Despite the small available working area, the artist insisted on sticking to his planned depiction. Because of the difficulty in executing such a miniature design some of the images are, however, incomplete and blurred. There are several possible explanations for this phenomenon. First, the patterns could have been incised into the mold and then unintentionally erased at the time of the engraving because of shortage of space, leaving smooth sections when the lamp was taken out of the mold. Another possibility is that the patterns could have been made by stamping into a softened limestone mold. The final option is that the pedestals were decorated by stamping onto the leather hard clay before firing. In all these scenarios, the decoration either was erased by the fingers of the potter, or he did not press the stamp hard enough to create the entire image.

Fig. 8.8. Section of the lamp from Fig. 1 from Tell en-Naṣbeh from Tomb 33 showing the pedestals of the lamp.

Fig. 8.9. Drawing of the decorated pedestals of the Tell en-Naṣbeh lamp (By R. Sussman).

It is very difficult to describe and decipher the depictions within the framed pedestals because the pedestals are very small and the decorations differ on each one. In addition, the motifs and scenes on the pedestals are hard to identify because no precise parallels to them could be found.

I suggest that the following patterns appear on the pedestals, from right to left (Figs. 8.8–9). Panel 1: portions of a column from which two stairs lead up; the top is roofed by an arch; the space is filled with marks that cannot be clearly identified. Panel 2: the clearest pedestal depicts an arcade that consists of three arches; under the central arch stands a tree with a wide crown bearing rounded fruit, perhaps an apple tree. Under both the left and right arches a human figure flanks the crown of the tree. The figure on the right is the clearer of the two. This figure stands with legs spread; the head is triangular and two pairs of dots may represent hands and feet. Below the figure there is a structure built of two squares (an altar). Another, smaller figure appears alongside the trunk on the right. This figure, while smaller, is drawn with the same elements as the first. The scene on the left side of the tree is not so clear; it may have been identical to the one on the right. Panel 3: On the central pedestal, which is the highest, I again propose identifying a central gabled arcade flanked by an arch on each side. Under the central arch may stand a human figure; it is unclear what stands below the left arch, and the space under the right arch appears to be empty. Panel 4: Another column seems to stand here, perhaps resembling the first panel. Panel 5: Another large tree, probably with rounded fruit, is depicted, with possibly a human figure to the right of its trunk.

DISCUSSION

This is not the only known multiple-nozzle lamp decorated with arcades, which was rather a common pattern of the period. After studying the arcades depicted on other lamps of this era the first conclusion that may be drawn is that this style of pedestal is typical only on the decorated oil lamps of the Beit Nattif type, especially those produced in the southern part of the country. They are known on both single-nozzle oil lamps and also on lamps with multiple-wick-holes (Figs. 8.2–3 and 8.6). The same style of pedestal depicted on the lamp under discussion was found on other lamps, each supporting a column of one of three different orders:

monolithic, with *annuli*, and twisted. Such lamps are known from a tomb at Gezer (Macalister 1912: pl. 77:17); from additional lamps found at Tell en-Naṣbeh (Fig. 8.2; McCown 1947: fig. 23:10, pl. 42:18); from Beit Nattif (Zissu and Klein 2011: fig. 2); and from a fragment recently found under the floor of a church at Shiloh (Magen and Aharonovich 2012: fig. 61).

The same type of pedestal, supporting columns upon which an arch rests, and below which stands a naked goddess (Fig. 8.7) is depicted on a terracotta found in Cistern I at Beit Nattif (mentioned above; Baramki 1936: pl. 9:5). The author suggests that the pedestals on that shrine are decorated as well. The type of column, however, differs; it is monolithic. Note that the capital on the left is decorated with pointed leafs, like the one in Fig. 8.11 from Syria, the capitals of the arcade depicted on the lamp found at Shiloh (Magen and Aharonovich 2012: fig. 61), and on the left capital on the lamp from Tell en-Naṣbeh (Fig. 8.1 right).

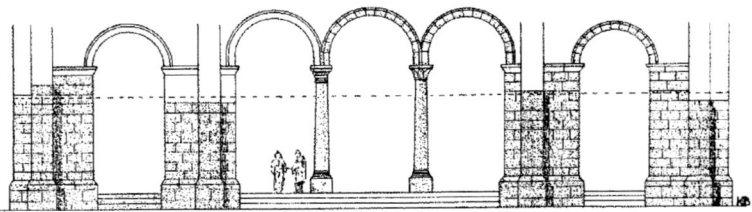

Fig. 8.10. Narthex from the Kerratin cathedral in Syria showing a similar type of pedestal (Butler 1929: ill. 169).

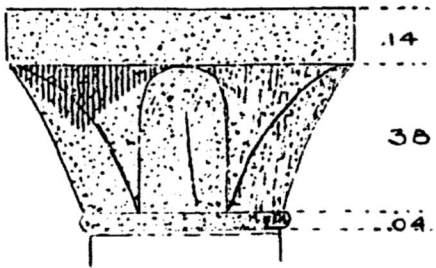

Fig. 8.11. The decorated capital from the same cathedral which resembles the capital on the left column on the Tell en-Naṣbeh lamp.

Among actual architectural remains, such four-cornered, straight-sided pedestals that would have supported columns are rare. Most of the square pedestals found in this country are recessed at the center. Some were also decorated, such as those from the Bet She'an region (Zori 1977: pl. A:1–2) and from Susita (Hippos) in the Golan Heights (Segal, Schuler and Eisenberg 2010: fig. 35).

Fig. 8.12. The city of Neapolis with square pedestals as depicted on the Madaba Map (Piccerillo and Aliata 1994: 177).

Pedestals resembling those depicted on the Beit Nattif lamps were popular in Syria during the Roman and Byzantine periods; they were employed within public buildings such as theaters, synagogues, churches and cathedrals (Fig. 8.10). The pedestals, however, were seldom decorated. When they were, it was with a single pattern, as found on a pedestal from a tomb in Syria (Butler 1903: 284). It is very interesting that on the Madaba Map the pedestals depicted as part of the church representing the city of Neapolis

(Shechem), in the Samaria region, resemble the pedestal on our lamp; the shape of the capitals is identical to the shape of the pedestals. This style differs from all the depictions of the rest of the cities that appear on the same map, where the columns stand on plain low drums (Fig. 8.12; Piccirillo and Aliata 1994: 177). Pedestals supporting twisted columns, found on the numerous Samaritan oil lamps depicting shrines, do not resemble those on the Beit Nattif type of lamps made in the same period (Sussman 2001: pl. 2). Decorated pedestals of the Roman period support mainly civic monuments such as the fourth-century Arch of Constantine near the Coliseum in Rome (Van der Meer and Mohrman 1958: fig. 120).

Other, comparable material may have appeared on altars, many of which bear decorations on their rectangular panels. In addition, framed, decorated wall panels were found in churches and synagogues, and became common in reliefs on stone work at Palmyra (Dunant and Stucky 2000: 83–84, pl. 3; after the first-century CE). The decorated panels on these ceramic lamps also resemble the panels on molded, six-faced glassware of the same period. On the latter, a different pattern appears on each panel, among them a shrine, menorah, rhomboids and plants (Goodenough 1953: 388–429). These patterns probably were employed for many decades from the late third to the fifth and sixth centuries CE.

Scenes under arcades were common already in the fifth-century CE. Depictions of trees bearing fruit, under which human figures stand, are abundant on mosaic floors especially in Jordan, as in the Church of St. Stephen at Umm Al-Rasas (Piccirillo and Aliata 1994: fig. 50), where the figures which originally stood between the trees were disfigured or erased during the iconoclastic Umayyad Period. The human figures were replaced by geometric chains, similar to those that hang on both sides of the fish on our lamp, or by floral designs.

The depiction of the arcade was probably intended to portray the interior arcade of a basilica, either the narthex or the arcades that separated the nave from the central hall. When a single arch is depicted it is meant to represent the shrine (as on Fig. 8.6). The arcade is found as a decorative element on many mosaic floors (Fig. 8.13). These arcades on mosaic floors resemble a lamp made in the shape of a basilica that emphasizes the interior arcade and the lamps hanging there (Fig. 8.14). In both examples three oil lamps are shown. In the former they are hanging, as on the lamp in Fig. 8.3; on the latter they project from the arched building—meant to show at the same time its interior as well. Colonnades of this type, where the pedestals were probably covered with paintings, may have been common features at the front of a sanctuary. It seems probable that the lamp artist either copied such real-world pedestals, or at least drew inspiration from them for his lamp.

Fig. 8.13. Mosaic floor from St. Stefano church at Umm al-Rasas, Jordan, showing both the cathedral and the interior with hanging lamps (Piccerillo and Aliata 1994: pl. 3).

Arcades, which were an important and impressive part of public structures, either on the exterior or the interior, also became a very important decorative element in various media, and were frequently depicted on mosaic floors, sarcophagi, minor art (e.g. ivories), and wall paintings. It is therefore no wonder that lamps were decorated in the same way, and also the pedestals.

Fig. 8.14. Bronze lamp in the form of a basilica with lamps at
the front, fifth century CE (Lowrie 1947: pl. 41:20).

The use of the twisted column, supported by the type of pedestal
depicted on the lamp under discussion, was popular in Syria (Butler
1903: 35, colonnade from Apamea). Such a twisted column was
also found at Sussita (Hippos) in the northern part of Israel; it consists of a stone covered with stucco (Segal, Schuler and Eisenberg
2010: figs. 34–35). The use of twisted columns points towards Syria
as the source of architectural inspiration chosen to adorn lamps
produced by local artists in the Holy Land, such as the Tell en-
Naṣbeh lamp. The twisted type of column is frequently depicted on
Samaritan oil lamps (Sussman 2001; pl. 2:6–9), though, as noted
above the supporting pedestals are different. Twisted columns are
also depicted on lead coffins made at Tyre in Lebanon/Phoenicia
(Rahmani 1999: figs. 83–84), and on the relief featuring the Menorah supported by a twisted column on the wall at Beit She'arim
(Goodenough 1953: 56).

The depiction of arches decorated with dots is also characteristic of Beit Nattif oil lamps (Sussman 2001: pl. 1:10–12 and 17–
20); the dots may stand for the blocks from which the arch was
built. Not all arches, however, were depicted resting on columns;
some are found that do not touch the capitals. This can be seen on
the fragment from Shiloh (Magen and Aharonovich 2012: fig. 61),
where the capitals are floating. In addition, as on the lamp in Fig.
8.3, the number of pedestals does not always match the number of
columns.

On the fragment found at nearby Shiloh there is a lintel at a
distance above the freestanding pedestals. A vertical line (column)

flanked by a zigzag descends from this lintel. This schematic drawing corresponds to the way in which the second inner row of pedestals supports columns as depicted in the church of Neapolis that
appears on the Madaba Map (Fig. 8.12), thus showing both central
arcades of the cathedral.

Fig. 8.15. Multiple-nozzle lamp with a pair of fish lamps
(Schloessinger 1950–1951: pl. 22).

Piccirillo pointed out the differences in the style of architecture
between that of Neapolis and the other cities on the Madaba Map.
He described the type of pedestal that matches the capital as the
old Doric order. Piccirillo states "For Neapolis; too, the mosaicist

used the colonnade façade of a building to represent the whole city, and this might be an allusion to the Theotokos Church built by Justin I (518–527 CE) on the top of Mount Gerizim," (1992: 344). We may suggest that the artist who decorated the lamp in Figs. 8.2 also intended to suggest two arcades, and that the amphorae represent the arcade on the other side of the central hall. A similar intention to show simultaneously both arcades flanking the central hall may explain the additional arches on the lamp in Fig. 8.3. The floating lintel and zigzag on the Shiloh fragment may likewise signify a second arcade.

The items that occupy the spaces between the columns of the shrines on oil lamps with a single-wick-hole include various elements, such as hanging lamps, doors, a screen or a curtain. On the multiple wick-hole oil lamps we find additional items within the arcades, such as amphorae, candelabras, and the cross (Magen 1990: fig. 97). For example, besides the pedestals that carry columns on the Tell en-Naṣbeh lamp in Fig. 8.2, as on the lamp from Shiloh, we are able to identify two additional pedestals; these instead support a pair of giant amphorae.

On the lamp from Tomb 33 at Tell en-Naṣbeh a pair of fish adorn the two central spaces. Fish also appear on pear-shaped lamps of the Beit Nattif type, but on those lamps they are styled differently. For example, scaled fish appear on the shoulders of a lamp arranged in a heraldic posture on both sides of a wreath, similar to how they are depicted on the shoulder of a lamp with multiple-wick-holes. On the lamp with multiple-wick-holes in Fig. 8.15 a pair of scaled fish are arranged lengthwise along the nozzle facing an eye pattern guarded by circles (Schloessinger 1950–51: pls. 22–23; Goodenough 1953: no. 545). A single highly stylized fish flanked by two dots is depicted within the channel of Late Byzantine oil lamps made in the Decapolis (Fig. 8.16). The shape of the lamp and its decoration resembles the shape and the depiction of the fish on the nozzle itself (fish on fish/lamp on lamp). Lamps themselves appear in the form of scaled fish (Schloessinger 1950–51: pl. 21: A; Figs. 8.4–5). Portraying lamps on oil lamps used at the time was common. These include authentic pottery lamps, the Jewish menorah, glass lamps, and also amphorae-shaped lamps or containers for oil used to fill the lamps (Fig. 8.2).

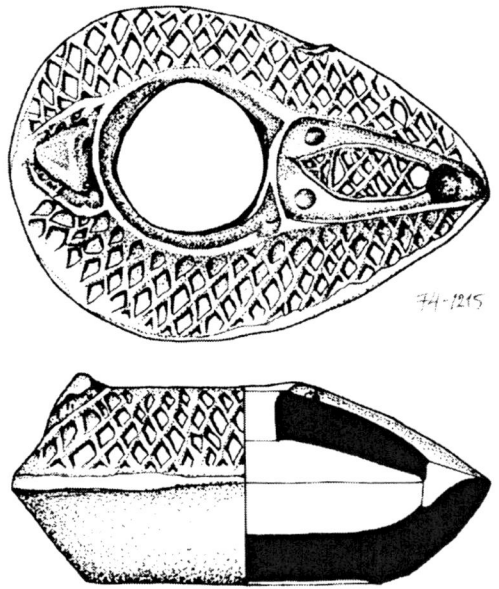

Fig. 8.16. Late Byzantine oil lamp from the excavations of Zori
at Bet Ha-shitta showing a fish in the channel along the nozzle.
Israel Department of Antiquities and Museums 74–1219
(Courtesy of the Israel Antiquities Authority).

The fish depicted on these lamps may also symbolize fertility or
may have been solely a decorative pattern, as on mosaic floors, as
has been discussed by Schloessinger (1950–1951). The possibility
that the entire assemblage of motifs on the lamp from Tomb 33 is
part of a scene may suggest an artist inspired by a Christian artistic
genre. Fish stood for Jesus as the messiah (YXTUS). Pairs of fish
became a common pattern on Western and North African oil
lamps thought to have been made for Christians, and also for Jewish communities that existed side by side. For example, a pair of
fish hang within an arcade on lamps of Red Slip Ware dated to the
fourth–fifth century CE from Carthage (Ennabli 1976: pl. 43: 760).

As mentioned above, four lamps with multiple-wick-holes,
three intact and another fragmentary, were found among the 22
lamps in Tomb 33 at Tell en-Naṣbeh. McCown suggested that
these four lamps belong to the early stage of burials (1947: 114)—

probably Jewish, pagan or Crypto-Christian of the Late Roman period, which shared similar funerary customs. None of the lamps found in burials C, E and F features a cross.

The second stage of burial in Tomb 33, however, contains oil lamps of the Candlestick type, among them lamps bearing crosses, which clearly belong to Christians of the later part of the Byzantine period. The lamps with crosses were found only in the center of the tomb, not in the earlier burials A–F.

On the lamp found at Hizme (Fig. 8.3), a site in the neighborhood of Tell en-Naṣbeh, I suggest that the central pedestal bears a cross. This lamp is the product of a less expert artist. The majority of the lamps that accompanied the Beit Nattif oil lamps at Hizme belong to the Candlestick type, identified as serving the community of converts to Christianity. Only a few multiple- and single-nozzle oil lamps of the Beit Nattif type bear crosses.

Whether or not the potters who produced oil lamps with multiple-wick-holes thought that the lamps would provide more powerful illumination, they certainly understood that the larger space on these lamps provided them the opportunity to express a culturally meaningful image in line with the period's fashion. Did the artist of our lamp intend to illustrate the interior of a specific church or synagogue that he had really seen? Or, was he simply following his imagination and his deep knowledge of Western and Eastern art and architecture?

We may infer once again that we may have evidence of strong cultural ties between the southern Levantine oil lamp workshops and the art and architecture of Syria, well expressed in the potters' artistic choice of patterns of decoration found on the Beit Nattif lamps and terracotta figurines. For example, Syrian architectural elements are found on the walls of a catacomb at Beit She'arim. There we also find incised arcades, which form a relief, and where the columns also stand on rectangular pedestals (Goodenough 1953: 53, 55, 62). The importance of the arcade as one of the major subjects fits well into the Byzantine media of mosaic pavements and cathedral facades, as is well illustrated on the mosaic pavements in Jordan. We know that Beit She'arim served as a burial ground for Jews of the Diaspora—mainly from Syria. The artist who produced the fine piece of art on this lamp from Tell en-Naṣbeh was well acquainted with the current patterns of Eastern art and adjusted them to the space available on the panel on the lamp.

The artistic interdependence between the decoration on the oil lamps and other media, among them the mosaic floors, is well attested. For example, the depiction of trees flanked by figures was probably adapted to the pedestals depicted on the lamps from another medium, such as mosaic floors. Trees bearing fruit are not abundant on mosaic floors in this country. One tree bearing fruit was a central piece of the mosaic floor uncovered in the church at Roglit (Khirbet Jufea) in the Judean Shephelah excavated by R. Gophna and the author (published by Yeivin 1960: pl. 5:3), dated to the fifth-century CE. Another pavement in the church at Shiloh, also dated to the fifth-century CE, shows a tree with a stag on either side; a figure of a fish is also depicted behind two quadrilateral pillars (Kjaer 1930: fig. 30). Most arboreal depictions, however, come from Byzantine era Jordan. One example is the row of apple trees on the mosaic floor of the nave in front of the sanctuary of the church of St. Stephen at Umm al-Rasas (Piccirillo and Aliata 1994: 126:6, 140; 30, 32 and 244). Here the figures that originally stood between the trees were replaced by geometric patterns identical to those between the outer columns in the lamp from Tell en-Naṣbeh. This was probably done in the eighth-century CE, after the Arab conquest, as a result of the iconoclastic movement of the time. Were the Muslim artisans aware of the earlier lamp and mosaic decorations?

Chronologically the Tell en-Naṣbeh lamp fits into the Late Roman period, when the use of *ovuli* to surround the filling-hole was still popular, and also when there were close cultural relations between the southern Levant, Syria, and Palmyra. The similar lamp found under the floor of the church at nearby Shiloh was dated to the fourth–fifth centuries CE. There is, however, a discrepancy between the fourth–fifth centuries CE date proposed for this Beit Nattif type of lamp and the various mosaic floors mentioned above, dated to the sixth-century CE. For example, the similarity of the pedestals on our lamps to the depiction of Neapolis on the Madaba Map of the Byzantine Period cannot be ignored (Fig. 8.12).

After checking other structures on lamps bearing similar pedestals, I have come to the conclusion that almost all of the pedestals depicted on the lamps of the Beit Nattif type with a wide filling hole were decorated, but less successfully than those on the Tell en-Naṣbeh lamp. This indicates that the use of such decorated pedestals was the leading fashion in Judean lamp workshops, and so may predate the mosaic floors. It might also mean that these lamps continued to be made during the entire fifth-century CE. For example, Hadad suggests that such lamps found at Bet She'an do not predate the fifth-century CE (2002: 35).

CONCLUSION

Unfortunately, we could not identify the ruins of a prominent structure of the type depicted on the lamp, especially one with decorated pedestals, in the area around Jerusalem or in the Judean region where the lamp was made, or anywhere else in the country.

Hopefully, someday such a structure will be found. Nevertheless, it seems obvious that we may also posit other, non-architectural media as sources of inspiration for the decoration on the Tell en-Naṣbeh lamp examined here. We emphasize again that the decorative elements adorning the lamp from Tomb 33 were probably common in mosaic pavements and other media already during the fifth-century CE. For example, the mosaic pavement of the church at Shiloh (a site not far from Tell en-Naṣbeh), may have served as the source of inspiration for the decoration on the lamp. As mentioned above, lamps with multiple-wick-holes decorated with a similar structure and columns and pedestals identical to those on the Tell en-Naṣbeh lamp, were found at Shiloh (Magen and Aharonovich 2012: fig. 61). We may even dare to suggest that artists who decorated both the mosaic pavement and lamps were inspired from a common source. As we have seen, however, lamps on which an arcade is depicted above other decorative elements were in fashion and common during the Byzantine Period, especially on lamps with multiple-wick-holes, and also on lamps with a single-wick-hole where the space was limited to a single vault—a shrine. It is difficult to ascertain for which community these lamps were intended, as noted by McCown (1947: 114), but that they differ from structures depicted on lamps made in the Samaria region suggests a different community. The mosaic floors in Israel dated to the fifth-century CE may thus support a similar date for the lamp from Tell en-Naṣbeh.

REFERENCES

Baramki, D. C.

1936 Two Roman Cisterns at Beit Nattif. *Quarterly of the Department of Antiquities in Palestine* 5: 3–10.

Butler, H. C.

1903 *Architecture and other Arts.* American Archaeological Expedition to Syria in 1899–1900 Publications 2. New York: The Century Company.

1929 *Early Churches in Syria, Fourth to Seventh Centuries,* ed. and completed by E. B. Smith. Princeton Monographs in Art and Architecture 1. Princeton: Department of Art and Archaeology of Princeton University.

Dunant, C., and Stucky, R. A.

2000 *Le sanctuaire de Baalshamîn à Palmyre,* Vol. 4: *Skulpturen/Sculptures.* Bibliotheca Helvetica Romana 10. Roma: Institut suisse de Rome.

Ennabli, A.

1976 *Lampes chrétiennes de Tunisie (musées du Bardo et de Carthage).* Etudes d'Antiquités africaines. Paris: Éditions du Centre national de la recherche scientifique

Goodenough, E. R.

1953 *Jewish Symbols in the Greco-Roman Period,* Vol. 3. Bollingen Series 37. New York: Pantheon Books.

Hadad, S.

2002 *The Oil Lamps from the Hebrew University Excavations at Bet Shean.* Qedem Reports 4. Excavations at Bet Shean 1. Jerusalem: Institute of Archaeology, Hebrew University of Jerusalem

Kjaer, H.

1930 The Excavations of Shiloh 1929: Preliminary Report. *Journal of the Palestine Oriental Society* 10: 87–174.

Lowrie, W.

1947 *Art in the Early Church.* New York: Pantheon Books.

Macalister, R. A. S.
1912   *The Excavations of Gezer 1902–1905 and 1907–1909.* 3 vols. London: Murray.

Mackay, D.
1949   The Jewelry of Palmyra and its Significance. *Iraq* 11: 160–87.

Magen Y.
1990   A Roman Fortress and a Byzantine Monastery at Khirbet el-Kiliya. Pp. 321–32 in *Christian Archaeology in the Holy Land, New Discoveries: Essays in Honour of Virgilio C. Corbo, OFM,* ed. G. C. Bottini, L. Di Segni, and E. Alliata. Collectio Maior 36. Jerusalem: Franciscan Printing Press.

Magen Y., and Aharonovich E.
2012   The Northern Churches at Shiloh. Pp. 209–18 in *Christians and Christianity,* Vol. 3, *Churches and Monasteries in Samaria and Northern Judea,* ed. N. Haimovich-Carmin. Judea and Samaria Publications 15. Jerusalem: Israel Antiquities Authority.

McCown, C. C.
1947   *Tell en-Naṣbeh,* Vol. 2: *The Pottery.* Berkeley, CA: The Palestine Institute of Pacific School of Religion.

Piccirillo, M.
1992   *The Mosaics of Jordan,* ed. P. M. Bikai and T. A. Dailey. American Center of Oriental Research Publications 1. Amman, Jordan: American Center of Oriental Research.

Piccirillo, M., and Aliata, E., ed.
1994   *Umm al-Rasas Mayfaʿah I, Gli Scavi del Complesso di Santo Stefano.* Collectio Maior 28. Jerusalem: Studium Biblicum Franciscanum.

Rahmani, L. Y.
1999   *A Catalogue of Roman and Byzantine Lead Coffins from Israel.* Jerusalem: Israel Antiquities Authority.

Schloessinger, M. S.
1950–1951   Five Lamps with Fish Reliefs from Israel and Other Mediterranean Countries. *Israel Exploration Journal* 1: 84–95.

Segal, A.; Schuler, M.; and Eisenberg, M.
2010   *Hippos – Sussita: Eleventh Season of Excavations (July 2010).*
        Haifa: Zinman Institute of Archaeology, University of Hai-
        fa.

Sussman, V.
1985–86 Ornamental Figures on "Beit Nattif" Type Oil Lamps
        from Northern and Southern Workshops. Pp. 63–86 in *Is-
        rael: People and Land,* ed. R. Zeevy. Haaretz Museum Year-
        book 2–3. Tel Aviv: Haaretz Museum (Hebrew).
2001   Structures Depicted on Oil Lamps of Eretz-Israel. Pp. 53–
        76 in *Judea and Samaria Research Studies* 10, ed. Y. Eshel. Ke-
        dumim – Ariel: The Research Institute, The College of Ju-
        dea and Samaria (Hebrew).

Van der Meer, F., and Mohrmann, C.
1958   *Atlas of the Early Christian World,* trans. and ed. M. F. Hed-
        lund and H. H. Rowley. London: Nelson.

Yeivin, S.
1960   *A Decade of Archaeology in Israel, 1948–1958.* Uitgaven van
        het Nederlands Historisch-Archaeologisch Instituut te
        Istanbul 8. Istanbul: Nederlands Historisch-
        Archaeologisch Instituut in het Nabije Oosten.

Zissu, B., and Klein, E.
2011   A Rock-Cut Burial Cave from the Roman Period at Beit
        Nattif, Judaean Foothills. *Israel Exploration Journal* 61: 196–
        216.

Zori, N.
1977   *The Land of Issachar, Archaeological Survey of the Gilboa and its
        Slopes.* Jerusalem: Israel Exploration Society (Hebrew).

On the Use and Reuse of Rock-Cut Tombs and a Ritual Bath at Tell en-Naṣbeh: New Perspectives on the Roman and Byzantine Necropoleis[1]

Boaz Zissu

Department of Land of Israel and Archaeology
Bar-Ilan University

Eitan Klein
Israel Antiquities Authority

Abstract

The article discusses a selection of archaeological remains from the Early Roman, Late Roman, and Byzantine periods uncovered by William F. Badè at Tell en-Naṣbeh between 1926 and 1935. The finds, such as rock-cut tombs, a ritual bath and archaeological assemblages are discussed in light of modern understandings of Second Temple Judaism and emergent Christianity. Ca. 40 tombs from the above mentioned periods discovered in the necropoleis surrounding the tell suggest that during these periods there was a settlement in the vicinity whose inhabitants created this

---

[1] All illustrations, unless otherwise noted, are courtesy of the Badè Museum of Biblical Archaeology of Pacific School of Religion in Berkeley, CA.

graveyard. Because the excavations on the tell did not un-cover significant finds from these late periods, it is likely that the tombs were used by the residents of Khirbet Shuweika or Khirbet 'Aṭṭara. The ritual bath with a dou-ble entrance/exit, and the few ossuaries that were discovered in some burial caves, indicate that these installations were initially used by a Jewish population that was careful about the laws of the Torah in the spirit of the times—the late Second Temple period. By contrast, the many objects discov-ered in the tombs, and especially lamps with crosses, attest to population changes in the region after the Bar Kokhba Revolt, when the Jewish inhabitants left and the vacuum was filled by pagans and later by Christians.

INTRODUCTION

Tell en-Naṣbeh covers an area of about 3.2 hectares in the hill country south of Ramallah (Map. Ref. OIG 1706/1143). On the tell, generally identified as biblical Mizpah of Benjamin, remains from various periods—discussed at length in this volume—have been discovered (McCown 1947; Wampler 1947; for a summary and literature, see Zorn 1993a). At the foot of the tell is the ancient Roman road connecting Jerusalem (Aelia Capitolina) with Shechem (Neapolis), following the ancient Ridge Route (Roll 1994: 21–22).

Excavations by an expedition from Pacific School of Religion in Berkeley, California, conducted between 1926 and 1935 under the supervision of William Frederic Badè, found remains from the Early Roman, Late Roman, and Byzantine periods on, and in the vicinity of, the tell. Most of these finds came from rock-cut fea-tures, mainly tombs, on the slopes surrounding the tell. This article will discuss a selection of these features and their finds from a new perspective, in accordance with the approaches and standards cus-tomary in current scholarship. The reader is referred to the 1947 reports by McCown and Wampler for detailed descriptions of the tombs and their contents.

NECROPOLEIS

The excavations by the American expedition at Tell en-Naṣbeh revealed a large number of tombs from various periods in the vi-cinity of the tell. A total of 71 tombs of various types and dating to various periods were discovered; more than 40 of these tombs had architectural features or contained archaeological finds typical of the Roman and Byzantine periods. Information about these tombs is found in the final excavation report written by a team under the direction of Chester C. McCown (1947: 109–24) while the pottery was presented by Joseph C. Wampler (1947).

The excavations on the tell did not uncover significant finds from the Early Roman, Late Roman, and Byzantine periods. Therefore, we will suggest that the tombs were used by the residents of a nearby settlement, perhaps located west of the tell.

TOMBS FROM THE EARLY ROMAN PERIOD (LATE SECOND TEMPLE PERIOD TO BAR KOKHBA REVOLT)

Eight tombs (nos. 2, 4, 6, 8, 13, 33, 56, 71) discovered by the Badè expedition in the vicinity of the tell contain rock-cut *kokhim* (*loculi*). A *kokh* (pl. *kokhim*) is a long and narrow niche (ca. two meters long, and ca. 0.7 meters wide), hewn usually perpendicular to the wall of a burial chamber. A *kokh* was originally intended to hold a single corpse in a primary burial. But in many cases a *kokh* may contain more than a single corpse; sometimes *kokhim* contain collected bones (secondary burials) or ossuaries. Ossuaries are small, rectangular covered receptacles made of soft limestone and sometimes painted or ornamented with carved or incised designs. They were typically used by Jews for secondary burial of human bones. Such ossuaries are found in rock-cut tombs in Judea, Galilee and also in Transjordan. The practice of collecting bones in ossuaries began in the late first century BCE and continued in Jerusalem until the destruction of 70 CE, and in Judaea until the end of the Bar Kokhba Revolt, and even afterwards (Rahmani 1994). Many ossuaries carry inscriptions in Hebrew, Greek or Aramaic. The presence of architectural components such as *kokhim* enables us to date the hewing of the Tell en-Naṣbeh tombs to the late Second Temple period, ca. second century BCE–first century CE (see plan of Tomb 4, Fig. 9.1, and discussion below). Another burial chamber, which was damaged in the course of development work, was documented by Rafa Abu Raya in 1993 southeast of the tell (OIG 171050.1143100). This cave has a rock-cut rectangular courtyard in front. Inside the cave is a rectangular burial chamber with a sunken floor (sometimes called a standing pit in the scholarly literature) hewn in its center and ten raised *kokhim* spaced along its walls. The cave had been looted and no artifacts remained, but its plan is typi-

cal of the first century BCE–first century CE (Abu Raya 1995:
114–5).

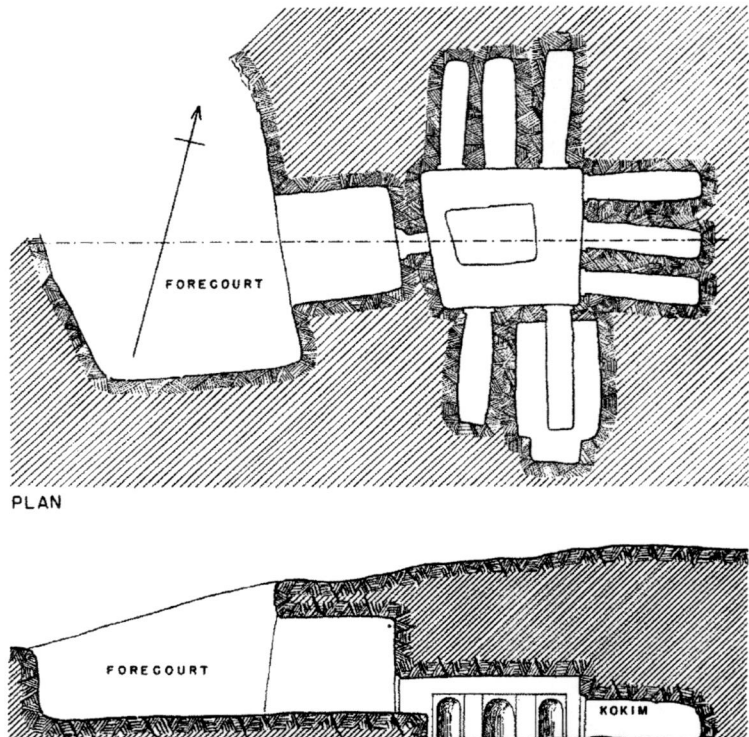

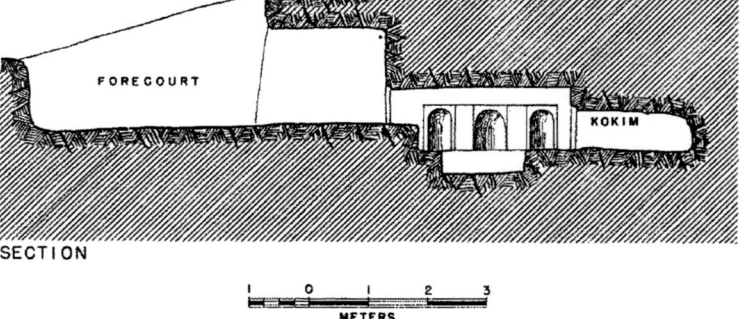

Fig. 9.1. Plan of Tomb 4 (McCown 1947, fig. 12).

Not all the tombs from the Early Roman period contained datable
finds. As noted above, some tombs were dated on the basis of their
architectural form, such as the presence of *kokhim*, and other elements. When datable objects were discovered, the tombs could be
assigned to the first and second centuries CE—up to the time of
the Bar Kokhba Revolt. For example, ossuaries were found in three

of the tombs (nos. 6, 14, and 71). Reuse of tombs is also attested for a number of burial chambers.

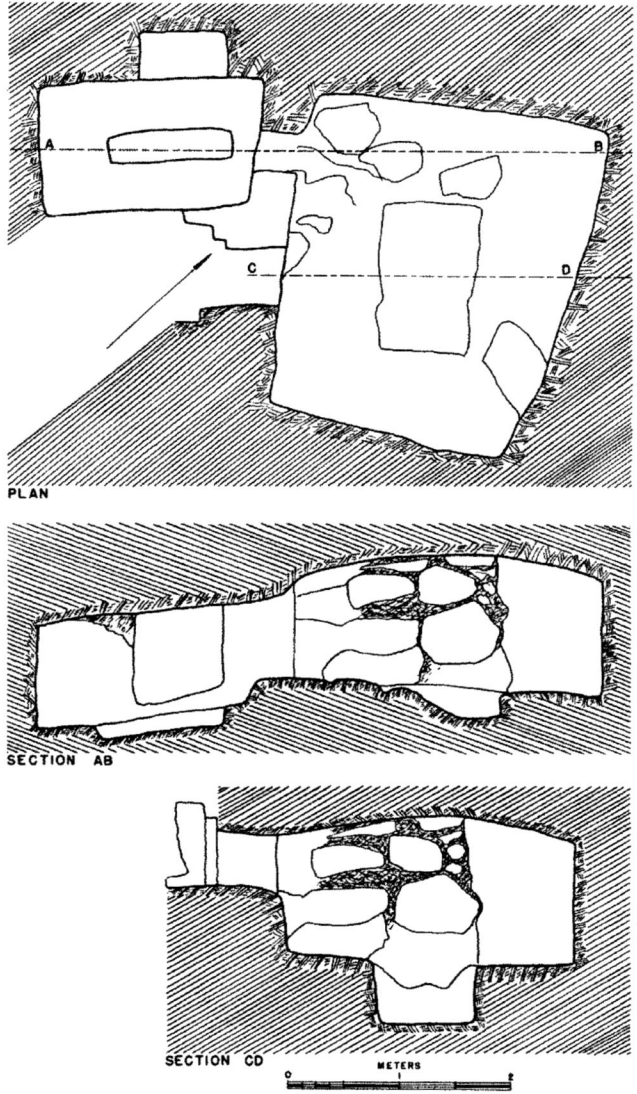

Fig. 9.2. Plan and section of Tomb 14 (McCown 1947, fig. 13).

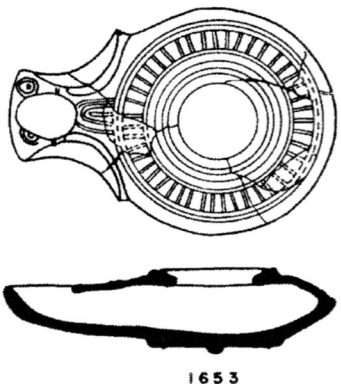

1653

Fig. 9.3. Darom oil-lamp, typical of the period 70–136 CE,
found in Tomb 14. This find shows that the tomb was used by
Jews until the Bar-Kokhba revolt (Wampler 1947: pl. 72:1653).

For example, Tomb 14 (McCown 1947: 104–06) was hewn in the
Iron Age or the Hellenistic period (Fig. 9.2). It was reused in the
Early Roman period up to the Bar Kokhba Revolt (132–136 CE) as
attested by a variety of finds. An intact ossuary, decorated with typical rosettes, flanking a schematic monument or column set on a
stepped base (Fig. 9.5) and fragments of additional ossuaries, were
found in Tomb 14. Unfortunately this ossuary has no inscription
on it. The "Darom" oil lamp also found in this tomb (Fig. 9.3) attests to its use until the Bar Kokhba Revolt; the decorated ossuary
shown in Fig. 9.5 is typical of the first century CE. Tomb 14 was
used again in the third and fourth centuries CE, as evidenced by
lamps typical of those periods (Figs. 9.4).

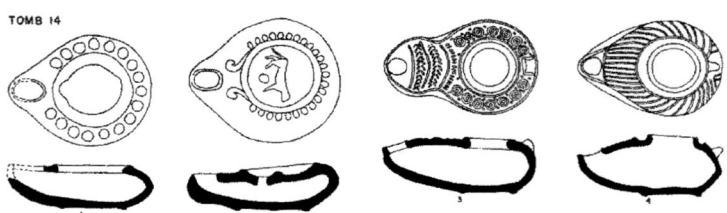

Fig. 9.4. Oil-lamps typical of the third and fourth centuries CE,
found in burial cave no. 14 (McCown 1947: fig. 21:1–4).

1. FRONT VIEW

2. BACK VIEW

3. INTERIOR OF OSSUARY AND LID

Fig. 9.5. Ossuary from Tomb 14 (McCown 1947: pl. 43).

TOMBS FROM THE LATE ROMAN AND BYZANTINE PERIODS

Objects from the Late Roman and Byzantine periods were discovered in at least 18 tombs around the site (nos. 2, 4, 6, 13, 14, 15, 16, 18, 19, 22, 23, 26, 27, 30, 31, 33, 56, 71) and in additional tombs at Khirbet ʿAṭṭara (McCown 1947: 101–28). Only four of these tombs (nos. 13, 19, 22, 30) had plans typical of the Late Roman and Byzantine periods. Others were cut in earlier times and were reused during the Late Roman and Byzantine periods. The typical Late Roman and Byzantine forms include rock-cut *arcosolia* cut in their walls with burial troughs underneath. An *arcosolium* (pl. *arcosolia*) is a recess hewn parallel to the wall of the burial chamber. They have the form of a bench and the space where the body lay may be sunken. The bottom of an *arcosolium* is a horizontal surface used for primary or secondary burials; its rear wall is vertical and its ceiling is arched. *Arcosolia* first appear in the first century CE and are prepared, in various forms, until the end of the Byzantine period. Also discovered were tombs of other types, common of the Late Roman and Byzantine periods; such as, simple cist graves (as nos. 20, 21, 28, 44) and shaft tombs with one or two *arcosolia* cut at the bottom of the shaft (as. nos. 17, 23, 24, 26, 27, 41). Some of the *kokhim* tombs, which were common in the Early Roman period, were reused in the Late Roman and Byzantine periods. Two tombs (nos. 2 and 6) in which this secondary use was observed, will be discussed here in more detail.

Tomb 2 (Fig. 9.6), located approximately 400 meters west of Tell en-Naṣbeh, southeast of Khirbet Shuweika, was excavated in 1929. Its plan includes a rock-cut vestibule, a small, framed opening for a rolling stone, and a main burial chamber with five *kokhim* in its walls. In the center of the burial chamber was a rectangular, sunken, rock-cut standing space. Changes seem to have been made at a later time, including what seems to be an enlargement of two *kokhim* (McCown 1947: 110, fig. 15). The form of the original chamber and the discovery of a knife-pared ("Herodian") oil-lamp demonstrate that the tomb was first used for burial in the late Second Temple period, probably the first century CE. The cave was used again during the third and fourth centuries CE, as is evidenced by two Karm esh-Sheikh lamps from this time (Rosenthal and Sivan 1978: 99–100).

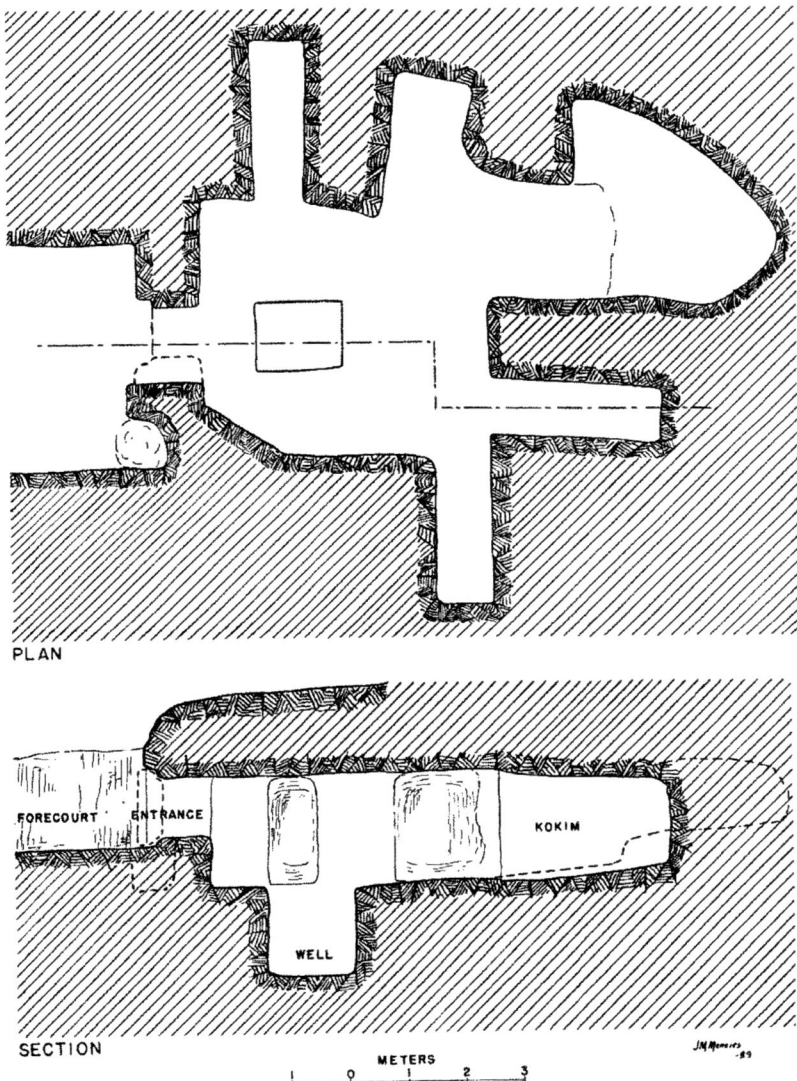

PLAN

SECTION

FORECOURT   ENTRANCE   KOKIM

WELL

METERS
0   1   2   3

Fig. 9.6. Plan and section of Tomb 2 (McCown 1947: fig. 15).

TOMB 6

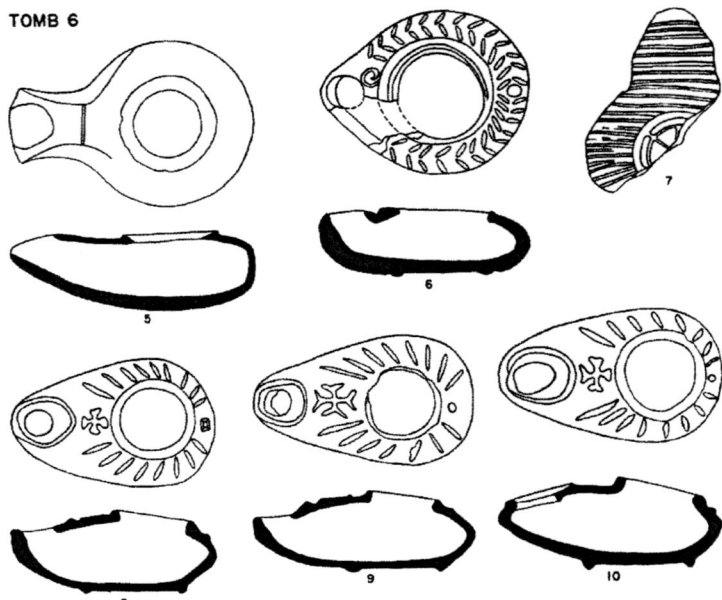

Fig. 9.7. Lamps discovered in Tomb 6 (McCown 1947: fig. 22:5–10).

Tomb 6, too, is located in the western necropolis of Tell en-Naṣbeh. The tomb, excavated in 1932, includes a main burial chamber with seven *kokhim* (for a somewhat schematic plan, see McCown 1947: 110–11, fig, 1:19). Ten knife-pared lamps (of the type shown in Fig. 9.7.5) and fragments of an ossuary attest that the tomb was first used for burial in the late Second Temple period, during the first century CE. Evidence of later use includes a fragment of a lamp from the second to fourth century CE (Fig. 9.7.6) and a variety of lamps dated to the fourth and fifth centuries CE, including lamps of the Ein Yabrud type, decorated with a cross (Iliffe 1935: 177–78; see also Figs. 9.7.8–10 below). The cross demonstrates that towards the beginning of the Byzantine period the tomb was used for the burial of Christians.

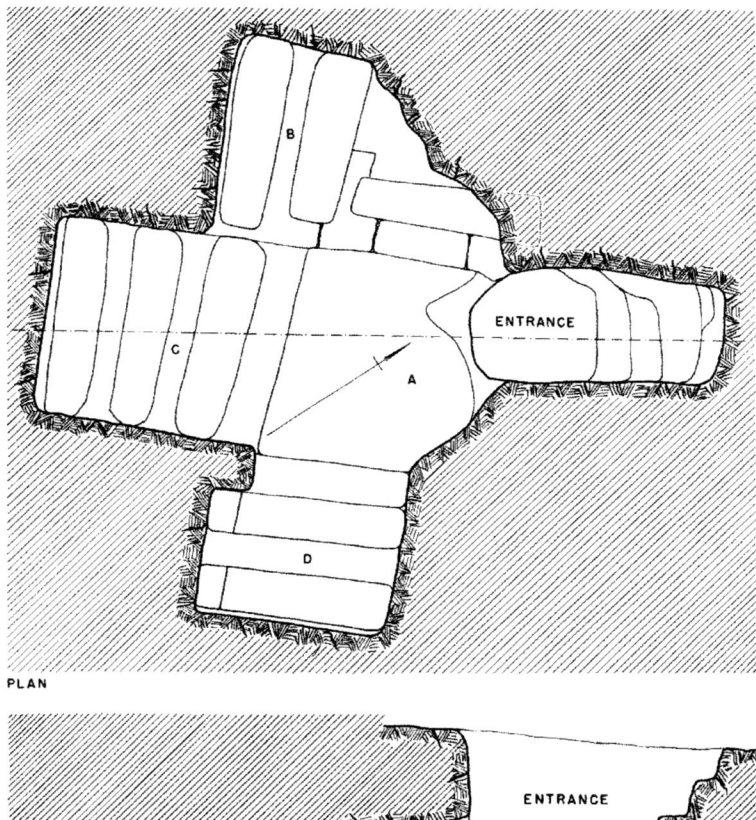

PLAN

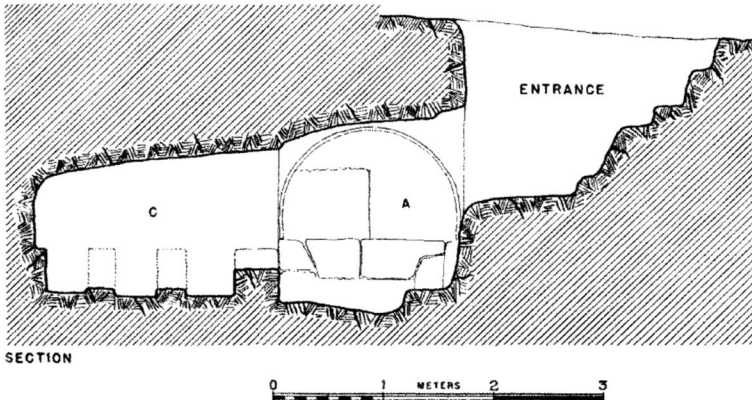

SECTION

Fig. 9.8. Plan and section of burial cave no. 19 (McCown 1947:
fig. 18).

Tomb 19 has a plan typical of the Byzantine period (see Fig. 9.8)
containing three *arcosolia* with rock-cut troughs at their bases. A

large number of ceramic lamps of various types from the fourth
through seventh centuries CE were discovered in the tomb. Particularly interesting is a late Iron Age II agate seal discovered in the
tomb with the words "Ja'azaniah servant of the King" written in
ancient Hebrew script above an image of a rooster in a combat
pose (see Fig. 9.9). One of the army captains who came to Geda-
liah ben Ahikam at Mizpah, following the destruction of Jerusalem
by the Babylonians in 586 BCE, was Ja'azaniah (2 Kings 25:23; Jer.
40:8), and this may very well be his seal. The discovery of a sixth-
century BCE seal in a tomb hewn and used more than a thousand
years later suggests that the seal was found in the Byzantine period,
kept as a precious personal belonging (nicely decorated and inscribed in the ancient and prestigious paleo-Hebrew script), and
buried with its new owners.

4   5

Fig.9.9. "Ja'azaniah servant of the King" seal from Tomb 19
(McCown 1947: pl. 57:4, 5).

It is worthwhile examining Tomb 33 in some detail here; it is an
arcosolium tomb containing a wealth of finds from these periods.
Tomb 33, excavated in 1932, is located in the western necropolis of
Tell en-Naṣbeh (Fig. 9.10). The tomb entrance on the northeast is
near the bottom of a deep rectangular shaft. A step leads from the
entrance to a square main burial chamber. In the wall to the right
of the entrance is an *arcosolium* with a burial trough at the bottom of
it (trough A). Three burial troughs were installed perpendicular in
each of the two remaining walls (B, C, and D opposite the entrance
and E, F, and G opposite trough A). Thirteen lamps of various
types were found in the main burial chamber (Fig. 9.11), including

two decorated multiple-nozzled lamps (of the Beit Nattif type, dated to the third and fourth centuries CE; see the chapter by Sussman in this volume), two single-nozzled lamps of the Beit Nattif type, and six of the 'Ain Yabrud type.

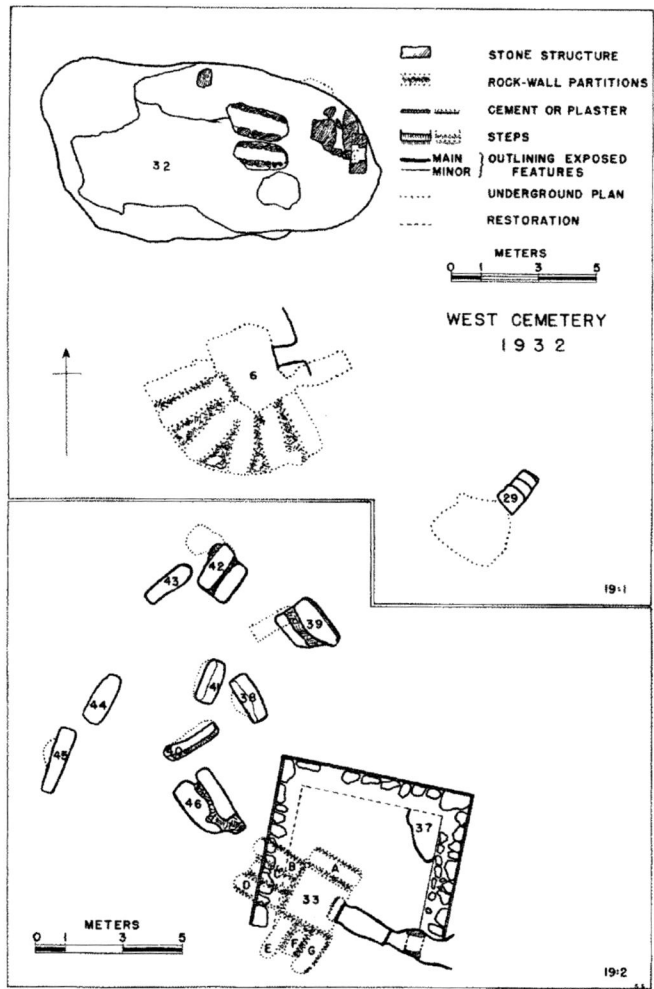

Fig. 9.10. Plan of the western necropolis. Note the plan of Tomb. 33 (McCown 1947: fig. 19).

Another two decorated multiple-nozzled lamps (Beit Nattif type, third and fourth centuries CE) and six decorated lamps of the Beit Nattif and Ramat Mamre types were found in troughs C, E, and F (McCown 1947: 114–16; Rosenthal and Sivan 1978, 103–09). Because no lamps with crosses were discovered in the burial troughs, McCown proposed that the tomb had undergone two stages of activity. In the first stage (third–fourth centuries CE), the tomb was hewn and burial was performed in the troughs; in the second stage the tomb was used by Christians. Also in the second stage (later fourth century?), lamps were placed only in the main burial chamber (McCown 1947: 114; see also discussion in Barag 1970, 43).

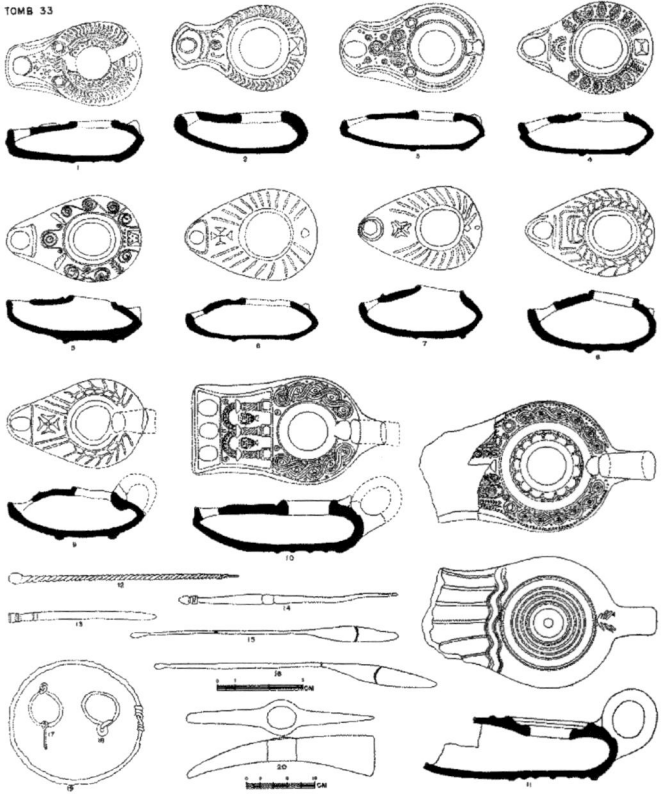

Fig. 9.11. Oil-lamps and additional finds from Tomb 33 (McCown 1947: fig. 23).

In our opinion, the chronological overlap between the types of lamps suggests that there is no real basis for distinguishing between two stages in the tomb. We therefore propose dating the tomb solely to the first half of the fourth century CE. This date is consistent with the excavators' assertions regarding tombs containing similar assemblages of lamps in other parts of the country, such as burial tomb no. 99 at Gezer (Macalister 1912: 338–39), the tomb at 'Ain Yabrud (Husseini 1938: 54–55), and the tomb at Beit Fajjar (Husseini 1935; Iliffe 1935). The finds do not supply definitive data regarding the religious beliefs of the owners: were they Christians or Pagans?

DISCUSSION: BURIAL IN JUDEA AND THE BENJAMIN REGION IN THE ROMAN AND BYZANTINE PERIODS

After the Bar Kokhba Revolt, Judea and the Benjamin region underwent changes in settlement and demography when the Jewish inhabitants left and a pagan, and later a Christian, population moved in. These demographic changes and the cultural and religious differences between the three societies were manifested in part in the architectural plans of their tombs and in different burial practices.

The Jewish inhabitants of the region in the Early Roman period buried their dead in family tombs, mostly ones with *kokhim*. These tombs have a typical architectural plan including a vestibule, a decorated façade, and a main burial chamber with *kokhim* in its walls. Tomb 4 at Tell en-Naṣbeh is a representative example. From the first century BCE to the first third of the second century CE, secondary burial of bones in niches and/or ossuaries was a common practice (Kloner and Zissu 2007: 15–56). Sometimes this practice also influenced the architectural form of tombs: *kokhim* were widened and chambers with shelves were added as storerooms for ossuaries (see, e.g., the double *kokh* in the eastern corner of Tomb 4 at Tell en-Naṣbeh).

In contrast to this single, almost uniform plan, in the Late Roman period (and the Byzantine period) the residents of Judea used a range of tomb types, such as those discovered in the Tell en-Naṣbeh necropoleis. These include simple cist graves (e.g. nos. 20, 21, and 28, in Fig. 9.12), tombs with two *arcosolia* (e.g. nos. 17, 27, and 23 in Fig. 9.12), and tombs with *arcosolia* and burial troughs (e.g. nos. 13, 19, and 33 above; McCown 1947: 101–28).

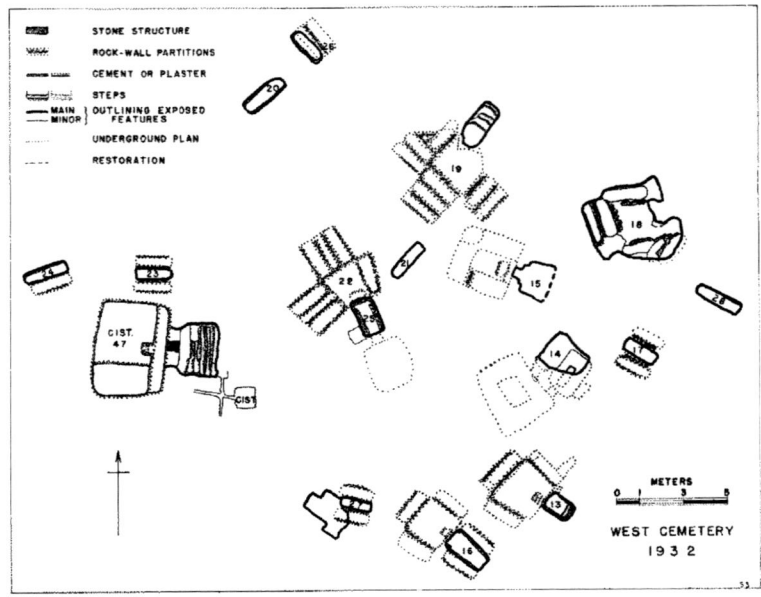

Fig. 9.12. Plan of the western portion of the western necropolis. Note the ritual bath with a double entrance/exit, identified as "Cistern 47" (McCown 1947: fig. 20).

In many cases, earlier tombs that could be modified without the expenditure of great effort and extensive resources were reused in the Late Roman and Byzantine periods. This is exemplified by Tombs 2, 6, and 14 at Tell en-Naṣbeh. It was commonly done— not only at the site under discussion—but also at dozens of sites in Judea and the Benjamin region (e.g., Ben Shemen, Horbat Kelah, Gezer, Khirbet Hayibe, Horbat Gader, Ramat Polin, Romema, the Knesset compound in western Jerusalem, Mt. Herzl, Arnona, Ramat Rahel, Beit Nattif, Khirbet Hubeila, and Horbat Burgin; see Klein 2011: 102–3). Reuse of burial caves has also been noted in Jerusalem at Dominus Flevit (Bagatti and Milik 1958), Akeldama (Avni 1993; Avni and Greenhut 1996), and additional sites.

Tombs of the type represented by Tomb 14 at Tell en-Naṣbeh, containing a square burial chamber with a standing space in the center surrounded by raised shelves, are generally dated to the Iron Age or the end of the Hellenistic period (Barkay 1994: 160–64). Some such burial caves continued to be used, without architectural changes, in the late Second Temple period and at the time of the Bar Kokhba Revolt (Kloner and Zelinger 2007). In addition to the clear case of Tell en-Naṣbeh, this phenomenon is known from four sites south of Jerusalem: Umm el-Asafir, Beit Einun, Zif, and Khirbet Aliya (Klein 2011: 103).

Tombs with *arcosolia* are represented at Tell en-Naṣbeh by Tombs 13, 19, and 33 (among others). These tombs are characterized by an entrance in one of the walls leading to a main burial chamber with *arcosolia* and burial troughs. This type of cave was extremely common throughout Eretz Israel in the Late Roman and Byzantine periods, and it seems to have begun as early as the Early Roman period. *Arcosolium* tombs are common, for example, in the urban necropoleis of Aelia Capitolina and Eleutheropolis (Avni 1997: 37–44). The number of burial troughs at the bottom of the *arcosolia* varies: *arcosolia* with between one and six troughs at the bottom are known. In addition to Tell en-Naṣbeh, tombs of this sort have been found at many Judean sites, including Horbat Zechariah, Gezer, Motza, el-Azariya, Beit Fajjar, Horbat Ethri, and Tel Eton (Klein 2011: 104–05).

A RITUAL BATH WITH A DOUBLE ENTRANCE/EXIT IN THE WESTERN NECROPOLIS

A stepped, plastered, rock-cut installation explored in the western portion of the western necropolis was defined by the excavators as a cistern (Cistern 47; Fig. 9.12). Ronny Reich, however, has identified it as a typical ritual bath with a double entrance (1990: 261–62). Zorn independently came to a similar conclusion in his PhD (1993b: 932; Zorn records that the installation appears in Badè Museum archival photographs A1151, A1153, A1154, A1124, A1127, A1128). A stepped corridor leads down to this double opening, on the other side of which is the immersion chamber (McCown 1947: 123, fig. 20). From there one walks down several wide steps to a stepped pool. Next to the corridor is a rock-cut cistern connected by a channel to the pool.

Ritual baths with a double entrance/exit are rare compared with simple ritual baths (with just one opening serving as both entrance and exit). Approximately sixty baths of the former type are currently known, most in Jerusalem and a few at Second Temple period sites in Judea (Adler 2011: 135–36). These include ones in the northern Hebron hills (Amit 1994, 1996), a few have been discovered in Jericho (Netzer 1982), Qumran (Reich 2000), the Benjamin region (Itah 2002), the Lod Shephelah (Reich 1981; Zelinger 2009: fig. 65), and the hills west of Jerusalem (Klein and Zissu 2012).

Reich was the first to discuss ritual baths containing a double entrance/exit; the basic explanation that he proposed is now accepted by scholars. Reich believed that the purpose of having two separate openings or staircases was to keep the ritually impure people going down into the bath away from the pure people coming up, so that the latter would not become impure again through physical contact with the former (Reich 1980; Reich 1990: 34–39). Reich added that there may have been additional reasons for the separation arrangements in ritual baths due to differing customs among Jews in the late Second Temple period (Reich 1990: 39). This means of separation is also reflected in the rabbinical literature: "All vessels found in Jerusalem on the way down to the place of immersion are impure, whereas those on the way up are pure, for they are not the same on their way down as on their way up" (M. Shekalim 8:2). Rashi explains: "They would go down to the place of immersion one way and come up a different way." Saul Lieberman suggested that this halachic situation is reflected in two external sources (Lieberman 1968). The first source, a "Fragment of an Uncanonical Gospel" known also as Papyrus no. 840 from Oxyrhynchus (Upper Egypt), presents a dialogue between Levi, a Pharisee high priest and Jesus (Grenfell and Hunt 1908: 1–10, pl. 1). Jesus asks the high priest whether he is ritually pure. Levi replies: "I am clean; for I washed in the pool of David, and having descended by one staircase I ascended by another …".

The second source is the letter from Aristeas to Philocrates in which he describes the Temple Mount: "There are steps too which lead up to the cross roads, and some people are always going up, and others down and they keep as far apart from each other as possible on the road because of those who are bound by the rules of purity, lest they should touch anything which is unlawful" (The Letter of Aristeas, 106–07). Scholars have noted, however, that the Letter of Aristeas is not necessarily relevant to our topic because it is not clear whether he is talking about immersion or some other activity taking place within the Temple precincts (see Regev 1996; Amit 1996).

Regev discusses the question of why the separation arrangements existed in only a small number of ritual baths from the Second Temple period. He suggests that these baths belonged to a priestly population, whereas the rest of the people immersed in ordinary ritual baths. Regev bases his opinion, which views the separate routes as characteristic of practices related to the Temple and the priestly class, on several halachic sources describing separation arrangements between the Temple entrance and exit. Given that the priests were particularly careful about matters of purity and impurity, Regev proposes that they used ritual baths with separation arrangements to prevent physical contact between the ritually pure and the impure (1996, 2006).

Amit, in contrast, shows that there is no overlap between the location of priestly settlements and the distribution of ritual baths with a double opening. Therefore, he believes that although ritual baths of this type indicate greater care with the laws of purity and impurity, they should not be attributed specifically to a priestly population. In his view, the entire aggregate of halachic and cultural-material factors should be taken into account when we consider the ritual baths with separation arrangements. He points out that there are three different hierarchies with respect to purity: a geographical hierarchy, from the Temple to Jerusalem to Eretz Israel; a human-cultural hierarchy, from the priests to the *haverim* (pious scholars) to the *amei ha-aretz* (common people); and a halachic hierarchy, from severe impurity conveyed by contact with the dead to the minor impurity caused by seminal emission (Amit 1996: 56–62).

Asher Grossberg, too, rejects Regev's argument that this type of ritual bath was associated with the priestly class. In contrast, he proposes that these baths were intended to serve all the pilgrims to Jerusalem, who had to purify themselves in crowded conditions before entering the Temple (Grossberg 1997). His proposal, however, relates only to ritual baths in Jerusalem and does not solve the problem of baths of this type in Second Temple period Jewish settlements scattered throughout rural Judea, such as Tell en-Naṣbeh.

Yonatan Adler recently summed up the discussion of the nature of these installations. Adler agrees with the basic assumption that the separation arrangements in ritual baths were meant to prevent contact between the ritually pure and the impure, but he examined the various possible ways of becoming impure through physical contact from a halachic standpoint. According to the Bible

and rabbinical literature, one cannot become impure through physical contact with an impure person except if the latter has one of
several types of impurity referred to as an *av tum'a* (principal cause
of defilement): a *zav* (a man who has experienced a certain kind of
discharge), a *zava* (a woman who has had non-menstrual bleeding),
a *niddah* (a menstrual or post-menstrual woman), a man who has
had relations with a *niddah*, someone who has come into contact
with a dead person, a woman following childbirth, and a *metzora*
(traditionally translated as a leper, but now understood to refer to a
different condition). Adler proposes a different explanation for the
separation arrangements in ritual baths based on the mishnaic passages at the end of the second chapter of the tractate Hagigah (M.
Hagigah 2:6–7). These passages describe an ascending hierarchy of
ritual purity and the practical consequences of this hierarchy:
someone who is careful to remain pure in order to engage in an
activity requiring a certain level of sanctity has to regard those who
were careful to remain pure in order to engage in an activity requiring a lesser level of sanctity as having the severe impurity of an *av
tum'a*. Hence, Adler suggests that the need to prevent contact between people who maintain different levels of purity is what led to
the separation arrangements in the ritual baths (Adler 2011: 142–
46).

Another matter worth discussing here is the specific location
of the ritual bath in question, within the necropolis. Ritual baths in
necropoleis or as part of monumental burial assemblages are
known from Jerusalem (e.g., the Tombs of the Kings), from the
tomb of the "Goliath family" in Jericho, and from other sites. But
there is a problem here for which a solution was only recently suggested: according to Jewish law as known today, one cannot purify
oneself from contact with the dead in the cemetery itself because it
takes a week to achieve purification. Adler has proposed that the
immersion in the cemetery was meant to allow immediate purification for those exposed to secondary impurity, i.e., contact with an
impure person (Adler 2009).

CONCLUSION

The numerous tombs from the Early Roman, Late Roman, and
Byzantine periods discovered in the necropolis west of the tell suggest that during these periods there was a settlement in the vicinity
whose inhabitants created and utilized this graveyard. Because the

excavations on the tell did not uncover significant finds from the Early Roman, Late Roman, or Byzantine periods we can suggest that the tombs were used by the residents of a nearby settlement instead. Because most of the tombs from these periods were found on the western slopes of the tell (Fig. 9.13), they may belong to residents of the Roman–Byzantine period settlement at Khirbet Shuweika, recently excavated by Marwan Abu Khalaf, Robert Hoyland and their team (Abu Khalaf et al. 2006; Hoyland 2001). This settlement is situated approximately 500 meters west of the tell. Another option is that the tombs were used by the residents of Khirbet ʿAṭṭara, located just south of the tell (for a survey report, see Feldstein et al. 1993: 160–62).

Fig. 9.13. View of Tell en-Naṣbeh from the southwest (Photograph courtesy of Shimon Gibson).

The ritual bath with a double entrance/exit and the few ossuaries that have been discovered in several burial caves indicate that these installations were used by a Jewish population that was careful about the laws of the Torah according to the spirit of the times. In contrast, the many objects discovered in the tombs, and especially lamps with crosses, attest to population changes in the region after the Bar Kokhba Revolt when the Jews left and the vacuum was filled by pagans who over time converted to Christianity.

REFERENCES

Abu Khalaf, M.; Abu Aʿmar, I.; Al-Houdalieh, S.; and Hoyland, R.
2006   The Byzantine and Early Islamic settlement of Khirbat Shuwayka. *Web Journal on Cultural Patrimony* 1.2: 47–76.

http://www.webjournal.unior.it/Dati/18/55/3.%20Palesti
na,%20Abu%20Khalaf.pdf

Abu Raya, R.
1996   Kafr 'Aqab. *Excavations and Surveys in Israel* 15: 129–30.

Adler, Y.
2009   Ritual Baths Adjacent to Tombs: An Analysis of the Archaeological Evidence in Light of the Halakhic Sources.
Journal for the Study of Judaism 40: 55–73.
2011   The Archaeology of Purity: Archaeological Evidence for
the Observation of Ritual Purity in Eretz-Israel from the
Hasmonean Period until the End of the Talmudic Era (164
BCE–400 CE), Ph.D. dissertation, Bar-Ilan University
(Hebrew).

Amit, D.
1994   Ritual Baths (Mikva'ot) from the Second Temple Period in
the Hebron Mountains. Pp. 157–189 in *Judea and Samaria
Research Studies: Proceedings of the Third Annual Meeting 1993*,
ed. Y. Eshel. Kedumim–Ariel: Judea and Samaria College
(Hebrew).
1996   Ritual Baths (Mikva'ot) from the Second Temple Period in
the Hebron Mountains. M.A. thesis, Hebrew University of
Jerusalem (Hebrew).

Avni, G.
1993   Christian Secondary Use of Jewish Burial Caves in Jerusalem in the Light of New Excavations at the Aceldama
Tombs. Pp. 265–76 in *Early Christianity in Context: Monuments and Documents*, ed. F. Manns, and E. Alliata. Studium Biblicum Franciscanum Collectio Maior 38. Jerusalem:
Franciscan Printing Press.
1997   The Necropoleis of Jerusalem and Beth Guvrin during the
4th –7th Centuries A.D. as a Model for Urban Cemeteries
in Palestine in the Late Roman and Byzantine Periods,
Ph.D. dissertation, Hebrew University of Jerusalem (Hebrew).

Avni, G., and Greenhut, Z.
1996   Architecture, Burial Customs and Chronology. Pp. 1–39 in
The Akeldama Tombs: Three Burial Caves in the Kidron

Valley, Jerusalem, ed. G. Avni and Z. Greenhut. Israel Antiquities Authority Reports 1. Jerusalem: Israel Antiquities Authority.

Bagatti, P. B., and Milik, J. T.
1958   *Gli Scavi del "Dominus Flevit" (Monte Oliveto, Gerusalemme)*, Part 1, *La Necropoli del Periodo Romano*. Publications of the Studium Biblicum Franciscanum 13. Jerusalem: Franciscan Printing Press.

Barag, D.
1970   Glass Vessels of the Roman and Byzantine Periods in Palestine, Ph.D. dissertation, Hebrew University of Jerusalem (Hebrew).

Barkay, G.
1994   Burial Caves and Burial Practices in Judah in the Iron Age. Pp. 96–164 in *Graves and Burial Practices in Israel in the Ancient Period*, ed. I. Singer. Jerusalem: Yad Ben Zvi (Hebrew).

Feldstein, A.; Kidron, G.; Hanin, N.; Kamaisky, Y.; and Eitam D.
1993   Southern Part of the Maps of Ramallah and el-Bireh and Northern Part of the Map of 'Ein Kerem (Sites 141–321). Pp. 133–264, in *Archaeological Survey of the Hill Country of Benjamin*, ed. I. Finkelstein and Y. Magen. Jerusalem: Israel Antiquities Authority and Civil Administration in Judea and Samaria, Staff Officer of Archaeology.

Grenfell, B. P. and Hunt, A. S.
1908   *The Oxyrhinchus Papyri*, Vol. 5. London: The Egypt Exploration Fund.

Grossberg, A.
1997   Ritual Baths in Second Temple Period Jerusalem and How They Were Ritually Prepared. *Cathedra* 83: 151–68 (Hebrew).

Hoyland, R.
2011   The Byzantine/Early Islamic Site of Khirbat Shuwayka in Palestine (The Monastery of the Prophet Samuel?). Pp. 219–32 in *Le Proche-Orient de Justinien aux Abbassides: peuplement et dynamiques spatiales; actes du Colloque "Continuites de l'occupation entre les periodes byzantine et abbasside au Proche-Orient,*

VIIe–IXe siècles, Paris, 18–20 Octobre 2007, ed. A. Borrut. Turnhout: Brepols.

Husseini, S. A. S.
1935   A Fourth-Century A.D Tomb at Beit Fajjar. *The Quarterly of the Department of Antiquities in Palestine* 4: 175–7.
1938   A Rock-Cut Tomb-Chamber at 'Ain Yabrud. *The Quarterly of the Department of Antiquities in Palestine* 6: 54–55.

Iliffe, J. H.
1935   Note on the Lamps from Tomb at Beit Fajjar. *The Quarterly of the Department of Antiquities in Palestine* 4: 177–78.

Itah, M.
2002   Ritual Baths in the Hill Country of the Benjamin Region. Pp. 81–90 in *Judea and Samaria Research Studies 11*, ed. Y. Eshel. Ariel: Eretz (Hebrew).

Klein, E.
2011   Aspects of the Material-Culture of Rural Judea during the Later Roman Period, Ph.D. dissertation, Bar-Ilan University (Hebrew).

Klein, E., and Zissu, B.
2012   Ritual Immersion Baths (Miqwa'ot) with Double Entrances in the Jerusalem Hills. Pp. 225–45 in *New Studies on Jerusalem*, Vol. 18, ed. E. Baruch, Y. Levin and A. Levy-Reifer. Ramat Gan: Ingeborg Rennert Center for Jerusalem Studies.

Kloner, A., and Zelinger, Y.
2007   The Evolution of Tombs from the Iron Age through the Second Temple Period. Pp. 209–20 in *"Up to the Gates of Ekron": Essays on the Archaeology and History of the Eastern Mediterranean in Honor of Seymour Gitin*, ed. S. White Crawford, A. Ben-Tor, J. P. Dessel, W. G. Dever, A. Mazar, and J. Aviram. Jerusalem: Israel Exploration Society.

Kloner, A. and Zissu, B.
2007   *The Necropolis of Jerusalem in the Second Temple Period*. Interdisciplinary Studies in Ancient Culture and Religion 8. Leuven: Peeters.

Lieberman, S.
1968   Notes, Pp. 97–98, in *P'raqim: Yearbook of the Schocken Institute for Jewish Research of the Jewish Theological Seminary of America*, Vol. 1, ed. E. S. Rosenthal. Jerusalem: Schocken Institute (Hebrew).

Macalister, R. A. S.
1912   *The Excavations of Gezer, 1902–1905 and 1907–1909*, Vol 1. London: Palestine Exploration Society.

McCown, C. C.
1947   *Tell en-Naṣbeh*, Vol. 1: *Archaeological and Historical Results*. Berkeley, CA: The Palestine Institute of Pacific School of Religion.

Netzer, E.
1982   Ancient Ritual Baths in Miqvaot in Jericho. *The Jerusalem Cathedra* 2: 106–19.

Rahmani, L.Y.
1994   *A Catalogue of Jewish Ossuaries, in the Collections of the State of Israel*. Jerusalem: Israel Antiquities Authority and the Academy of Science.

Regev, E.
1996   Ritual Baths of Jewish Groups and Sects in the Second Temple Period. *Cathedra* 79: 3–21 (Hebrew).

2006   Archaeology and the Mishnah's Halakhic Tradition: The Case of Stone Vessels and Ritual Baths. Pp. 136–52 in *The Mishnah in Contemporary Perspective*, Vol. 2, ed. A. J. Avery-Peck and J. Neusner. Handbook of Oriental Studies, Section 1, the Near and Middle East 87. Leiden: Brill.

Reich, R.
1980   Mishnah, Sheqalim 8:2 and the Archaeological Evidence. Pp. 225–56 in *Jerusalem in the Second Temple Period: Abraham Schalit Memorial Volume*, ed. A. Oppenheimer, U. Rapaport, and M. Shtern. Sifriyah le-toldot ha-yishuv ha-Yehudi be-Erets-Yiśra'el. Jerusalem: Yad Ben Zvi (Hebrew).
1981   Archaeological Evidence of the Jewish Population at Hasmonean Gezer. *Israel Exploration Journal* 31: 48–52.

1990   Miqwa'ot (Jewish Ritual Immersion Baths) in Eretz-Israel in the Second Temple and the Mishna and Talmud Periods, Ph.D. dissertation, The Hebrew University of Jerusalem (Hebrew).

2000   Miqwa'ot at Khirbet Qumran and the Jerusalem Connection, Pp. 728–31 in *The Dead Sea Scrolls Fifty Years after Their Discovery: Proceedings of the Jerusalem Congress, July 20–25, 1997*, ed. L. H. Schiffman, E. Tov and J. C. VanderKam. Jerusalem: Israel Exploration Society.

Roll, I.
1994   Roman Roads, Pp. 21–22 in *Tabula Imperii Romani. Iudaea, Palaestina: Eretz Israel in the Hellenistic, Roman and Byzantine Periods*, ed. Y. Tsafrir, L. Di Segni, and J. Green Jerusalem: The Israel Academy of Science and Humanities.

Rosenthal, R., and Sivan, R.
1978   *Ancient Lamps in the Schloessinger Collection*. Qedem, 8. Jerusalem: Institute of Archaeology, The Hebrew University of Jerusalem.

Thackeray, H. St. J. trans.
1918   *The Letter of Aristeas*. London: Society for Promoting Christian Knowledge.

Wampler, J. C.
1947   *Tell en-Naṣbeh*, Vol. 2: *The Pottery*. Berkeley, CA: The Palestine Institute of Pacific School of Religion.

Zelinger, Y.
2009   *The Rural Settlements in the Shephela of Lod (Lydda) during the Second Temple Period*, Ph.D. dissertation, Bar-Ilan University (Hebrew).

Zorn, J. R.,
1988   William Frederic Badè. *Biblical Archaeologist* 3: 28–35.

1993a   Naṣbeh, Tell en-, Pp. 1098–1102 in *The New Encyclopedia of Archaeological Excavations in the Holy Land*, Vol. 3, ed. E. Stern. Jerusalem: The Israel Exploration Society and Carta.

1993b   Tell en-Nasbeh: A Re-evaluation of the Architecture and Stratigraphy of the Early Bronze Age, Iron Age and Later Periods. Ph.D. dissertation, University of California, Berkeley.

Tell en-Naṣbeh's Contributions to Understanding Iron Age Israelite Water Systems[1]

Jeffrey R. Zorn
Department of Near Eastern Studies
Cornell University

Abstract

Because of the wide exposure of its excavated architectural remains Tell en-Naṣbeh has played a significant role in studies involving Iron Age Israelite town and house planning and the nature of the Israelite family. This essay examines a seldom explored aspect of settlement structure and planning: the manipulation of water resources. It shows how Tell en-Naṣbeh's streets and alleys were used to direct water runoff either to cisterns inside of individual houses, or to the

[1] Most of the data used in this study may be found in the author's 1993 dissertation, especially pp. 259–89 in Volume I, Section C3 "Drains, Cisterns and Other Water Installations." Some of the estimates have been slightly revised from that earlier work. Detailed discussions of individual drains may be found in Volume II of the same work in the chapters that cover individual map sections. Metric data, such as lengths, widths, elevations, etc. are derived from the 1:100 site plans archived in the Badè Museum Biblical Archaeology of Pacific School of Religion in Berkeley, CA. Photographs were provided courtesy of the Badè Museum through the kind efforts of Kiersten Neumann (Associate Curator) and the plans were adapted from the 1:100 scale plans in the Museum's archives. The author thanks the Badè Museum for permission to use these illustrations here.

periphery of the town where a system of drains channeled unwanted water through the offset-inset wall or through the inner-outer gate complex. The study then examines the number and nature of cisterns at Tell en-Naṣbeh. Special attention is paid to the volume and distribution of cisterns in a study area in the south-west corner of the site. Cisterns in that area vary considerably in size, and not every dwelling possesses its own cistern. It is suggested that the existence of cisterns with capacities far beyond the needs of a typical nuclear family in some houses, and the lack of cisterns in adjoining dwellings, may be connected with the role of extended families. Finally, the seldom discussed but important role Israelite girls/women played in transporting water from sources beyond the town walls is briefly explored.

INTRODUCTION

Sunlight, air, land and water are the key ingredients for life on Earth. The land of ancient Israel is abundantly supplied with the first three. It is the fourth resource, water, which has historically been more of a problem, and has become an increasingly pressing issue in the modern world (Zizola and Faris 2011). Unlike Egypt and Mesopotamia, which rely almost entirely on their rivers, the Nile and the Tigris and Euphrates, and systems of canals for water, the inhabitants of the land of Israel have had to rely on a variety of different water sources to meet their needs (Tsuk 1997b; King and Stager 2001: 122–23). These sources include a few small rivers and streams (e.g. the Jordan, Yarkon and Kishon), a large number of springs, rainfall, and a variety of manmade systems such as wells, cisterns and some truly monumental systems (e.g. the large Iron Age systems and the aqueducts of the Roman era). In the central highlands, the core area of Israelite settlement, the location of natural springs often dictated where settlements were constructed. However, since springs were usually located outside of the settlements they served they could be an inconvenient water source; some family member would have to be tasked with drawing water from the spring and bringing it back to the house (Gen. 24:10–15; see below). In addition, because they are dependent on the amount of water in their aquifers for their flow, the volume of water that springs deliver can vary based on the season and whether the year was wet or dry (Tsuk 1997b: 132). Finally, because of the usual location of springs outside a settlement's fortifications, access to such sources could be cut off completely during a time of war.

However, just as too little water was a concern, an overabundance of water at one time, usually in the form of rain, could also cause problems (contra Neufeld 1970: 415). Water flowing swiftly down a sloping street could cut ruts into the surface, making walking more difficult. Conversely, this same flow could lead to unwanted silt accumulation in other locations (McClellan 1984: 64) and such muddy conditions could make walking difficult (Mic. 7:10; Ps. 18:43; 2 Sam. 22:43; Zech. 9:3, 10:5). Water could flow into houses and ruin materials kept on the floor. If the mud plaster used on the walls and roof of a building was not kept in good repair water could damage the structure. For example, quickly flowing water could undercut the base of a wall leading to its subsequent collapse. A factor outside the knowledge of the Israelites was that standing pools of water, and even water kept in cisterns, could foster the spread of diseases by providing homes for mosquitos and microbes found in human and animal waste (Rosen and Greenberg 2002: 287–91; Bradley 1977: 5–15; Carson 1919: 351; International Public Health 1914: 594).

The Israelites of the Iron Age often went to great lengths to construct systems that allowed them to store or access water resources from within their fortified settlements. They were especially adept at creating huge systems at major sites like Hazor, Megiddo, Jerusalem and others, or at important administrative centers like Beer Sheba, which allowed them to access water from adjacent springs, aquifers and wadis. These systems have been studied at great length (e.g. Shiloh 1992; Kaplan 2010; King and Stager 2001: 210–23). Less studied are the ways in which water was procured, stored and otherwise manipulated in smaller, less important settlements, or by individual households. However, those responsible for planning and constructing the walls, roads and open places of a settlement, be they members of the community itself or royal officials, had to take into account such water related factors as they constructed, rebuilt or otherwise modified their settlements. This is not to say that all settlements show evidence of such planning. Some grew in a more agglutinative manner with little, if any advance planning. Some sites were so small that collecting or removing water was purely a household level issue.

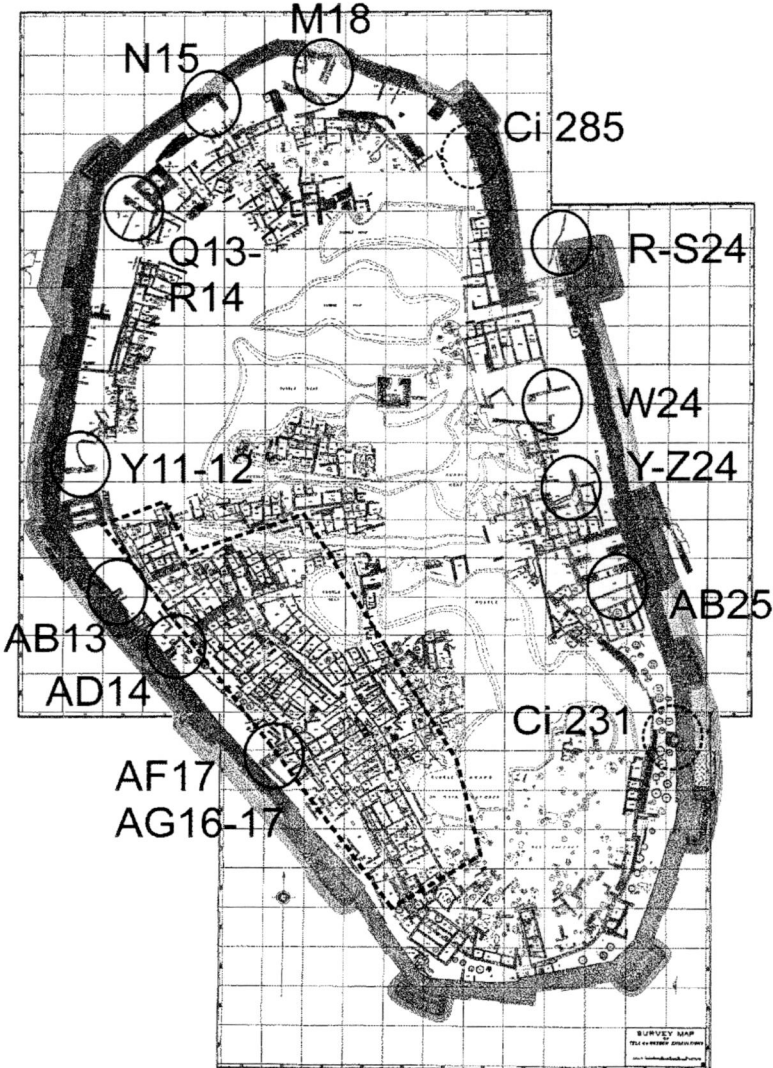

Fig. 10.1. Plan of Tell en-Naṣbeh showing areas discussed in this essay. Solid circles are locations of drains. Dashed circles are locations of Cisterns 285 and 231. Polygonal dashed line marks the area examined for water flow along roads and cistern size and distribution. Each grid square is 10 x 10 m.

However, some sites clearly attest to at least some planning, as witnessed by subsurface drains. An understanding of how the Israelites could manipulate water resources requires not only knowledge of the layout of individual houses, but also of adjoining houses, streets, neighborhoods and even the layout of the entire settlement. Such a study in turn requires a site with fairly extensively excavated remains. This makes Tell en-Naṣbeh, approximately two thirds of which was excavated, a prime candidate for such an endeavor.

This study will document the structural remains at Tell en-Naṣbeh devoted to the manipulation of the town's water resources (Fig. 10.1). In the course of the investigation certain assumptions, estimates, and scenarios will be offered to clarify some of the issues faced by the town's inhabitants. For example, this study suggests an average daily water consumption of 10 or 15 liters per person (Zorn 1993: 302–03). Similarly, it is assumed that the average size of a nuclear family is about 5 individuals in a single dwelling (Zorn 1994: 32–33; in contrast Schloen suggests a mean household size of 6–7; 2001: 136). The outcomes of scenarios based on such assumptions will differ if another scholar works from a different set of metric assumptions. The point of such exercises, however, is twofold. First, they help bracket, at least broadly, some of the issues faced by the Israelites themselves. Second, they will encourage others to think more about the amount of effort average Israelites of towns and villages put into dealing with this most important resource. While the systems they created for this purpose were not as monumental as the huge shafts, galleries and tunnel systems found in major Iron Age sites they do reveal a certain level of national, communal, and individual planning. For example, drains that fed out below a building's walls had to be constructed before those walls. If a drain was to run through or below the settlement's wall, or below some part of the gate other than its passageway, the drain had to go in first. This was a decision that had to be implemented by the royal engineers who laid out such major fortifications, such as those at Tell en-Naṣbeh. Similarly, the town's buildings and roads could be laid out so that water did not collect in unwanted areas, but flowed towards outlets or storage installations. This is more a community scale issue. Exactly where a cistern would be located in any given house would be up to its owner. Yet, the engineers, community leaders, and individual homeowners were all dealing with the same resource.

BENEFITS AND PROBLEMS OF WORKING WITH OLD SITES

A significant problem with most excavations of the last few decades is that complete plans of individual Iron Age houses, let alone the neighborhoods in which they were located, are becoming increasingly difficult to come by. This is due to the much slower and more careful excavation and recording techniques in use today. Modern excavations at multi-strata sites with deposits of significant depths are often lucky to excavate a significant part of a single building. Site wide plans, or even plans of neighborhoods, are almost impossible to achieve anymore except at single period sites, or at sites where the latest occupation stratum is the one being studied. Even in these more ideal situations widespread exposures of more than just a few houses are difficult to achieve. While it may be possible to say that a house had a cistern, it is usually not possible to determine how that cistern related to all relevant adjacent spaces. Thus, analysis of how water was manipulated on a site-wide basis is usually impossible in recently excavated sites. However, this is where the old excavations conducted during the period of the British Mandate (and even earlier) can be of great use. These sites (e.g. Megiddo, Tell Beit Mirsim) were often excavated on a vast scale, dwarfing the exposures visible today. While many kinds of detailed information (e.g. animal bones, pollen, micro artifacts) were undoubtedly missed, macro information regarding town plans is available, and this is exactly the information necessary for understanding how water was manipulated. Tell en-Naṣbeh is a perfect candidate for studying the kind of macro social activity that can be garnered from these old reports. The deposits there are relatively shallow and, with the large labor force employed at that time, approximately two thirds of the site was excavated, much of it to bedrock. Because it is a fortified rural town it provides evidence of how water was manipulated outside of the major urban centers excavated on a similarly large scale in the same era (Megiddo, Lachish, Samaria, Gezer).

The problems of working with data from these early excavations (and Tell en-Naṣbeh is no exception) are well known and only a brief summary is required here (Zorn 1999). Elevations on walls, especially along their bases, are usually sparse or non-existent. Floors (especially dirt floors) were often missed, leading to mixing of artifacts of different periods. Intrusive features, like pits, were often not noticed or recorded. Photographic documentation may be sparse, or even non-existent for certain features, and the features themselves may not have been well cleaned for those photographs. The exact location of even in situ floor assemblages may not be recorded. For these reasons, and others, site stratigraphy may be confused and chronology imprecise.

At Tell en-Naṣbeh there is another significant issue, the longevity of the site. The main Iron Age phase at the site, with its three sub-phases (Strata 3C–3A according to the revised stratigraphy in Zorn 1993: 88–93), likely covers a period from the tenth century through beginning of the sixth century BCE. Over this period it is clear from changes in wall construction techniques (e.g. single stone walls early, double stone walls later) that houses were modified in a variety of ways. For this reason, it is usually impossible to know when one house was modified internally in comparison with its neighbors. Thus the plan of Stratum 3 is something of a chronological pastiche. Nevertheless most house plans are very complete and clear, exhibit a mixing of wall construction techniques, and the buildings usually follow typical three- and four-room plans, cohering with neighboring structures into readily observable architectural or neighborhood blocks. This suggests that the basic plan of the settlement changed relatively little over the centuries. Of course, the plan primarily represents the appearance of the town in its final phase at the beginning of the sixth century.

WATER MANIPULATION: INTRODUCTION

There are three basic factors that determine the character of any drainage system: the natural slope of the site; natural or man-made obstacles to water flow; and whether the area through which the water was to flow was also used for human or animal traffic. The most obvious example of a man-made obstacle is a town wall. Drainage in a small, unwalled settlement is a much smaller problem than in a walled town. A wall turns a town into a sort of reservoir which traps and holds in water. Examples of smaller man-made obstacles include architectural terraces, stairways and thresholds. Natural obstacles include high and low points in the bedrock.

Fig. 10.2. Looking north along drain in M18; the drain enters
the town wall where the man is standing (Badè Museum of
Biblical Archaeology photograph #693).

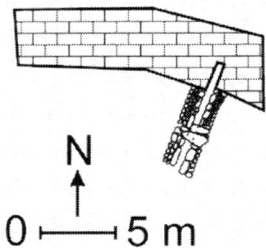

Fig. 10.3. Schematic plan of drain in M18; 1:500.

The natural slope of the site is of great importance. At a site built on a ridge, like Tell en-Naṣbeh, water will run off on both sides of the ridge. Because of the natural weathering and erosion of the underlying limestone bedrock hill country sites typically have a terraced appearance that falls away from the central high point. A settlement built on a reasonably flat plain will not have either this natural bi-furcation or terracing. Also, a site built on a terraced hilltop is not usually level from one end to the other; there is usually some slope along the hill. Water pouring downslope perpendicular to the crest of the ridge will eventually have to flow parallel to it once it meets a natural or man-made obstacle, such as the town wall, or else collect in a pool. At Tell en-Naṣbeh the slope is downward from south to north.

Site-wide sub-floor drainage did not exist in Iron Age Israel; water had to be channeled above ground most of the time, going underground only when practical or necessary. The only real avenue for extensive aboveground drainage was a town's road system. However, these same roads had to remain serviceable for human and animal traffic. The water could not be allowed to impede movement by either collecting in extensive pools or too badly eroding the dirt surface of the roads.

SITE WIDE DRAINAGE

Tell en-Naṣbeh follows the classic ring-road structure characteristics of many Israelite hill country sites (Shiloh 1987). Houses along the periphery form a band facing inward onto a road that rings the settlement. Across the road and up slope is another band of houses facing outward and downward. The ring-road at Tell en-Naṣbeh is not continuous around the site; it is interrupted by a block of houses at least at one point on the west (the area east of the drains in AB13 and AD14 in Fig. 10.1), but the underlying principle of a ring-road is clear. In order to facilitate ease of movement through the settlement, the town is crossed by several roads that run perpendicular to the ring-road. The inhabitants of Tell en-Naṣbeh used the ring-road and cross-roads as part of their settlement's drainage system.[2] They intended to move water away from where it was not wanted, to places where it was needed, or to remove it from the town into the area beyond the settlement's wall.

One of the most striking aspects of the layout of Tell en-Naṣbeh is the number and location of drain channels found in the intra-mural area associated with the offset-inset wall and how these features are related to the nearby road system. Eight such drains were identified, extending in a band from about the middle of the western side of the town to its northern end. An analysis of the interplay of these drains and the nearby road system reveals how the engineers who oversaw the construction of Tell en-Naṣbeh's massive fortifications took into account the pre-existing road system constructed by the town's inhabitants.

The drain in M18 is constructed in the intramural fill poured up against the town wall (Figs. 10.2–3), is about 7.5 m long by 2.3 m wide, and has walls ranging from ca. 60 to 90 cm thick. An elevation on the floor of the drain where it meets the town wall is 775.98, another on its east wall near its south end is 777.61. The inner channel walls are made of large, rough ashlar blocks set stretcher fashion. These are up to ca. 1.3 m long and 35 cm wide. The external part of the drain walls is composed of smaller cobbles. The floor of the channel may have been stone lined, though this is uncertain due to incomplete documentation. The drain clearly runs up to and into the city wall. Unfortunately the architectural remains in the vicinity of the drain are not especially clear, so how water was fed to the drain from within the town cannot be determined.

---

[2] See already McClellan 1984: 64–65 for insightful comments about the importance of drainage, in general, in Levantine settlements, and drainage at Tell en-Naṣbeh in particular.

Fig. 10.4. View of larger drain in N15 looking north as the drain begins to pass through the offset-inset wall (Badè Museum of Biblical Archaeology photograph #356).

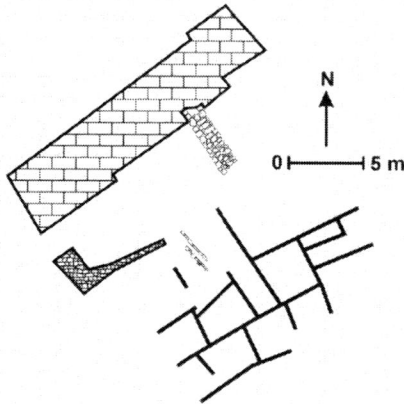

Fig. 10.5. Schematic plan of drains in N15; 1:500.

In N15 two drains were found (Figs. 10.4–5). The smaller drain is clearly built over Room 213 (shown on McCown 1947: fig. 41) that was part of the casemate-like fortifications of the original Stratum 3C town. The larger drain is also built over an earlier wall (also shown on McCown 1947: fig. 41). Both are built in the fill deposited against the offset-inset wall. The larger drain leads directly into the town wall. The plan shows this more substantial drain to be about 6 m long by 1.5 m wide; top and bottom elevations on the south drain wall are 776.71 and 776.19. Several capstones seem to have been found in situ. The drain walls are fieldstones and it may have had a plastered floor, though this is not certain. The relations of this drain to the architecture to its south are not clear. The smaller drain in N15 is to the southwest of the larger one just described and is not as well preserved. It is about 3.2 m long by 0.6 m wide. Its walls are constructed of narrow stones set lengthwise. The elevation of the channel is about 776.69. It is not clear if the small drain originally fed into its larger neighbor in some way, though this seems doubtful given the locations of the preserved segments, or simply directed water into the intramural zone which then flowed on its own into the larger drain.

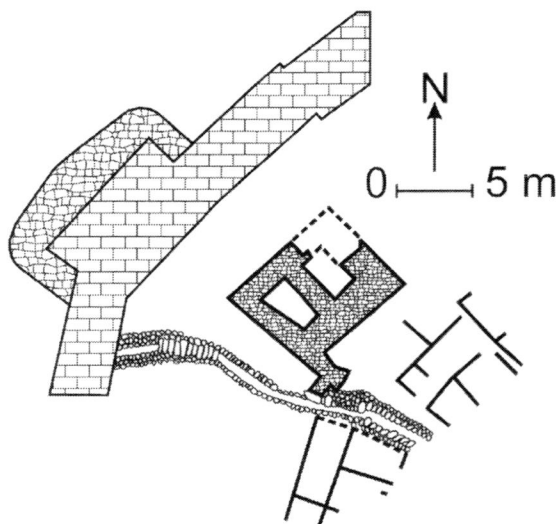

Fig. 10.6. Schematic plan of drain in Q13–R14; 1:500.

The drain in Q13–R14 (Fig. 10.6), approximately 20 m long, sits southwest of a small tower. Its remains were not represented on the 1:400 site plan of the 1947 report and it is not mentioned in the text of the publication, but it does appear on fig. 41 (McCown 1947: 181); it is briefly mentioned by McClellan (1984: 65). No photographs were taken of the drain. The construction of the drain is not uniform. Adjacent to the city wall, the walls of the drain channel are three stones thick, about 1 m wide, with an overall width of about 2.3 m; in the intramural area the walls narrow to a single stone in width, about 0.8 m wide, with an overall width of about 1.4 m; they widen to two stones in R14, about 0.8 m wide with an overall width of about 2.4 m, where the channel is alongside the tower. Ten capstones were preserved. The top elevations of the capstones are 776.19 and 775.73, and the lowest point in the channel is 774.90. The drain runs up to the 3B offset-inset wall, but could not be traced through it. Clearly, since the drain runs from inside the ring-road town of Stratum 3 up to the offset-inset wall the drain is contemporary with both. Perhaps the section of drain walls two stones thick belongs to the original 3C town and the drain was later modified and lengthened when the offset-inset wall was added. Water was likely fed into this drain from the presumed ring-road to the east.

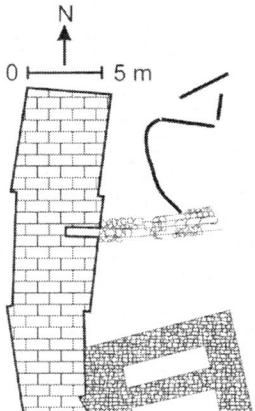

Fig. 10.7. Schematic plan of drain in drain in Y12; 1:500.

The next drain along the western side of the town is in Y11–12. The plan of the drain channel is not very clear (Fig. 10.7). The only available photograph (Fig. 10.8) shows a close up view of the drain; there it seems that a later wall is built partially over the south wall of the drain, obscuring its construction. It almost gives the impression that there are two drains, one above the other. The preserved remains of the drain are about 10 m long and 1.5 m wide. The visible drain wall is two stones wide, and the drain had a stone-paved floor. It may be that two capstones survived. An elevation on what may be a capstone is at 776.44; the base of the drain wall is at about 775.60. Both the plan and photograph show the drain crossing the offset-inset wall. The area to the east of the drain was not excavated, so how it related to the town's layout is unknown.

Fig. 10.8. Looking south at drain in Y12 (Badè Museum of Biblical Archaeology photograph #791b).

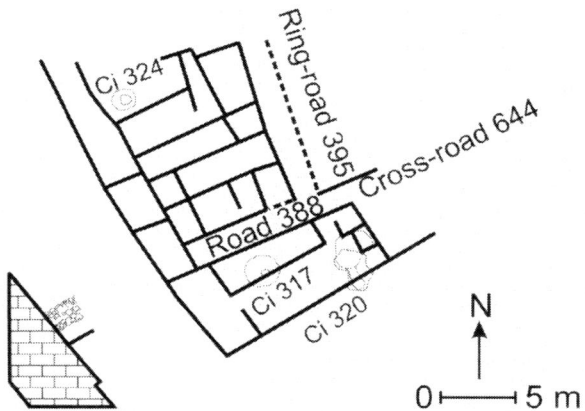

Fig. 10.9. Schematic plan of drain in drain in AB13; 1:500.

To the south and east is what appears to be a drain in AB13 (Fig. 10.9). Unfortunately there is no photograph of this feature. Here there are two narrow stone walls made of small to medium sized fieldstones, with what look like stone paving between them. The top elevation on the south wall is 775.75 and the base elevation of the north wall is 775.18. McClellan also recognized this feature as a possible drain (1984: 59). How water was fed to this possible drain from the town is unclear. To the east is a space designated as Room 388 (McClellan 1984: 59). Like road 541 to the southeast, which clearly does direct water into a drain channel, 388 is paved with stone cobbles and is not part of any adjacent building. Moreover, it aligns with cross-road 644, just as 541 aligns with cross-road 627. However, unlike 541 that clearly opens into the intra-mural space beyond, 388 seems to be blocked on the southwest by the walls of a casemate room. The plan does not show a passage from 388 to the intramural space. However, it is also clear from the plan that there were two or three stages of construction in this area, so it may be that at some point there was such an opening. Also, unlike 541, none of the adjacent structures seem to be oriented to open on to 388; rather, they seem to open onto the ring-road.

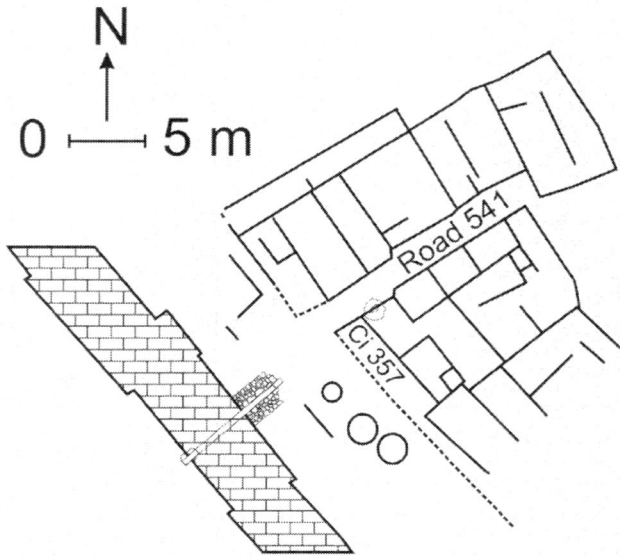

Fig. 10.10. Schematic plan of drain in drain in AD14; 1:500.

Because of its similarity with 541, and because it does not seem to serve for access to the buildings to either side, it seems quite possible that 388 did funnel water into the intramural area at some point in the town's history.

The next drain is in AD14 (Fig. 10.10). There is no photograph of this drain. However, it was well enough preserved that the plan shows its channel running completely through the offset-inset wall. Its preserved length is 8.4 m and the width of the channel is ca. 30 cm. The top of its north wall is at 776.28, with a base of 775.53; what seems to be a capstone is at 776.70 and the floor of the channel is at 775.75. The drain walls are ca. 1.0 m wide and composed of small to medium fieldstones three to four stones wide. It is uncertain how far to the northeast the channel extended. The channel is aligned with road 541 to the east. This cobblestone paved road provides drainage for water flowing along ring-road 514 and cross-road 627 and channels it into the intramural area. The drain in AD14 is the obvious destination even though the original site plan shows several later walls in the intramural area.

Fig. 10.11. View to west of drains in AF17 and AG16–17.
Most of the capstones have been removed (Badè Museum of
Biblical Archaeology photograph #1363).

Fig. 10.12. View to east of drains in AF17 and AG16–17.
Road 517, which fed these drains, lies under the debris, behind
the pile of baskets right of center (Badè Museum of Biblical
Archaeology photograph #1370).

The final two intramural drains are found in AF17 and AG16–17
(Figs. 10.11–13).[3] The southern, larger drain was about 9.0 m long,
2.5 wide, has walls up to 1 m thick, and the channel is about 60 cm

---

[3] McClellan (1984: 65, fig. 4) reconstructed a side-road (his road 505)
similar to roads 541 and 517 in the long, narrow string of rooms southeast
of Ci 358 (a suggestion also made by Badè in his diary; Zorn 1993: 762).
His reconstruction of this space as a road leaves out the walls which separate the rooms along this narrow space, but the only explanation offered
for these cross walls is that they prevented excessive drainage through this
space. While it is possible that McClellan's road 505 was an alley used to
channel water into the intramural area, it is troubling that there is no drain
located beyond its southwestern end; such drains are the norm with all
other such side-roads. Unfortunately the relation of this string of rooms
to the large structure to their southeast is not clear. If this space was a
side-road it is unclear if the water flow was directed north to the drain in
AD14, or south to the drains in AF17 and AG16–17.

wide. Six capstones were preserved; the easternmost is at 779.04. One elevation on the north wall is at 778.74. The floor of the drain is at 778.39 on the east and 777.92 on the west. It runs up to, but not through the offset-inset wall. The northern, smaller drain has walls 20 to 40 cm thick with a channel about 20 cm wide. Only one capstone was preserved and has an elevation of 778.09. An elevation on the north wall is at 777.95. The floor of the channel on the east is at 777.39 and 777.25 on the west. Photographs also suggest that the northern drain may be a bit lower than its southern neighbor. The plan gives the impression that the two drains converge toward the west, but there is no sign that they actually met. In fact, the southern drain seems to occupy space towards the offset-inset wall that the northern drain might have passed through, at least partially. Since the northern drain is not preserved in the vicinity of the offset-inset wall it seems likely that the northern drain was the original drain, which was eventually replaced by its larger neighbor.

Understanding the relationship of these two drains to the town plan is complicated by several factors. First, on the original site plan only the larger, southern drain is depicted. More important, the town architecture around and east of the drain is muddled on the plan. The rooms presented on the published 1:400 site plan in AF/AG17–18 (generally numbered in the 400–430 range) represent structures both of the Iron Age Stratum 3 town, and walls of the later Stratum 2 (Babylonian–Persian periods). The Stratum 2 walls are especially evident around the drains. The walls of Stratum 3 in this area are actually found on fig. 42 of the site report (McCown 1947: 182). When the Stratum 2 walls are removed from the site plan, and the earlier walls of Stratum 3 from fig. 42 are inserted, a clearer picture of the Iron Age II town in this area emerges (Fig. 10.13; also McClellan 1984: 55, fig. 4). Similar to the situation with road 541 to the north, road 517 fed water from the ring-road 514 and cross-road 563 into the intramural area. As with road 388 and its drain, it is uncertain how water crossed the area of the casemate-like wall to reach the drains. However, the presence of two drains to the west of road 517, and the similarity of the situation here to road 541 and its drain, suggest that some arrangement for drainage through the wall must have existed.

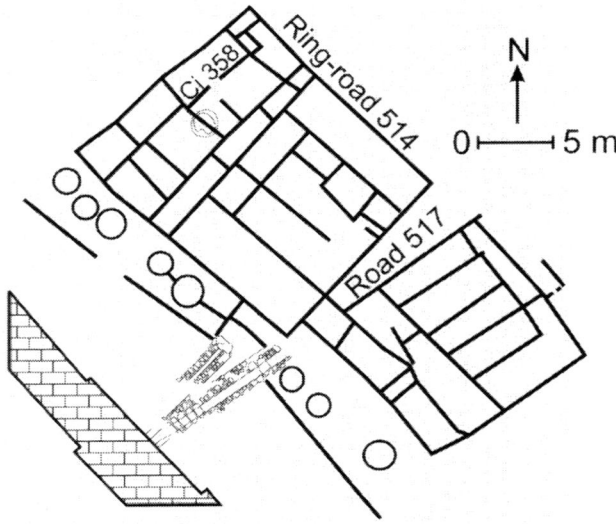

Fig. 10.13. Schematic plan of drain in AF17 and AG16–17;
1:500.

From the above discussion several points regarding the drains
along the north and west sides of the town become apparent. The
drains are built in the fill piled up against the inner face of the offset-inset wall. The drains are not of uniform construction. Several
of the channels demonstrably continue into the offset-inset wall
itself, and one can be seen to continue all the way through the wall.
It is clear from the drain in Q13–R14, the most completely preserved channel that runs from inside the original casemate-like wall,
through the intramural area, and up to the offset-inset wall, that
these drains were all probably integrated into the plan of the Stratum 3 ring-road town, even if in most cases their preserved remains
preclude definitive assessments (contra McCown 1947: 185, 202).
Wherever the excavated adjacent architectural remains are substantial enough to establish their plans, these drains align with spaces in
the town that seem to be roads which create breaks in the peripheral band of houses. In at least two cases these feeder roads were
paved with cobbles, perhaps as a way to combat erosion, and thus
suggesting heavy water flow through these areas. It seems likely
that wherever understanding the local architecture is problematic it
may be possible to reconstruct similar lanes likewise providing ac-

cess from the interior of the town to the intramural space inside the offset-inset wall (Isserlin 1998: 121, for general comments on drainage patterns in Iron Age towns). Finally, it is clear that those responsible for the construction of the drains in the intramural areas did face some difficulties. The superposition of certain drains (M18, N15) over some of the original casemate-like wall, and the free flow of water along one cobbled alley (AD14), while a similar nearby cobbled alley shows some blockage (AB13) are evidence of these difficulties. The construction of the new town wall, the pouring of a massive leveling fill between the original casemate-like town wall and new solid fortification system, and the need to run drains from inside the original town through the new fill and the new offset-inset wall required modifications to existing structures in some cases. It is not surprising that the integration of the old settlement with its new fortifications raised such problems for those responsible for its construction.

Given these data it seems likely that the drains were constructed at the same time as the city wall. This massive project probably took place in the time of King Asa of Judah who is said to have constructed Mizpah's walls in the early 9th century (1 Kings 15: 22; contra Finkelstein 2012), and not in the sixth–fifth centuries, as is stated in the original site report (McCown 1947: 185).

DIVERTERS/CURBS IN ROADS

There are clues in the site plan that the slope of a street and door thresholds were not always sufficient to prevent unwanted water from entering adjacent dwellings. In certain locations the town's inhabitants constructed single stone wide curbs in front of their houses to divert water away from their doors (McClellan 1984: 65; Isserlin 1998: 121; Fig. 10.24 below). These are either C- or L-shaped in form. Two such diverters can be seen on the north side of cross-road 563 (one is labeled Bin 352 on the site plan). Two similar diverters are found along the ring-road. The first is adjacent to Cistern 165, and what may be another is to the west, where it may be protecting what appears to be an oven that was also constructed in the road. The southwestern end of road 563 extends beyond the front wall of the adjacent building, apparently to direct the flow of water from road 563 into the northern part of road 514 instead of into road 517 (McClellan 1984: 65). As will be seen below, some homeowners created ways to capture water from adjacent roads to fill their cisterns. These curbs clearly show that other homeowners also strove to keep unwanted water out of their dwellings.

GATE DRAINAGE SYSTEM

In many sites the gate area was very often the site of a drain because the gate was the major natural break in a settlement's defenses and was also often a low point in the site's fortifications. That is, the gate was in an area that sloped down, which facilitated drainage. For this reason the construction of a drain in such an area made practical sense. Some examples of sites with gate drainage systems include Megiddo, Gezer, Lachish and Beer Sheba. The gate complex at Tell en-Naṣbeh provides another example of such a system.

Because of its position on the main north–south road on Judah's northern border Tell en-Naṣbeh was especially well protected, with defenses more typical of a major urban center then a rural agricultural town. The entry into the town was defended by an inner-outer gate complex (four-chamber inner gate and two-chamber outer gate), a feature that is paralleled at a number of prominent sites (e.g. Megiddo, Lachish). Because of the local topography on the eastern side of the settlement the gate complex was especially long, almost 90 m from north to south (see Zorn 1997 for a detailed discussion of this gate complex). Four sections of drains were found in the vicinity of this gate system (Fig. 10.14).

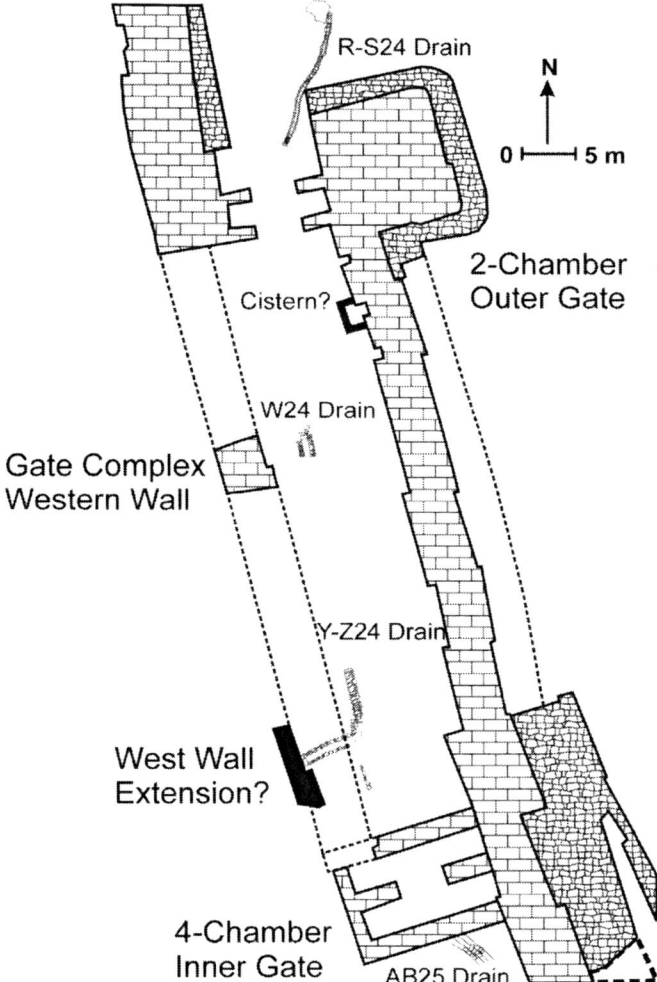

Fig. 10.14. Schematic plan showing drain segments in area of inner-outer gate complex; 1:700.

Fig. 10.15. View to southeast at drain channel leading away
from outer two-chamber gate in R–S24 (Badè Museum of Biblical Archaeology photograph #992).

The best preserved and documented drain segment is found just
outside the outer gate (R–S24; Fig. 10.15). From just outside the
gate's threshold on the south it follows a slightly curving path for a
distance of about 14.5 m to the north. The overall width of the
drain is about 50 cm and the interior channel is only slightly more
than 20 cm wide. The drain's walls are constructed of small, mostly
rectangular fieldstones laid stretcher fashion. A total of twenty-nine
capstones were preserved. An elevation on a capstone at the south
end is 773.99. The nearby drain wall is at 773.88 and an elevation
on the drain floor here is at 773.64. An elevation on the drain floor
not far from its midpoint is 773.45; about one third of the distance
to its northern end is a floor elevation at 773.16. On the north the
drain ends on the east side of what seems to be a rock-cut installation. This feature is roughly 2.0 m on a side and 1.5 m deep (773.29
to 771.83). There is no photograph of this feature. Possibly the
installation is a kind of cistern into which the drain emptied. This
would have provided water outside the town for arriving people
and animals. However, if there was once a direct connection between the drain and the installation it was not preserved. Unfortunately the floor of the outer gate and the area immediately to the
south of the gate inside the town were not excavated down to the

depth of the drain, so the feature's nature in these areas is un-known.

Two sections of drain are preserved in the space between the inner and outer gates. The section in W24 was uncovered in a test trench dug in 1927. For some unexplained reason many of the ar-chitectural remains from this trench, including the drain, were not reproduced on the original 1:400 site plan; they only appear in fig-ure 57 of the site report (McCown 1947: 220). The drain was also not photographed. The walls of the drain are constructed of small fieldstones and are two to three stones wide. The drain's preserved length is 2.7 m and its overall width is 1.4 m. The drain walls are about 45 cm wide and the channel is 50 cm wide. Two capstones were preserved. An elevation on one capstone is at 775.14 and an elevation on the floor of the drain is at 774.69.

Fig. 10.16. View to south of east-west portion of drain in Z24 near four-chamber inner gate (Badè Museum of Biblical Ar-chaeology photograph # 837b).

The third section of drain is in Y–Z24, just north of the inner gate (Fig. 10.16). The northern half of the drain runs north to south while the southern part bends to run to the west. The preserved length of the drain is 12 m, with an overall width of 1.2 m. The walls of the drain are about 30 cm thick and constructed of fieldstones one or two stones wide; the channel width is 60 cm wide. The eastern wall of the drain, where it bends to the west, is not preserved. Approximately 18 capstones were preserved along the northern stretch of drain, but none were preserved on its western extension. Elevations on the northern and western walls are at 778.09 and 778.06. No elevations are preserved for the northern half of the drain, but the floor of the southern half sloped down from 777.84 on the west to 777.44.

How this section of drain functioned in conjunction with the other sections of drain found in the gate area is a bit problematic because of its westward bend. The drain is well below all the other walls (Stratum 2) preserved in its vicinity, except for a section of wall in Z23–24 against which the western extension of the drain ends. This fieldstone wall is 8.3 m long, 1.7 m wide on the north and about 2.4 wide on the south; the place where the wall widens is hidden under a later wall. This wall partially overlies a projected continuation of the western wall of the outer gate complex and its southward extension uncovered in W23. The wall in Z23–24 is only about half as wide as the wall in W23, but has similar thicker and thinner sections (an offset-inset?). This wall also lines up well with the western wall of the inner gate. It may be then that the wall in Z23–24 is a narrower continuation of the wall in W23 that connected the two gates. If this is the case perhaps this section of drain collected and drained at least some of the water that accumulated in the space between the two gates. It is also possible that the western extension of the drain was installed in Stratum 2 and was used to drain runoff away from the new buildings constructed to the northwest of the then abandoned inner gate. Finally, a short section of a narrow fieldstone wall was found south of the drain. It appears to be below an adjacent wall of Stratum 2, but there are no elevations on it. This possible section of wall is about the same width as the walls of the drain in Y–Z24 and roughly lines up with the north–south course of the drain and with the space where the opening would have been in the inner gate. It is possible that this fragment represents a southward extension of the drain in Z24.

Fig. 10.17. View to east in deep trench in AB25 showing short segment of drain channel at the bottom of the trench. To the left is the four-chamber inner gate. To the left is a four-room house of Stratum 2. In the background is a section of the off-set-inset wall (Badè Museum of Biblical Archaeology photograph #819).

Finally, a short fragment of a drain channel was found in AB25, just south of the inner four-chamber gate (Fig. 10.17). This drain, like that in W24, was not reproduced on the original 1:400 site plan but does appear in fig. 52A of the report (McCown 1947: 210). Its preserved length is 1.5 m and overall width is 1.3 m. The walls are 35–45 cm thick and the channel is about 45 cm wide. Three or four capstones were preserved. An elevation on the west wall of the drain is at 776.84; what seems to be an elevation on the floor of the channel is at 776.60. Its elevations are one or two meters below those of the adjacent foundations of the four-chamber gate to the north. A systematic error of 1.0 m was made in many of the elevations on the 1:100 plan that documents the drain, including features adjacent to the drain, so the precise depth of the drain below the gate is uncertain; the photograph suggests a depth greater than one meter. The orientation of the drain would lead it through the central opening in the gate. Probably it was part of a larger system that drained a small plaza inside the inner gate. It is unclear whether it connected with the drain channel north of the four-chamber gate in Y–Z24 described above. The floor of the drain in Z24 is at 777.44 and 777.84, about a meter higher than the drain fragment in AB25; this would make a direct connection unlikely. However, as noted, there was a one meter error in recorded elevations in parts of the inner gate area. The elevations on the plan for the drain were not corrected upwards by that amount; if they were adjusted the drain in AB25 might have connected with that in Z24.

Some general observations on the gate drainage system can now be made. The drain sections in W24, Y–Z24, and AB25 were all constructed in the intramural fill poured up against the offset-inset wall of Stratum 3B. The two sections within the gate complex are below walls of Stratum 2. The drain sections are of various construction techniques, their walls are not of uniform thickness and their channels are not of the same width. The section of drain north of the outer gate is smaller than those within the gate complex. Since the outer gate is the only part of the gate system which continued in use into Stratum 2 it may be that an earlier drain channel, comparable in size to those inside the gate complex, once existed in this area in Stratum 3 and was replaced by a smaller drain in Stratum 2. There is a downward slope from south (776.60) to north (773.16) between the existing drain sections, assuming that the elevations of the drain in AB25 are adjusted by one meter; this is about 3.4 m over 100 m. Even if the drain section north of the inner gate belongs to Stratum 2, the visible drain sections nicely represent a single system that served to drain the area of the inner-outer gate complex of Stratum 3. It is likely that other sections of drain channels still lie hidden in unexcavated areas of the gate complex.

INTRAMURAL CISTERNS

The town's street system and wall drains were not the only means the inhabitants of Tell en-Naṣbeh had for dealing with excess water. Another method was the use of intramural cisterns. Two such cisterns are known. One is Cistern 285 located in the northeast in AP22 (Fig. 10.18); the other is Cistern 231 in the southeast in AF27 (Fig. 10.19). Both cisterns predate the offset-inset wall. The wall was built part way through the entrance to Cistern 285, while a niche was left in the wall to accommodate Cistern 231 (McCown 1947: 217). There is a niche in the offset-inset wall in V24, just inside the outer gate, which has a narrow enclosing wall similar to the wall enclosing the mouth of the Cistern 231, so perhaps this marks the location of a third unexcavated cistern. Herzog (1992: 263) claims that there were six intramural cisterns fed by drain channels, but does not give their number designations, so it is impossible to know which cisterns he intends. None of the drain channels discussed above feeds into a cistern, and neither Cistern 285 nor 231 is fed by a drain.

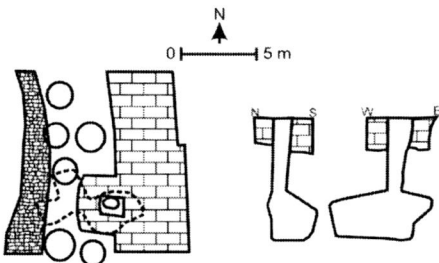

Fig. 10.18. Cistern 285; 1:500.

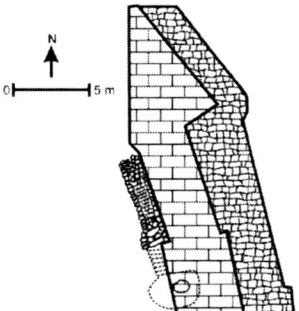

Fig. 10.19. Cistern 231; 1:500.

HOUSEHOLD CISTERNS AT TELL EN-NAṢBEH

Israel's Mediterranean climate has two main seasons, a cool wet winter when most of the rain falls (October to April) and a warm dry summer in which there is little to no rain (May to September). Tell en-Naṣbeh is in an area that receives about 50 cm of rainfall per year. Clearly, given the long dry season, it was in the best interests of the community to capture and store as much of this half meter of rainfall as possible. One of the most important techniques for capturing and storing rainfall for later use was the cistern, a usually rock-cut, sub-surface storage chamber. While cisterns had been used to some extent since the Bronze Age (Miller 1980) their use begins to become more pronounced in the hill country in Iron Age I, and greatly proliferates in Iron Age II (King and Stager 2001: 126; Zertal 1988: 348–50; Faust 2005: 207–08; Tsuk 1997b: 130–31). However, it is incorrect to claim that most Iron Age II houses had cisterns (King and Stager 2001: 126; see Hopkins 1985: 151–52, 265–66; Isserlin 1998: 121), as is clear from the remains at Tell en-Naṣbeh.

Fig. 10.20. Floral motif in plaster in Cistern 33. Note the stippling in the lower plaster layer used to help bind layers together (Badè Museum of Biblical Archaeology photograph #A70).

Cisterns (*bôr, bō'r*) are mentioned in twenty-two verses in the Hebrew Bible (Stager and King 2011: 122–23). Several of these passages indicate that the possession of one's own cistern was very desirable, a sign of the good life (Deut. 6:11; 2 Kings 18:31; Isa. 36:16; Neh. 9:25; Prov. 5:15). The construction of cisterns by kings was occasionally noted (2 Chr. 26:30; Jer. 41:9). However, water from a cistern was seen as inferior to spring water (Jer. 2:11) and was subject to ritual corpse contamination, which water from a spring was not (Lev. 11:36). A cistern might also be used as a hiding place during war (1 Sam. 13:6), as a prison (Jer. 37:16, 38:6–13), and as an impromptu burial site (Jer. 41:7–9).

The original Tell en-Naṣbeh report identified 53 cisterns based on the presence of "water-proofing cement" (McCown 1947: 129). Plaster on the wall of Cistern 33 preserves stippling marks used to key layers of plaster together; it also preserves an impressed floral design (Fig. 10.20; McCown 1947: pl. 44.1–2). Cistern 159 preserved three layers of plaster (McCown 1947: pl. 45.2) However, 53 cisterns is a minimal estimate because such plaster may not have survived in all cisterns, and not all cisterns cut into limestone need such plastering to make them water tight (King and Stager 2001: 126). The main distinction between the two types of rock-cut features identified at Tell en-Naṣbeh, cisterns and silos, is shape (for additional details on Tell en-Naṣbeh cisterns see Zorn 1993: 275–85). Cisterns tend to have narrow circular mouths which can easily be sealed to help prevent large debris, animals, and humans from falling in, and also to reduce evaporation (eight Tell en-Naṣbeh cisterns were found still sealed; e.g. McCown 1947: pl. 95.1). Cisterns also tend to widen out substantially below ground while silos tend to have mouths that are about the same diameter as their shafts (the roofs of some cisterns may have collapsed, making them seem more like silos). On the basis of form, the previous number of identified cisterns has been increased from 53 to 101 site wide. Some number of these may not have been in use simultaneously with others, and some number must certainly have existed in the one third of the site that was not excavated. An estimate of roughly 110 cisterns for the entire site at any moment seems appropriate for Stratum 3 (Zorn 1993: 283). A similar estimation of the total number of dwellings in Stratum 3 amounts to about 200 (Zorn 1993: 116). In other words, it may be suggested that somewhat more than half of all houses had any sort of cistern.

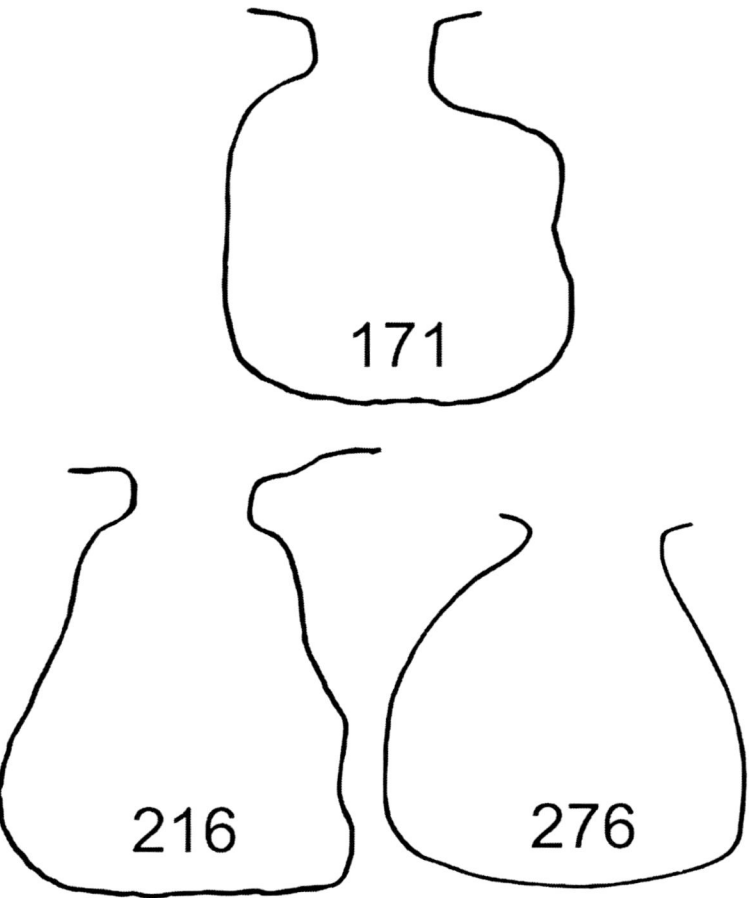

Fig. 10.21. Example cross sections of selected cisterns. Cylindrical-shaped Cistern 171 (Top); Bottle-shape Cisterns 216 (bottom left) and 276 (bottom right). Not to scale (Adapted from plans in Badè Museum of Biblical Archaeology).

Forty-four of the 53 originally identified cisterns were grouped into two types (Fig. 10.21). The more numerous type (39 examples recorded, 89% of total) is bottle-shaped, that is, below their necks they broaden out in rough trapezoidal forms. Fewer in number (5 recorded, 11% of total recorded) are those that fall into the cylinder-shaped variety.

Fig. 10.22. Covered mouth of Cistern 363 (left) fed by drain channel (right) in Room 617. Note the low wall surrounding the mouth of the cistern. The junction of roads 514, 541 and 627 is just beyond the wall behind the squatting figure. Looking northeast (Badè Museum of Biblical Archaeology photograph #1433).

In most cases no obvious channels used to fill the Tell en-Naṣbeh cisterns remain. The best preserved example feeds water from the intersection of roads 514, 627 and 541 into Cistern 363 by way of a stone-lined and covered channel (Fig. 10.22). Drains were also found feeding Cistern 119 (unfortunately there were are no other surrounding architectural remains; McCown 1947: pl. 79.3–4) and Cistern 326, found inside the 4-room house of Stratum 2 inside the outer gate. Cistern mouths were cut into bedrock, but over time, as floor accumulations increased in depth, it seems that the construction of narrow stone walls around them raised the mouths of cisterns. Some examples include Cisterns 176 (McCown 1947: pl. 101.4), 165 in the southern part of the study area (McCown 1947: pl. 44.5), and 363 (Fig. 10.22). Presumably most cisterns were sited at low spots in floors and water simply flowed in from the surrounding space. McClellan (1984:61) noted the large number of cisterns at the lower western end of cross-road 644 where it connect to road 388 (Ci 364a and others around it), and suggested they were so sited in order to capture runoff from that street. There has been much debate over whether three- and four-room houses were completely roofed over or contained an open courtyard (e.g. Stager 1985: 15; Netzer 1992: 195–97; Mazar 1990: 485–86; Holladay 2009: 69–70). It perhaps makes more sense that the mouth of a cistern would be located in a space open to the elements in which water collected, rather than in a roofed over space, especially if there is no evidence that water was fed into the cistern from an adjacent road. Of course, the presence of such a channel providing water from beyond the room in which the cistern was located, such as for Cistern 363, obviates any need for placing it in an open space. Water from such open and public spaces was not, however, of the highest quality (Rosen and Greenberg 2002: 286).

Evidence that cisterns were sited so that they might be filled directly from street runoff does, however, exist. Cistern 363 has already been mentioned. Cistern 380 has two mouths; one is located inside the house, the other, beyond the house wall, is located in the adjacent ring-road 514 (Fig. 10.23). A low wall also cuts across the interior of the cistern, perhaps suggesting that one part of the cistern was a settling basin for street debris. Cistern 380 is thus the clearest example of a cistern constructed to make use of street runoff. However, there are indications that other cisterns made similar use of street runoff, though in a less sophisticated manner. In the study area the mouths of several cisterns were found cut across by house walls that separated the dwelling from an adjacent road (357, 359). Several other cisterns also seem to lie along the projected line of similar front house walls (146, 160, 161, 163; McClellan 1984: 65), though the walls themselves were not preserved. It is possible that the cisterns cut across by walls in this fashion allowed water to flow into them from the street and be drawn from inside the house.

Fig. 10.23. Looking north along ring-road 514. The mouth of Cistern 380 in the road is on the right, while the opening on the left is inside the house (Badè Museum of Biblical Archaeology photograph #1294).

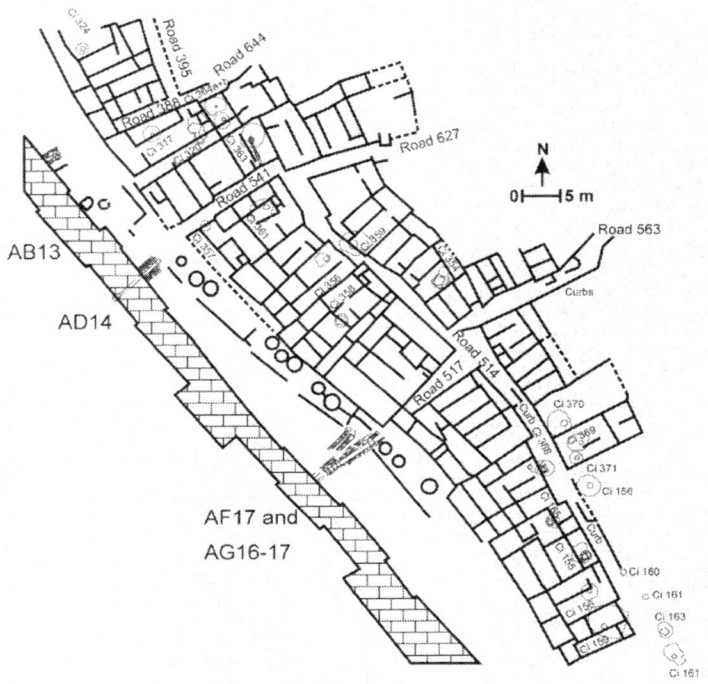

Fig. 10.24. Schematic plan of study area along southwestern
side of site; 1:1000.

What does the ratio of cisterns to houses say about how water was
manipulated at Tell en-Naṣbeh? In the study area there are substantial remains of 31 buildings that seem to be dwellings, mostly of the
three- and four-room variety (Fig. 10.24). As indicated by squiggly
lines on the 1:100 plans these structures were almost all excavated
down to bedrock. A total of 20 cisterns were found in these dwellings. However, four of the dwellings had two cisterns each. Thus,
of the 31 dwellings 15 did not possess their own cistern, while 16
had one or two cisterns, a ratio of almost 1:2. The possession of
one's own cistern was a clear desideratum for the biblical authors
(who were no doubt upper class and might well have been able to
afford the construction of a cistern). In some sites (probably small
ones) and in some periods every house may have had one. It is
clear, however, that even in the hill country not every house necessarily had one (Isserlin 1998: 125, 139).

If access to, and storage of, water was a significant concern to the ancient Israelites why did every house in the hill country not have a cistern? As shown above, a well-sited cistern could be fed from roof, courtyard and street runoff, obviating the need for carrying water from a spring every day (more on this below). A cistern could also provide a certain amount of water independence. If a large cistern were full at the end of the rainy season its owners knew how much water they had available to last them through the summer. During a siege access to a settlement's spring might be cut off and a cistern might be its owner's only source of water. During the summer or a period of drought the flow of local springs might be severely diminished, which would also affect how much water was captured in cisterns, but some could, at least, be captured. However, cisterns do have their own drawbacks. Cisterns also contain debris from human and possibly animal activities in courtyards and streets and so are likely less healthy than water drawn daily from a spring, though springs can also contain varied contaminants (Rosen and Greenberg 2002: 291–92). Also, the hewing of a cistern is not a trivial matter. The construction by hand of a cistern with a capacity of 20 m^3 could require the removal of solid limestone weighing 50 tons, and the huge Cistern 159 might have required the removal of over 140 tons of solid rock (Walker 2011). Once hewn a cistern would likely require some maintenance, either in the form of occasional plastering or cleaning. However, how often, if ever, a cistern was cleaned out is not clear. For example, Cisterns 361 and 369 each contained over 100 recorded finds of all types, and Cistern 370 contained 275+ objects, including bones, suggesting that cleaning could be rare in some instances.

However, as is clear from the number of cisterns found at Tell en-Naṣbeh, the town's inhabitants believed that the hewing of a certain number of cisterns was desirable. That is, the benefits were thought to largely outweigh the disadvantages. Why then do only about half the houses have cisterns? After all, the Stratum 3 settlement existed for over 300 years, so there was a great deal of time in which to undertake the work. The answer may be tied in to the capacity and distribution of the cisterns themselves.

Cistern	Shape	Base	Depth	Volume	Individuals
Ci 155	B	4.6	3.0	10.2	6/4/7/5
Ci 156	B	3.1	2.2	5.0	3/2/3/2
Ci 159	B	22.1	3.5	57.5	32/21/38/26
Ci 165	B	-	-	-	-
Ci 166	B	-	-	-	-
Ci 317	B?	3.5	-	-	-
Ci 320	?	6.8	4.2	21.3	12/8/14/9
Ci 324	?	1.5	0.1	0.1	0/0/0/0
Ci 354	B	5.2	3.0	11.6	6/4/8/5
Ci 356	B	3.1	3.9	9.0	5/3/6/4
Ci 357	B	1.3	2.3	2.2	1/1/1/1
Ci 358	B?	2.5	2.9	5.4	3/2/4/2
Ci 359	B	12.6	3.9	36.6	20/14/24/16
Ci 361	B	7.1	-	-	-
Ci 363	C	8.5	4.8	40.5	23/15/27/18
Ci 364a	B	3.1	-	-	-
Ci 364b	B	5.4	2.0	8.0	4/3/5/4
Ci 368	B	6.8	3.5	17.7	10/7/12/8
Ci 369	B	6.6	2.0	9.8	5/4/7/4
Ci 370	C	8	4.7	37.4	21/14/25/17
Ci 371	B	2	-	-	6/4/7/5
Average		6.0	3.0	18.1	
Standard Deviation		4.7	1.2	16.4	

Notes:

Shape: B = Bottle; C = Cylinder; ? = Shaped not recorded.

Base: Approximate area of base of cistern in m^2.

Depth: Depth of cistern based on elevations at bottom and mouth of cistern minus 53 cm for thickness of roof.

Volume: Volume of cistern in m^3; multiply Volume by 1000 for number of liters. Bottle shaped cisterns are calculated at 75% of a cylindrical shape and cylinders are calculated as cylinders.

Individuals: Number of people able to be supplied by the cistern in #1/#2/#3/#4 format

#1 = 10 liters per day for 180 days

#2 = 15 liters per day for 180 days

#3 = 10 liters per day for 150 days

#4 = 15 liters per day for 150 days

Table 10.1. Cistern Capacities in Study Area

An attempt to estimate the capacities of these cisterns does, however, face several difficulties. First, information or indications for the shapes of the cisterns is limited. Dotted lines on the 1:100 site plans are usually used to indicate the subsurface extent of each cistern. However, such dotted lines are not always used, especially at the southern end of the site that was excavated in the first two seasons when recording standards were more rudimentary. These dotted lines do provide a rough idea of the maximum internal floor area of each cistern, but not of their exact shapes. Second, only ten cistern sections were published in the 1947 report; drawings of a few others exist on the site's 1:100 plans. This lack of cistern sections hampers efforts to reconstruct cistern capacities. Finally, bedrock elevations are usually recorded near the mouths of cisterns, usually with another elevation at the base of the cistern. The thickness of the rock roof of the cistern is usually not directly available (only as can be estimated from a few section drawings). For most cisterns it is unclear how much of the total height of the cistern (based on the difference between the elevation at its mouth and the one at its base) is made up by the roof. Even given these caveats it is still possible to offer some tentative estimate of cistern capacities.[4]

In the study area 21 cisterns likely in use during the time of Stratum 3 were examined (Table 10.1). Of this total, 15 provided data that allowed their internal floor area to be estimated; they also provided elevations near their mouths and at their bases. Section drawings of four cisterns at the northern end of the site (171, 173, 183, and 216) suggest an average roof thickness of 53 cm. The height of each cistern was adjusted downward by this amount. This adjusted height was used to calculate the cylindrical cisterns as cylinders, while the bottle-shaped cisterns were calculated at 75% of a cylinder's capacity. The average capacity of the 15 measurable cisterns was about 18 m^3 or 18,000 liters. At 10 liters of water per day per person over a five month dry season (150 days) a cistern of this capacity could store enough water for the needs of 12 individuals (for data on 10 liters of water per day per person see Zorn 1993:

---

[4] The volumes used here are more conservative estimates than those found in Zorn 1993: 277–81.

302–03). At 15 liters per day per person a cistern of this capacity could supply eight individuals over the same period. If the known 53 cisterns had an average capacity of 18 m³ they could have supplied water for between approximately 350 to 640 people, depending on whether 10 or 15 liters per day is used, and whether 180 or 150 days is the time span. According to the same metrics, the estimated 110 total cisterns for the site could have supplied between about 730 and 1300 inhabitants. If the estimated 200 houses on the site contained an average of 5 inhabitants the cisterns could meet this total demand.

The cisterns do, however, vary greatly in capacity. The smallest have a capacity of only one or two cubic meters while the largest has a capacity of around 58 m³ (58,000 liters). This is also reflected in the standard deviation of the measured volumes. The standard deviation of 16 m³ is almost as much as the average capacity of the measured cisterns. Put another way, two thirds of the measured cisterns should lie within a range between 2 m³ and 34 m³. Using the above figures it is possible to suggest that a cistern with a capacity of 9.0 m³ would provide enough stored water for a family of 5 for 6 months at 10 liters per day, or a family of 6 for 5 months. At 15 liters per day the cistern would have to be 12.5 m³ for the same periods and family sizes. Cisterns with a capacity below that amount could not store enough water for a family of that size, and were thus likely meant to supplement other sources of water, or were filled by hand when it was thought necessary. Six of the measurable cisterns (40%; 156, 324, 357, 358, 364b) are below the 9.0 m³ threshold. Four cisterns (27%; 155, 354, 356, 369) fall in the range of 9.0–12.5 m³ figure, and five others (33%; 159, 320, 359, 363, 370) greatly exceed that figure. Cisterns 359, 363 and 370 could provide water for 20–25 individuals at 10 liters per day for 5–6 months, or for 14–18 people at 15 liters per day. Cistern 159 had sufficient capacity for 32–38 people at 10 liters per day for 5–6 months, or 21–26 people at 15 liters per day. In other words, the first three cisterns were sufficient for the needs of 3–5 families of 5 people each, and the largest cistern could supply water for 4–8 families.

Understanding water storage at Tell en-Naṣbeh is clearly more complicated than simply totaling up the estimated average capacities of the site's cisterns. Almost half of the dwellings had no cisterns at all; some had cisterns, but not with enough capacity to support a typical family through to the end of the dry summer months; some had cisterns with capacities greatly beyond the needs of a typical family; only a modest fraction (about 20% in the study area) had cisterns of a size suitable for the demands of a single family. So, while the total capacity of all the cisterns could have supported the town's likely population, direct access to cistern water was very uneven.

What could account for the hewing of such large cisterns, no trivial matter as shown above, which far exceed the needs of a typical size family in such domestic contexts? One possibility is that these large cisterns were meant to supply the needs of extended families inhabiting nearby houses, rather than only nuclear families.

Much has been written lately about the roles and history of extended and nuclear families in ancient Israel (see Faust 2012 for discussion and recent bibliography). Some posit (though there is disagreement) that before the rise of the monarchies extended families were the norm, but that as society became more urban and socially stratified such larger family groups disappeared and nuclear families were the rule. Some also see a difference between social structures in urban centers (more nuclear families) as compared to rural settings (preservation of extended families). The presence of a handful of cisterns in late Iron Age Tell en-Naṣbeh with a capacity far exceeding the needs of a nuclear family cannot prove that they were used by extended families at that time. They may, in fact, have been hewn much earlier in the life of the stratum. There is, in fact, no way to date when they were hewn. Still, that such large cisterns were hewn at all, at some point in the life span of Stratum 3, indicates that water storage installations of that size were desired and were in use. The possibility that they served extended families should be factored in to future discussions of family structure in ancient Israel.

The block of houses northeast of road 514 containing Cisterns 359 (36.6 m³) and 354 (11.6 m³) may represent evidence of water resources shared by an extended family or families (see the discussions by Brody 2009 and 2011, and by Faust 2012: 111 n. 53 and 163 n. 17 for additional data and debate over the existence of extended families in this block of buildings). Unfortunately, the area further upslope to the east was not excavated, so the number of additional houses and cisterns there is unknown, so the scenario offered here can only be suggestive of possibilities. The two cisterns together have a capacity of 48 m³. Depending on the amount of water used per day (10 or 15 liters) and length of the dry season (150 or 180 days) they could hold water for 18–32 individuals. This seems enough to support roughly 4–6 nuclear families. If each dwelling in this block (average total ground floor area, including walls but excluding possible upper floors, being 45 m²; Zorn 1993: 118) were occupied by a nuclear family (though the building northwest of Cistern 359 may have been used for olive pressing) these two cisterns seem capable of supplying their water storage needs. Water might be kept in storage jars (see below), but one is then left to explain the tremendous size of Cistern 359, with its capacity far beyond the needs of a nuclear family. Note also that these buildings all share walls, indicating that this block was constructed at one time as an architectural unit, another possible indication of cooperation and planning across an extended family. In order to facilitate site drainage this block was laid out in conjunction with the architectural units and roads surrounding it, suggestive of community level planning.

As mentioned above, some of the town's inhabitants may not have had access to sufficient cistern water to meet their needs. Many of these may have had to rely on water drawn from a spring on a daily basis. Even owners of cisterns may have felt the need to "top up" up at times. There are four springs within 1.5 km of Tell en-Naṣbeh (Mapping Center of Israel; straight line distances; actual distances navigating the settlement's streets and fortifications, along with local topography, would have been greater). Unfortunately the amount of water produced by these springs is not known, though hill country springs in general seem to have a flow of 10,000 to 350,000 m³ per year. This flow can drop off considerably during the summer and fall (Tsuk 1997c: 132). Even at the minimum flow, though, these four springs may have provided over 10,000 liters of water per day, which at 10–15 liters of water per person would suffice for around 670–1000 people. Since these springs all lie beyond the walls of the town, water from them had to be carried in. It is thus worthwhile to briefly explore some of the ramifications of the need to supply a family with spring or well water on a daily basis.

One liter of water weighs one kilogram. A family of five might require 50–75 liters of water on average each day. On an average daily basis this same weight in kilograms, along with the weight of appropriate containers, would need to be brought to a home which did not have access to a cistern. There are two ways that water could be transported: by animal or by human. The most typical beast of burden in ancient Israel was the donkey. A lower end estimate for a donkey's carrying capacity is about 45 kg (*Animal Management* 1914: 274). However, donkeys in use in the Old Assyrian trade with Anatolia carried about twice that weight, about 90–100 kg (Veenhof 1972: 45; Lewy 1964: 186), which matches modern usage in Ethiopia (Gebreab et al. 2004: 49). A round trip journey to a spring about 1 km a way was estimated to take about 2 hours for a donkey (Zertal 1988: 344). It seems that a single trip by a typical donkey could supply the average needs of a nuclear family. If a family did not have a donkey or other beast of burden the water would have to be carried by a member of the family.

A large cross-cultural study of traditional societies showed that the fetching of water was the third most common task performed by women (after preparing vegetables and cooking, but before tasks involved in cloth production) and was seldom a male task (Murdock and Provost 1973: 207). The same is suggested for Israel based on a variety of sources and parallels. One is the famous story of Rebekah in Gen. 24:10–22, who carries a vessel called a *kad*. There are also reports from early twentieth century researchers documenting the role of women in fetching water (e.g. Grant 1907: 92, also the top illustration on the plate entitled Women's Work between pages 48–49). This usually took place twice a day, in the morning and evening (Wilson 1906: 128). Fetching water is also the most commonly depicted female activity in classical Greek art (Durand, Frontisi-Ducroux, and Lissarrgue 1989: 122).

The roles of women in ancient Israel have been the subject of lively study, especially over the last 20 years (for recent bibliography see Ebeling 2010). These have tended to focus on the importance of women in grain processing/distribution, cloth production (e.g. Meyers 2007), and ritual activities, and how these were important mechanisms for creating and maintaining the female social networks which were crucial to a settlement's well-being (Meyers 2013: 141–46). So far, however, relatively little attention has been paid to the important social role Israelite women and girls played in fetching water for their households. Most often tasks and activities using water are mentioned, but not how the water itself was procured.

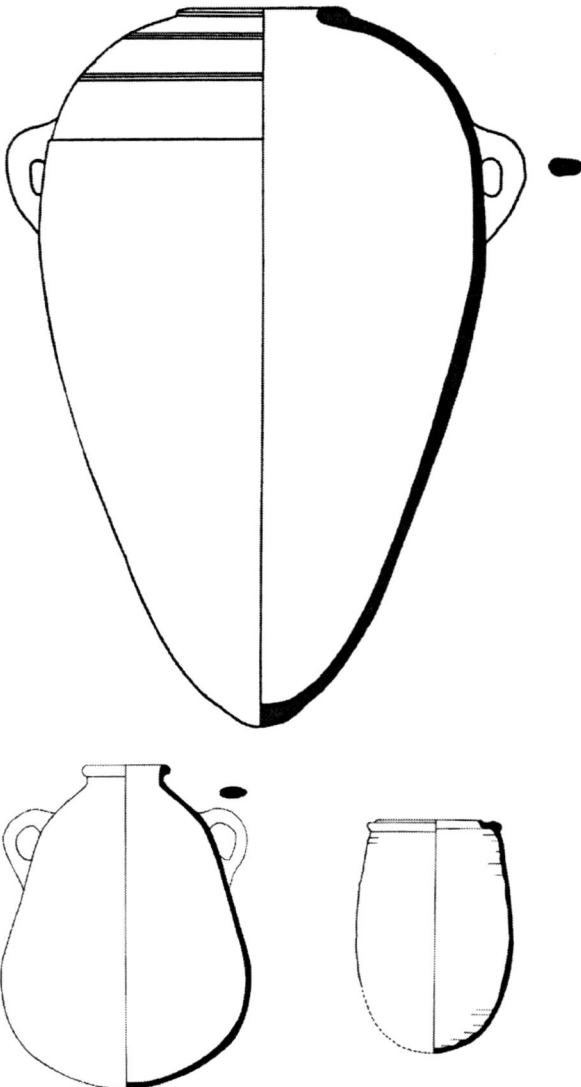

Fig. 10.25. Tell en-Naṣbeh jars 56 (top), 239 (bottom left) and 387 (bottom right) 1:10 (Wampler 1947: pls. 4, 14, and 24).

Heavy loads can be carried on the back or on the head (Lloyd et al. 2010: 528).[5] Head-loading of bulky and heavy burdens, such as water, seems fairly typical (Lloyd et al. 2010: 529). Studies have shown that people who have been trained from youth to bear loads in such a fashion can carry 70% of their own weight on their heads (Lloyd et al. 2010: 528; Maloy et al. 1986), though the most energy efficient weight was 20% of body weight. Girls in the range of 10 to 12 years were able to carry 20 liter buckets of water in this way (Lloyd et al. 2010: 528). One study suggested that the maximum weight an adult male Indian worker should carry on his head was 30 kg (Datta, Chatterjee, and Roy 1975). Thus, the amount an individual could carry on his/her head is quite substantial, but also quite variable. Much depends on an individual's age, strength, size, tolerance of pain, expertise in bearing such burdens and other factors.

The capacities of two typical small jars from Tell en-Naṣbeh were calculated (Fig. 10.25). Holemouth jar 387, found in Cistern 363 in the study area, had a capacity of 7.8 liters, while the more sack-shaped jar 239 had a capacity of 22.2 liters. Unfortunately jar 387 itself could not be located, but a jar of the same type, from the same cistern weighed 3.2 kg. Jar 387 full of water weighed about 11 kg. Jar 239 weighed 5.1 kg.[6] Full of water it weighed about 29.3 kg. The weight of the smaller jar and the water it could hold is within the range of around 20 liters that the 10–12 year old girls mentioned above could carry, while the larger jar is almost half again heavier than 20 liters. Wilson noted that Palestinian women normally carried one to two gallons of water (ca. 3.8–7.6 liters) in ce-

---

[5] It would be useful to study human skeletal remains from Iron Age Israel to identify markers indicative of head-loading. Such markers have been documented in a variety of cultures where head-loading is practiced (Capasso, Kennedy and Wilczak 1999: 14, possibly 31, 33–35, possibly 71; Lovell 1994: 161–62; Echarri and Forriol 2005)

[6] Joseph Greene of the Harvard Semitic Museum, where these vessels are currently on display, provided the weights for these two jars. Avshalom Karasik of the Israel Antiquities Authority calculated the volumes of the jars. I thank both these colleagues for their assistance with the metrics for these jars.

ramic jars on their heads, less than the capacity of jar 387. Use of this smaller jar would necessitate 6–10 round trips to a spring. Use of the larger jar would reduce the number of trips to 3–4. Fetching water from a spring each day for a family of five could thus be a significant investment in time for an individual, but was also crucial for the survival of the family.

If any animals had to be watered at the home this would affect how many people a cistern could support, though most likely animals were watered outside the settlement itself. It would also increase the number of daily trips to a spring required to provide for the entire household.

Where was spring water stored in an Israelite house if it did not possess a cistern? Was water kept in storage jars in homes? Such a practice is not mentioned in the biblical text. There are references to jars (*kad*) used to draw and transport water (Gen. 24:14–46; 1 Kings 18:33; Kelso and Albright 1948: 19; King and Stager 2001: 143–45; Dever 2001: 232–33). There are also references to water kept in containers, but it is not clear from the contexts what type of ceramic containers these were. For example, in 1 Kings 19:6 Elijah is provided with water in a vessel by an angel. In 1 Sam. 26:11–16 David is able to steal a water container from near Saul's head as he slept. Presumably since Saul was on campaign, and Elijah was on a journey, these were small, easily transportable jars, not massive pithoi. King and Stager (2001: 144) understand this small, portable container (*ṣappaḥat*) to be a pilgrim flask, which fits the above two contexts well (Kelso and Albright 1948: 30).

The absence of evidence for the use of large water storage jars from the texts does not, however, mean they did not exist; their absence from the texts may only be an artifact of the writers' interests. In fact, one scholar has argued, on the basis of the relative lack of cisterns in Iron Age I hill country sites, that the ubiquitous collar-rim jars of the period may have been used, at least in part, for water storage (Zertal 1988: 350–51). Thus, water storage in jars may have sufficed for houses that did not possess a cistern.

The ability to store water in jars would obviate the need to rely on cisterns. However, storage of water in jars has several drawbacks when compared with cisterns. First, as noted above, cisterns can be filled by using sloping surfaces and channels. Jars can be used to fill cisterns, but for large cisterns this was likely more of a supplementary procedure because of the great capacity of many cisterns as compared to the much smaller capacity of the jars used to fill them (to fill the ca. 58,000 liter capacity Cistern 159 by hand with the 7.8 liter capacity jar 387 would require over 7300 trips to a spring). On the other hand, storage jars have to be filled by hand with water brought from a spring. Moreover, cisterns take up very little floor space; only their mouths need to be taken in to consideration. The average capacity of a cistern in the study area was 18,000 liters. At Tell en-Naṣbeh a typical large jar (Fig. 10.25, jar 56 at top) had a capacity of 153 liters, which would likely suffice for a single family for 2–3 days. Each such jar had a diameter of 57 cm. In order to duplicate the storage capacity of an average cistern about 118 jars of this type would be required and would occupy 30–40 m² of floor space. Clearly storing that much water in jars was impractical. Unfortunately it is not possible to know how much water a typical family might keep on hand in storage jars. Was one day's worth of water considered sufficient? A week's? A month's? A household that relied exclusively on storing a few days' worth of water in jars would be at a great disadvantage during a siege when access to springs was cut off.

WATER USE AT TELL EN-NAṢBEH: SUMMARY AND CONCLUSION

It is clear from this discussion that the inhabitants of Tell en-Naṣbeh in Iron Age II Stratum 3 went to some lengths to lay out their dwellings, road system and cisterns both to capture what water they could, and also to channel excess water beyond the settlement's peripheral band of houses. The 3A settlement's road system was laid out to make use of the generally downward south to north slope of the bedrock (e.g. ca. 780.70 along the ring-road in AJ21 in the south and ca. 776.50 in Q15 in the north; also McClellan 1984: 65). Water flowed down from the crest of the hill to the ring-road and then north along the ring-road. When possible, street runoff was diverted into cisterns of dwellings that fronted on these streets. Along the northern and western sides of the town the remaining runoff was channeled from the ring-road into side-roads, through the line of casemate-like fortifications. This is evidence of a degree of local civic cooperation and planning.

At the height of the Tell en-Naṣbeh's expansion in Stratum 3B–C an elaborate drainage system had been developed. With the addition of the massive offset-inset wall and the creation of an intramural zone, drains were added to the existing street drainage system on the northern and western sides of the town to channel water through the intramural zone and out beyond the wall itself. On the eastern side such runoff was directed through a drain in the town gate, or into two known cisterns (see Zorn 1993: 269–75 for drainage systems known at other Iron Age sites published up to that time). This is not to say that the system as it evolved was perfect. For example, there were no doubt always some areas where unwanted water pooled, and a system designed for typical amounts of water could be overwhelmed by a 500 year flood.

Why was such effort expended to direct water away from the southern part of the town? The answer is clear from the nature of the installations found in the southern intramural zone. A total of 61 storage pits (called bins in the 1947 report) were uncovered on the south side of the town, from just south of the inner gate in AC24–25 on the east, to AD15 on the west (Zorn 1993: 251–57). They were constructed in the same fill poured up against the off-set-inset wall as the drains to the north and so postdate the construction of the wall. Such bins were used to store grain. Keeping the ground around these bins as dry as possible to minimize loss of food to rot was thus a significant concern. There is only a small area on the west where both drains and bins are found (AF–AG17 and AD15). The fact that the intramural storage system and wall drains seem to be part of a single, purposefully designed system intended to keep the southern bin area as dry as possible, suggests that the town wall and gate system, intramural fill, drains, intramural cisterns, and bins were integrated into a single system at the same time. Presumably the intramural fill was likewise sloped to the north to facilitate drainage away from the bins in the south. This was a tremendous construction project, certainly undertaken under royal direction.

Slightly more than half the town's dwellings had cisterns. As a whole, these cisterns could provide for the site's total population. However, not every house had a cistern of sufficient size to meet the needs of a typical family, while some contained cisterns with capacities far in excess of a single family's needs. This suggests that the largest cisterns may have served the needs of extended families. Conversely, some families may have had to rely on water drawn from springs or wells and transported laboriously to the town, probably by a female member of the family, and stored there in jars.

Tell en-Naṣbeh thus provides important evidence of how water manipulation at a small Judean border town evolved over time. However, Tell en-Naṣbeh cannot be used uncritically as a template to explain how other sites manipulated local water resources. Each site must be studied on the basis of its own local setting, including site topography, local hydrology, and even political history. Nevertheless, this study does serve as a valuable example for how local and national planning strategies for water manipulation at a modest Iron Age II hill country site could be integrated, and suggests some social implications that "flow" from the previous observations.

REFERENCES

1914 International Public Health in Jerusalem. *Journal of the American Medical Association* 63: 593–94.

Angelakis A. N.; Mays, L. W.; and Koutsoyiannis, D. ed.
2012 *Evolution of Water Supply Through the Millennia.* London: IWA Publishing.

Bradley, D. J.
1977 Health Aspects of Water Supplies in Tropical Countries. Pp. 3–17 in *Water, Wastes and Health in Hot Climates*, ed. R. Reachem, M. McGarry, and D. Mara. Chichester: John Wiley & Sons.

Brody, A. J.
2009 "Those Who Add House to House": Household Archaeology and the Use of Domestic Space in an Iron II Residential Compound at Tell en-Naṣbeh. Pp. 45–56 in *Exploring the Longue Durée: Essays in Honor of Lawrence E. Stager*, ed. J. D. Schloen. Winona Lake, IN: Eisenbrauns.
2011 The Archaeology of the Extended Family: A Household Compound from Iron II Tell en-Naṣbeh. Pp. 237–54 in *Household Archaeology in Ancient Israel and Beyond*, ed. A. Yasur-Landau; J. R. Ebeling; and L. B. Mazow. Leiden & Boston: Brill.

Capasso, L.; Kennedy, K. A. R.; and Wilczak, C. A.
1999   *Atlas of Occupational Markers on Human Remains.* Journal of Paleopathology, Monographic Publications 3. Teramo: Edigrafial.

Carson, H. Y.
1919   Restoring Sanitation in Palestine. *American City* 21: 349–51.

Datta, S. R.; Chatterjee, B. B.; and Roy, B. N.
1975   Maximum Permissible Weight to be Carried on the Head by a Male Worker from Eastern India. *Journal of Applied Physiology* 38: 132–35.

Dever, W. G.
2001   *What Did the Biblical Writers Know & When Did They Know It?* Grand Rapids, MI: Eerdmans.

Durand, J.-L.; Frontisi-Ducroux, F.; and Lissarrgue, F.
1989   Wine: Human and Divine. Pp. 121–30 in *A City of Images: Iconography and Society in Ancient Greece.* ed. C. Bérard, C. Bron, J.-L. Durand, F. Frontisi-Ducroux, F. Lissarrgue, A. Schnapp, and J.-P. Vernant, trans. D. Lyons, from the French. Princeton, NJ: Princeton University.

Ebeling, J. R.
2010   *Women's Lives in Biblical Times.* London: T & T Clark.

Faust, A.
2005   The Israelite Village: Cultural Conservatism and Technological Innovation. *Tel Aviv* 32: 204–19.
2012   *The Archaeology of Israelite Society in Iron Age II.* Winona Lake, IN: Eisenbrauns.

Finkelstein, I.
2012   The Great Wall of Tell en-Nasbeh (Mizpah), The First Fortifications in Judah, and 1 Kings 15:16–22 *Vetus Testamentum* 62: 14–28.

Gebreab, F.; Wold, A. G.; Kelemu, F.; Ibro, A.; and Yilma, K.
2004   Donkey Utilisation and Management in Ethiopia. Pp. 46–52 in *Donkeys, People and Development: A Resource Book of the Animal Traction Network for Eastern and Southern Africa (AT-NESA),* ed. P. Starkey and D. Fielding. Wageningen: ACP-EU Technical Centre for Agricultural and Rural Coopera-

tion (CTA). http://www.atnesa.org/donkeys/donkeys-feseha-utilisation-ET.pdf.

Grant, E.
1907 *The Peasantry of Palestine; The Life, Manners and Customs of the Village.* Boston: The Pilgrim Press.

Great Britain. War Office. Veterinary Department
1914 *Animal Management. 1908: Prepared in the Veterinary Department for General Staff, War Office.* London: Printed under the Authority of His Majesty's Stationary Office. Reprinted 1914.

Herzog, Z.
1992 Settlement and Fortification Planning in the Iron Age. Pp. 231–74 in *The Architecture of Ancient Israel: From the Prehistoric to the Persian periods: In Memory of Immanuel (Munya) Dunayevsky,* ed. A. Kempinski and R. Reich, Jerusalem: Israel Exploration Society.

Holladay, J. S., Jr.
2009 "Home Economics 1407" and the Israelite Family and their Neighbors: An Anthropological/Archaeological Exploration. Pp. 59–88 in *The Family in Life and in Death: The Family in Ancient Israel, Sociological and Archaeological Perspectives,* ed. P. Dutcher-Walls. Library of Hebrew Bible/Old Testament Studies 504. New York: T & T Clark.

Hopkins, D. C.
1985 *The Highlands of Canaan: Agriculture in the Early Iron Age.* The Social Word of Biblical Antiquity Series 3. Sheffield: Almond.

Isserlin, B. S. J.
1998 *The Israelites.* London: Thames and Hudson.

Kaplan, J.
2010 The Mesha Inscription and Iron Age II Water Systems. *Journal of Near Eastern Studies* 69: 23–9.

Kelso, J. L., and Albright, W. F.
1948 *The Ceramic Vocabulary of the Old Testament.* Bulletin of the American Schools of Oriental Research Supplementary

Studies 5/6. New Haven, CT: American Schools of Oriental Research.

King, P. J., and Stager, L. E.
2001   *Life in Biblical Israel.* Louisville, KY: Westminster John Knox.

Lewy, H.
1964   The Assload, the Sack and Other Measures of Capacity. *Rivista Degli Studi Orientali* 39: 181–97

Lloyd, R.; Parr, B.; Davies, S.; and Cooke, C.
2010   Subjective Perceptions of Load Carriage on the Head and Back in Xhosa Women. *Applied Ergonomics* 41: 522–29

Malony, G. M. O.; Heglund, N. C.; Prager, L. M.; Cavagna, G. A.; and Taylor, C. R.
1986   Energetic Cost of Carrying Loads: Have African Women Discovered an Economic Way? *Nature* 319: 668–69.

Mays, L. W.; Koutsoyiannis, D.; and Angelakis, A. N.
2007   A Brief History of Urban Water Supply in Antiquity. *Water Science and Technology: Water Supply* 7.1: 1–12.

Mazar, A.
1990   *Archaeology of the Land of the Bible, 10,000–586 B. C. E.* New York: Doubleday.

McClellan, T. L.
1984   Town Planning at Tell en-Naṣbeh. *Zeitschrift des Deutschen Palästina-Vereins* 100: 53–69.

McCown, C.C.
1947   *Tell en-Naṣbeh,* Vol. 1: *Archaeological and Historical Results.* Berkeley, CA: Palestine Institute of Pacific School of Religion.

Meyers, C. L.
2007   From Field Crops to Food: Attributing Gender and Meaning to Bread Production in Iron Age Israel. Pp. 67–84 in *The Archaeology of Difference: Gender, Ethnicity, Class and the "Other" in Antiquity,* ed. D. R. Edwards and C. T. McCollough. Winona Lake, IN: Eisenbrauns.
2013   *Rediscovering Eve: Ancient Israelite Women in Context.* New York: Oxford University Press.

Miller, R.
1980   Water Use in Syria and Palestine from the Neolithic to the Bronze Age. *World Archaeology* 11: 331–41.

Murdock, G. P., and Provost, C.
1973   Factors in the Division of Labor by Sex: A Cross-Cultural Analysis. *Ethnology* 12: 203–25.

Netzer, E.
1992   Domestic Architecture in the Iron Age. Pp. 193–201. in *The Architecture of Ancient Israel: From the Prehistoric to the Persian periods: In Memory of Immanuel (Munya) Dunayevsky*, ed. A. Kempinski and R. Reich, Jerusalem: Israel Exploration Society.

Neufeld, N.
1970   Hygiene Conditions in Ancient Israel (Iron Age). *Journal of the History of Medicine* 25: 414–37.

Rosen, B., and Greenberg, Z.
2002   Water Sanitation in Pre-modern Jerusalem. Pp. 285–93 in *Cura Aquarum in Israel: In Memoriam Dr. Ya'kov Eren*, ed. C. Ohlig, Y. Peleg and T. Tsuk. Proceeding of the 11th International Conference on the History of Water Management and Hydraulic Engineering in the Mediterranean Region, Israel 7–12 May 2001. Schriften der Deustschen Wasserhistorsichen Gesellschaft 1. Siegburg: DWhG

Shiloh, Y.
1987   The Casemate Wall, the Four Room House, and Early Planning in the Israelite City. *Bulletin of the American Schools of Oriental Research* 268: 3–15
1992   Underground Water Systems in the Land of Israel in the Iron Age. Pp. 275–93 in *The Architecture of Ancient Israel: From the Prehistoric to the Persian periods: In Memory of Immanuel (Munya) Dunayevsky*, ed. A. Kempinski and R. Reich, Jerusalem: Israel Exploration Society.

Schloen, J. D.
2001   *The House of the Father as Fact and Symbol: Patrimonialism in Ugarit and the Ancient Near East*. Studies in the Archaeology and History of the Levant 2. Harvard Semitic Museum Publications. Winona Lake, IN: Eisenbrauns.

Stager, L. E.
1985   The Archaeology of the Family in Ancient Israel. *Bulletin of the American Schools of Oriental Research* 260: 1–35.

Tsuk, T.
1997a Cisterns. Pp. 12–13 in *The Oxford Encyclopedia of Archaeology in the Near East*, Vol. 2, ed. E. M. Meyers. New York, NY: Oxford University.
1997b Hydraulics. Pp. 130–32 in *The Oxford Encyclopedia of Archaeology in the Near East*, Vol. 3, ed. E. M. Meyers. New York, NY: Oxford University.
1997c Hydrology. Pp. 132–33 in *The Oxford Encyclopedia of Archaeology in the Near East*, Vol. 3, ed. E. M. Meyers. New York, NY: Oxford University.

Veenhof, K. R.
1972   *Aspects of Old Assyrian Trade and it Terminology.* Studia et Documenta ad Iura Orientis Antiqui Pertinentia 10. Leiden: Brill.

Walker, R.
2011   *Density of Materials.* http://www.simetric.co.uk/si_materials.htm (accessed May 27 2013).

Wampler, J. C.
1947   *Tell en-Naṣbeh*, Vol. 2: *The Pottery.* Berkeley, CA: Palestine Institute of Pacific School of Religion.

Weinberger, R.; Sneh, A.; and Shalev, E.
2008   Hydrogeological Insights in Antiquity as Indicated by Canaanite and Israelite Water Systems. *Journal of Archaeological Science* 35: 3035–42.

Wilson, C. T.
1906   *Peasant Life in the Holy Land.* London: John Murray.

Zertal, A.
1988   The Water Factor during the Israelite Settlement Process in Canaan. Pp. 341–52 in *Society and Economy in the Eastern Mediterranean (c. 1500–1000 B.C.)*, ed. M. Heltzer and E. Lipinski. Orientalia Lovaniensia Analecta 23. Leuven: Uitgeverij Peeters.

Zizola, F., and Faris, S.
2011   Holy Water: A Precious Commodity in a Region of Con-
        flict. *Orion*, November/December, 2011. http://www.ori
        onmagazine.org/index.php/articles/article/6473.

Zorn, J. R.
1993   Tell en-Nasbeh: A Re-evaluation of the Architecture and
        Stratigraphy of the Early Bronze Age, Iron Age and Later
        Periods. Ph.D. dissertation, University of California,
        Berkeley.
1994   Estimating the Population Size of Ancient Settlements:
        Methods, Problems, Solutions and a Case Study. *Bulletin of
        the American Schools of Oriental Research* 295: 31–48
1997   An Inner and Outer Gate Complex at Tell en-Nasbeh.
        Bulletin of the American Schools of Oriental Research 307: 53–66.
1999   This Old Site: Issues in the Reappraisal of Early Excava-
        tions. Pp. 59–70 in *Archaeology's Publication Problem: Volume
        2*, ed. H. Shanks. Washington, DC: Biblical Archaeology
        Society.

A BIBLIOGRAPHY OF TELL EN-NAṢBEH

Archaeological Work in Palestine and Syria during 1932.
1933   *Bulletin of the American Schools of Oriental Research* 49: 15–19.

The Excavations at Tell en-Nasbeh.
1929   *Bulletin of the American Schools of Oriental Research* 35: 24–25.

Cave Found in Bible City Recalls Burial of Sarah.
1935   *The Science News-Letter* 27: 349–50.

Chickens Were Known in Old Testament Days, Art Reveals.
1934   *The Science News-Letter* 25: 167.

Excavations in Palestine 1931–1932.
1932   *The Quarterly of the Department of Antiquities in Palestine* 2: 184–94.

Fingerprints on Pottery Aid in Tracing Past.
1934   *The Science News-Letter* 26: 260–61.

"King of the World" Unknown for 2500 Years.
1943   *The Science News-Letter* 43: 24–25.

Tell en-Nasbeh.
1929   *Syria* 10: 81.

Tell en-Nasbeh.
1947   *Bulletin of the American Schools of Oriental Research* 107: 17.

The Badè Memorial for Biblical Archaeology.
1942   *Bulletin of the American Schools of Oriental Research* 85: 1–3.

Abu Khalaf, M.; Abu A'mar, I.; Al-Houdalieh, S.; and Hoyland, R.
2006 The Byzantine and Early Islamic settlement of Khirbat Shuwayka. Pp. 47–76 in *Web Journal on Cultural Patrimony*. http://www.webjournal.unior.it/Dati/18/55/3.%20Palesti na,%20Abu%20Khalaf.pdf.

Albright, W. F.
1926 Report of the Director of the School in Jerusalem. *Bulletin of the American Schools of Oriental Research* 24: 9–17.
1929 Letter from the School in Jerusalem. *American Journal of Archaeology* 32: 117–21.
1932 Review of *Some Tombs of Tell en-Nasbeh Discovered in 1929* by William F. Badè. *Journal of the American Oriental Society* 52: 52–53.
1936 William Frederick Badè (Jan. 22, 1871–March 4, 1936). *Bulletin of the American Schools of Oriental Research* 62: 4–5.
1936 Archaeological Exploration and Excavation in Palestine and Syria, 1935. *American Journal of Archaeology* 40: 154–67.
1948 Review of *Tell en-Naṣbeh: Excavated Under the Direction of the Late William Frederic Badè*, Vol. 1, *Archaeological and Historical Results* by Chester Charlton McCown; Vol. 2, *The Pottery* by Joseph Carson Wampler. *Journal of Near Eastern Studies* 7: 202–05.

Arnold, P. M.
1992 Mizpah. Pp. 879–81 in *Anchor Bible Dictionary*, ed. D. N. Freedman. New York: Doubleday.

Avigad, N.
1958 New Light on the MSH Impressions. *Israel Exploration Journal* 8: 113–19.

Badè, W. F.
1927 Excavation of Tell en-Nasbeh. *Bulletin of the American Schools of Oriental Research* 26: 1–7.
1927 The Excavations at Tell en-Nasbeh. *Palestine Exploration Fund Quarterly Statement*: 7–13.
1928 *Excavations at Tell en-Nasbeh, 1926 and 1927: A Preliminary Report*. Palestine Institute Publications 1. Berkeley, CA.
1929 Excavations at Tell en-Nasbeh. *Revue biblique* 38: 317–19.

1929   Tell en-Nasbeh in 1929. *Bulletin of Pacific School of Religion* 8: 3–12.

1930   The Tell en-Nasbeh Excavations of 1929, A Preliminary Report. *Palestine Exploration Fund Quarterly Statement*: 8–19.

1930   The Tell en-Nasbeh Excavations of 1929, A Preliminary Report. *Annual Report of the Board of Regents of the Smithsonian Institution*: 483–94.

1931   *Some Tombs of Tell en-Nasbeh Discovered in 1929.* Palestine Institute Publications 2. Berkeley, CA.

1931   Ceramics and History in Palestine. *Journal of Biblical Literature* 50: 1–19.

1932   A Jar Handle from Tell en-Nasbeh. *Zeitschrift für die alttestamentliche Wissenschaft* 50: 89–90.

1932   Tall en Nasba. *The Quarterly of the Department of Antiquities in Palestine* 2: 192–93.

1933   The Seal of Jaazaniah. *Zeitschrift für die alttestamentliche Wissenschaft* 51: 150–56.

1934   *A Manual of Excavation in the Near East: Methods of Digging and Recording of the Tell en-Naṣbeh Expedition in Palestine.* Berkeley, CA: University of California.

1935   New Discoveries at Tell en-Nasbeh. Pp. 30–36 in *Werden und Wesen des Alten Testaments: Vorträge gehalten auf der internationalen Tagung alttestamentlicher Forscher zu Göttingen vom 4.–10. September 1935* ed. P. Volz, F. Stummer, and J. Hempel. Beihefte zur Zeitschrift für die alttestamentliche Wissenschaft 66. Berlin: A. Töpelmann.

Boutin, A. T.; McClellan, W. R.; and Cusimano, D. A.
2014   Life and Death at Tell en-Naṣbeh: A Bioarchaeological Analysis. Pp. 31–58 in *"As for me, I will dwell at Mizpah …"*: *The Tell en-Nasbeh Excavations after 85 Years*, ed. J. R. Zorn and A. J. Brody. Piscataway, NJ: Gorgias.

Branigan, K.
1966   The Four-Room Buildings of Tell en-Naṣbeh. *Israel Exploration Journal* 16: 206–08.

Brody, A. J.
2009   Mizpah, Mizpeh. Pp. 116–17 in *The New Interpreter's Dictionary of the Bible, Me–R*, Vol. 4, ed. K. D. Sakenfeld. Nash-

ville, TN: Abingdon.

2009 "Those Who Add House to House": Household Archaeology and the Use of Domestic Space in an Iron II Residential Compound at Tell en-Naṣbeh. Pp. 45–56 in *Exploring the Longue Durée: Essays in Honor of Lawrence E. Stager*, ed. J. D. Schloen. Winona Lake, IN: Eisenbrauns.

2011 The Archaeology of the Extended Family: A Household Compound from Iron II Tell en-Naṣbeh. Pp. 237–54 in *Household Archaeology in Ancient Israel and Beyond*, ed. A. Yasur-Landau, J. R. Ebeling, and L. B. Mazow. Leiden and Boston: Brill.

2014 Interregional Interaction in the Late Iron Age: Phoenician and Other Foreign Goods from Tell en-Nasbeh. Pp. 55–69 in *Material Culture Matters: Essays on the Archaeology of the Southern Levant in Honor of Seymour Gitin*, ed. J. R. Spencer, R. A. Mullins, and A. J. Brody. Winona Lake, IN: Eisenbrauns.

2014 Phoenician Imports to Tell en-Nasbeh: Indicators for Interregional Interaction in the Iron IIB–IIC Southern Levant. Pp. 133–42 in *Les Produits de luxe au Proche-Orient ancien aux âges du Bronze et du Fer*, ed. M. Casanova and M. Feldman. Paris: Maison René Ginouvès.

2014 Transjordanian Commerce with Northern Judah in the Iron IIC–Persian period: Ceramic Indicators, Interregional Interaction, and Modes of Exchange at Tell en-Naṣbeh. Pp. 59–93 in *"As for me, I will dwell at Mizpah ..."*: *The Tell en-Nasbeh Excavations after 85 Years*, ed. J. R. Zorn and A. J. Brody. Piscataway, NJ: Gorgias.

Brody, A. J., and Friedman, E.
2007 Bronze Bangles from Tell en-Nasbeh: Cultural and Economic Observations on an Artifact Type from the Time of the Prophets. Pp. 97–114 in *To Break Every Yoke: Essays in Honor of Marvin L. Chaney*, ed. R. B. Coote and N. K. Gottwald. The Social World of Biblical Antiquity, Second Series 3. Sheffield: Sheffield Phoenix.

Broshi, M.
1977 Naṣbeh, Tell en-. Pp. 912–16, 17 in *Encyclopedia of Archaeological Excavations in the Holy Land*, Vol. 3, ed. M. Avi-Yonah

and E. Stern. Jerusalem: Massada.

1992   Naṣbeh, Tell en-. Pp. 1027–29 in *Anchor Bible Dictionary*, Vol. 4, ed. D. N. Freedman. New York: Doubleday.

Brown, S. H.

2014   Iron in the Iron Age: The Life-Cycle of Agricultural Implements from Tell en-Naṣbeh. Pp. 95–122 in *"As for me, I will dwell at Mizpah ...": The Tell en-Nasbeh Excavations after 85 Years*, ed. J. R. Zorn and A. J. Brody. Piscataway, NJ: Gorgias.

Burrows, M.

1935   Review of *A Manual of Excavation in the Near East. Methods of Digging and Recording of the Tell en-Naṣbeh Expedition in Palestine* by William Frederic Badè. *Journal of Biblical Literature* 15: 349.

Cross, F. M.

1969   Two Notes on Palestinian Inscriptions of the Persian Age. *Bulletin of the American Schools of Oriental Research* 193: 19–24.

Dalley, S.

2013   Gods from North-eastern and North-western Arabia in Cuneiform Texts from the First Sealand Dynasty, and a Cuneiform Inscription from Tell en-Naṣbeh, c.1500 BC. *Arabian Archaeology and Epigraphy* 24: 177–85.

Diringer, D.

1967   Mizpah. Pp. 309–28 in *Archaeology and Old Testament Study*, ed. D. W. Thomas. Oxford: Clarendon.

Dougherty, R. P.

1929   Review of *Excavations at Tell en-Nasbeh, 1926 and 1927. A Preliminary Report* by William Frederic Badè. *American Journal of Archaeology* 33: 455.

Duncan, G. S.

1935   Review of *A Manual of Excavation in the Near East. Methods of Digging and Recording of the Tell en-Nasbeh Expedition in Palestine* by William Frederic Badè. *Journal of the National Asso-*

ciation of Biblical Instructors 3: 61–62.

Dussaud, R.
1932   Review of *Some Tombs of Tell en-Nasbeh Discovered in 1929. A Special Report* by William Frederic Badè. *Syria* 13: 214.
1935   Review of *A Manual of Excavation in the Near East. Methods of Digging and Recording of the Tell en-Naṣbeh Expedition in Palestine* by William Frederic Badè. *Syria* 16: 409.

Edelman, D.
2006   The Function of the *mw(ṣ)h*-Stamped Jars Revisited. Pp. 659–71 in *"I Will Speak the Riddle of Ancient Times": Archaeological and Historical Studies in Honor of Amihai Mazar on the Occasion of His Sixtieth Birthday*, Vol. 2, ed. A. M. Maeir and P. d. Miroschedji. Winona Lake, IN: Eisenbrauns.

Finkelstein, I.
2012   The Great Wall of Tell en-Nasbeh (Mizpah), The First Fortifications in Judah, and 1 Kings 15:16–22. *Vetus Testamentum* 62: 14–28.

Foster, C. P.
2009   *Digging Up a Buried Town: The Excavations of Tell en-Nasbeh.* DVD. Berkeley: Badè Museum of Biblical Archaeology.
2013   Beyond the Display Case: Creating a Multisensory Museum Experience. Pp. 371–89 in *Making Senses of the Past: Toward a Sensory Archaeology*, Center for Archaeological Investigations Occasional Paper 40, ed. J. Day. Carbondale, IL: Southern Illinois University.
2014   Curating Badè's Legacy: Management of the Tell en-Naṣbeh Collection. Pp. 123–144 in *"As for me, I will dwell at Mizpah …": The Tell en-Nasbeh Excavations after 85 Years*, ed. J. R. Zorn and A. J. Brody. Piscataway, NJ: Gorgias.

Friedman, E. S.; Brody, A. J.; Young, M. L.; Almer, J. D.; Segre, C. U.; and Mini, S. M.
2008   Synchrotron Radiation-based X-ray Analysis of Bronze Artifacts from an Iron Age Site in the Judean Hills. *Journal of Archaeological Science* 35: 1951–60.

Ginsberg, H. L.
1948   MMŠT and MṢH. *Bulletin of the American Schools of Oriental Research* 109: 20–22.

Glueck, N.
1933   Palestinian and Syrian Archaeology in 1932. *American Journal of Archaeology* 37: 160–72.
1937   Review of *A Manual of Excavation in the Near East. Methods of Digging and Recording of the Tell en-Naṣbeh Expedition in Palestine* by William Frederic Badè. *Jewish Quarterly Review* 28: 89–90.

Grant, E.
1927   Tell en-Nasbeh Expedition of the Pacific School of Religion. *Palestine Exploration Fund Quarterly Statement*: 159–61.
1936   Review of *A Manual of Excavation in the Near East. Methods of Digging and Recording of the Tell en-Naṣbeh Expedition in Palestine* by William Frederic Badè. *American Journal of Archaeology* 40: 273–74.

Gunneweg, J.; Asaro, F.; Michel, H. V.; and Perlman, I.
1994   Interregional Contacts between Tell en-Nasbeh and Littoral Philistine Centres in Canaan during Early Iron I. *Archaeometry* 36: 227–40.

Heffner, E. H.
1927   Archaeological News — Tell en-Nasbeh. *American Journal of Archaeology* 31: 103.
1927   Archaeological News — Excavations of Tell en-Nasbeh. *American Journal of Archaeology* 31: 362.
1928   Archaeological News — Tell en-Nasbeh. *American Journal of Archaeology* 32: 75–76.
1929   Archaeological News — Tell en-Nasbeh. *American Journal of Archaeology* 33: 411–12.
1930   Archaeological News — Tell en-Nasbeh. *American Journal of Archaeology* 34: 71–72.
1931   Archaeological News — Tell en-Nasbeh. *American Journal of Archaeology* 35: 71.

Hempel, J.

1945–48 Review of W. F. Albright, *The Excavations of Tell Beit Mirsim, Vol. III: The Iron Age. Tell en-Nasbeh: Excavated Under the Direction of the Late William Frederic Badè*, Vol. 1, *Archaeological and Historical Results*, Vol. 2, *The Pottery. Zeitschrift für die alttestamentliche Wissenschaft* 61: 232–39.

Hoyland, R.

2011 The Byzantine/Early Islamic Site of Khirbat Shuwayka in Palestine (The Monastery of the Prophet Samuel?). Pp. 219–32 in *Le Proche-Orient de Justinien aux Abbassides: peuplement et dynamiques spatiales; actes du Colloque "Continuites de l'occupation entre les periodes byzantine et abbasside au Proche-Orient, VIIe–IXe siècles,"* Paris, 18–20 Octobre 2007, ed. A. Borrut. Turnhout: Brepols.

Katz, H.

1998 A Note on the Date of the 'Great Wall' of Tell en-Naṣbeh. *Tel Aviv* 25: 131–33.

Kenyon, K. M.

1950 Palestinian Excavations. *Antiquity* 24: 196–200.

Larkum, M.

2014 "Let me eat some of that red stuff, for I am famished!" (Gen. 25:30): Preliminary Insights into Iron Age Cooking Practices at Tell en-Naṣbeh Resulting from Gas Chromatography/Mass Spectrometry Analyses. Pp. 145–173 in *"As for me, I will dwell at Mizpah ...": The Tell en-Nasbeh Excavations after 85 Years*, ed. J. R. Zorn and A. J. Brody. Piscataway, NJ: Gorgias.

Lipschits, O., and Vanderhooft, D. S.

2011 *The Yehud Impressions: A Corpus of Inscribed Impressions from the Persian and Hellenistic Periods in Judah*. Winona Lake, IN: Eisenbrauns.

Masterman, E. W. G.

1929 Excavations at Tell en-Nasbeh, 1926–7. *Palestine Exploration Fund Quarterly Statement*: 56–57.

May, H. G.
1948   Review of *Tell en-Naṣbeh: Excavated Under the Direction of the Late William Frederic Badè*, Vol. 1, *Archaeological and Historical Results* by Chester Charlton McCown; Vol. 2, *The Pottery* by Joseph Carson Wampler. *Journal of Religion* 28: 134–35.

McClellan, T. L.
1984   Town Planning at Tell en-Naṣbeh. *Zeitschrift des Deutschen Palästina-Vereins* 100: 53–69.

McCown, C. C.
1929   Letter from Director McCown. *Bulletin of the American Schools of Oriental Research* 35: 14–15, 18.
1929   News Items from Jerusalem: Palestinian Archaeology in 1929 — Tell en-Nasbeh. *American Journal of Archaeology* 34: 93–94.
1930   Palestinian Archaeology in 1929. *Bulletin of the American Schools of Oriental Research* 37: 2–20.
1945   The Long-Room House at Tell en-Naṣbeh. *Bulletin of the American Schools of Oriental Research* 98: 2–15.
1947   *Tell en-Naṣbeh: Excavated Under the Direction of the Late William Frederic Badè*, Vol. 1: *Archaeological and Historical Results*. Berkeley, CA and New Haven, CT: Palestine Institute of Pacific School of Religion and American Schools of Oriental Research.
1950   Hebrew High Places and Cult Remains. *Journal of Biblical Literature* 63: 205–19.

Montgomery, J. A.
1933   Review of *Some Tombs of Tell en-Nasbeh Discovered in 1929, a Special Report* by William Frederic Badè; *The Citadel of Beth-Zur* by Ovid Rogers Sellers. *American Journal of Archaeology* 37: 511–12.

Muilenburg, J.
1954–55 Mizpah of Benjamin. *Studia Theologica* 8: 25–42.

Naish, J. P.
1932   Tell en-Nasbeh. *Palestine Exploration Fund Quarterly Statement*: 204–09.

Perkins, A. L.
1948   Review of *Tell en-Naṣbeh: Excavated Under the Direction of the Late William Frederic* Badè, Vol. 1, *Archaeological and Historical Results* by Chester Charlton McCown; Vol. 2, *The Pottery* by Joseph Carson Wampler. *Journal of the American Oriental Society* 68: 196–99.

Roberts, F. H. H. Jr.
1935   Review of *A Manual of Excavation in the Near East. Methods of Digging and Recording of the Tell en-Naṣbeh Expedition in Palestine* by William Frederic Badè. *American Anthropologist* 37: 692–94.

Robinson, D. M.
1933   Archaeological News and Discussions: Excavations at Tell en-Nasbeh. *American Journal of Archaeology* 37: 124.
1936   Archaeological News and Discussions: Necrology — William Frederic Badè. *American Journal of Archaeology* 40: 247.

Sellers, O. R.
1948   Review of *Tell en-Naṣbeh: Excavated Under the Direction of the Late William Frederic* Badè, Vol. 1, *Archaeological and Historical Results* by Chester Charlton McCown; Vol. 2, *The Pottery* by Joseph Carson Wampler. *Journal of Biblical Literature* 57: 392–93.

Simons, J. J.
1948   Review of *Tell en-Naṣbeh: Excavated Under the Direction of the Late William Frederic* Badè, Vol. 1, *Archaeological and Historical Results* by Chester Charlton McCown; Vol. 2, *The Pottery* by Joseph Carson Wampler. *Bibliotheca Orientalis* 7: 104–07.

Sussman, V.
2014   Observations Regarding an Oil Lamp of the Late Roman–Byzantine Period from Tell en-Naṣbeh. Pp. 175–97 in *"As for me, I will dwell at Mizpah ...": The Tell en-Nasbeh Excavations after 85 Years*, ed. J. R. Zorn and A. J. Brody. Piscataway, NJ: Gorgias.

Tufnell, O.
1948   Review of *Tell en-Naşbeh: Excavated Under the Direction of the Late William Frederic Badè*, Vol. 1, *Archaeological and Historical Results* by Chester Charlton McCown; Vol. 2, *The Pottery* by Joseph Carson Wampler. *Palestine Exploration Quarterly* 80: 145–50.

Vanderhooft, D., and Horowitz, W.
2002   The Cuneiform Inscription from Tell en-Naşbeh: The Demise of an Unknown King. *Tel Aviv* 29: 318–27.

Vincent, L. H.
1948   Review of *Tell en-Naşbeh: Excavated Under the Direction of the Late William Frederic Badè*, Vol. 1, *Archaeological and Historical Results* by Chester Charlton McCown; Vol. 2, *The Pottery* by Joseph Carson Wampler. *Revue biblique* 55: 287–97.

von Bothmer, D.
1941   Greek Pottery from Tell en-Naşbeh. *Bulletin of the American Schools of Oriental Research* 83: 25–30.

Wampler, J. C.
1940   Triangular Impressed Design in Palestinian Pottery. *Bulletin of the American Schools of Oriental Research* 80: 13–16.
1941   Three Cistern Groups from Tell en-Naşbeh. *Bulletin of the American Schools of Oriental Research* 82: 25–43.
1947   *Tell en-Naşbeh: Excavated Under the Direction of the Late William Frederic Badè*, Vol. 2: *The Pottery*. Berkeley, CA and New Haven, CT: Palestine Institute of Pacific School of Religion and American Schools of Oriental Research.

Wright, G. E.
1947   Tell en-Nasbeh. *Biblical Archaeologist* 10: 69–77.
1948   Review of *Tell en-Naşbeh: Excavated Under the Direction of the Late William Frederic Badè*, Vol. 1, *Archaeological and Historical Results* by Chester Charlton McCown; Vol. 2, *The Pottery* by Joseph Carson Wampler. *American Journal of Archaeology* 52: 470–72.

Zink, J. H.
1966   Tell en-Nasbeh. Pp. 569–71 in *The Biblical World*. Grand Rapids, MI: Baker Books.

Zissu, B., and Klein, E.
2014   On the Use and Reuse of Rock-Cut Tombs and a Ritual Bath at Tel en-Naṣbeh: New Perspectives on the Roman and Byzantine Necropoleis. Pp. 199–224 in *"As for me, I will dwell at Mizpah …": The Tell en-Nasbeh Excavations after 85 Years*, ed. J. R. Zorn and A. J. Brody. Piscataway, NJ: Gorgias.

Zorn, J. R.
1987   *The Secret of a Tell*. Berkeley, CA: Badè Institute of Biblical Archaeology.
1988   The Museum Trail: The Badè Institute of Biblical Archaeology. *Biblical Archaeologist* 51: 36–45.
1988   William Frederic Badè. *Biblical Archaeologist* 51: 28–35.
1990   Ascii-yahu son of Bit-el; Computerizing an Archaeological Data Base. *Journal of the Association of Graduate Near Eastern Students* 1: 55–59.
1993   Mesopotamian-style Ceramic "Bathtub" Coffins from Tell en-Nasbeh. *Tel Aviv* 20: 216–24.
1993   Naṣbeh, Tell en-. Pp. 1098–1102 in *The New Encyclopedia of Archaeological Excavations in the Holy Land*, ed. E. Stern. Jerusalem: Carta.
1993   Tell en-Nasbeh: A Re-evaluation of the Architecture and Stratigraphy of the Early Bronze Age, Iron Age and Later Periods. Ph.D. dissertation, University of California, Berkeley.
1994   Estimating the Population Size of Ancient Settlements: Methods, Problems, Solutions and a Case Study. *Bulletin of the American Schools of Oriental Research* 295: 31–48.
1994   Two Rosette Stamp Impressions from Tell en-Nasbeh. *Bulletin of the American Schools of Oriental Research* 293: 81–82.
1995   Scanning Pottery Profiles. *Center for the Study of Architecture Newsletter* 7: 7–9.
1995   Three Cross-Shaped "Ṭet" Stamp Impressions from Tell en-Nasbeh. *Tel Aviv* 22: 98–106.
1996   Tell en-Nasbeh: Ceramic Dating of Strata 1 through 5.

Bulletin of the American Schools of Oriental Research 303: 81–82.

1996   The Date of a Bronze Vase from Tell en-Naṣbeh. *Tel Aviv* 23: 209–12.

1997   A Legacy of Publication: William F. Badè and Tell en-Nasbeh. *Biblical Archaeology Review* 23: 68–69.

1997   An Inner and Outer Gate Complex at Tell en-Nasbeh. *Bulletin of the American Schools of Oriental Research* 307: 53–66.

1997   Badè, William F. P. 262 in *The Oxford Encyclopedia of the Ancient Near East*, ed. E. Meyers. Oxford: Oxford University.

1997   Mizpah: Newly Discovered Stratum Reveals Judah's other Capital. *Biblical Archaeology Review* 23: 28–38, 66.

1997   Naṣbeh, Tell en-. Pp. 101–03 in *The Oxford Encyclopedia of the Ancient Near East*, ed. E. Meyers. Oxford: Oxford University.

1998   Indiana Zorn and the Web Site of Tell en-Nasbeh. *Near Eastern Archaeology* 61: 257.

1998   The Dating of an Early Iron Age Kiln from Tell en-Nasbah. *Levant* 30: 199–202.

1999   A Note on the Date of the 'Great Wall' of Tell en-Naṣbeh: A Rejoinder. *Tel Aviv* 26: 146–50.

1999   This Old Site: Issues in the Reappraisal of Early Excavations. Pp. 59–70 in *Archaeology's Publication Problem: Volume 2*, ed. H. Shanks. Washington, DC: Biblical Archaeology Society.

2000   Mizpah. Pp. 908–09 in *Eerdmans Dictionary of the Bible*, ed. D. N. Freedman. Grand Rapids, MI: Eerdmans.

2001   Wedge- and Circle-Impressed Pottery: An Arabian Connection. Pp. 689–98 in *Studies in the Archaeology of Israel and Neighboring Lands in Memory of Douglas L. Esse*, ed. S. R. Wolff. Studies in Ancient Oriental Civilizations 59. Chicago: Oriental Institute.

2003   Tell en-Naṣbeh and the Problem of the Material Culture of the 6th Century. Pp. 413–47 in *Judah and the Judeans in the Neo-Babylonian Period*, ed. O. Lipschits and J. Blenkinsopp. Winona Lake, IN: Eisenbrauns.

2005   Mizpah. Pp. 701–05 in *Dictionary of the Old Testament: Historical Books*, ed. B. T. Arnold and H. G. M. Williamson. Downers Grove, IL: InterVaristy.

2008   Mizpah, Mizpah Wherefore Art Thou Mizpah? Tell en-Naṣbeh, Nebi Samwil and the Identification of a Biblical

Site. In *BAR Web Extra.* http://www.bib-arch.org/bar/extra.asp?ArticleID=12&ParentArticleID=3.

2013   Tell en-Naṣbeh. Pp. 400–08 in *The Oxford Encyclopedia of the Bible and Archaeology*, ed. D. Master. New York: Oxford University.

2014   *Photo Essay: Tell en Naṣbeh.* Oxford Biblical Studies Online. http://global.oup.com/obso/peNasbeh/.

2014   Tell en-Naṣbeh's Contributions to Understanding Iron Age Israelite Water Systems. Pp. 225–279 in *"As for me, I will dwell at Mizpah …": The Tell en-Nasbeh Excavations after 85 Years*, ed. J. R. Zorn and A. J. Brody. Piscataway, NJ: Gorgias.

Zorn, J. R., and Walsh, C.
1998   New Insights from Old Wine Presses. *Palestine Exploration Quarterly* 130: 154–61.

Zorn, J. R.; Yellin, J.; and Hayes, J.
1994   The m(w)ṣh Stamp Impressions and the Neo-Babylonian Period. *Israel Exploration Journal* 44: 161–83.

INDEX

BIBLICAL REFERENCES

GENERAL TERMS

AUTHORS AND INDIVIDUALS

SITES/GEOGRAPHIC TERMS

Lightning Source UK Ltd.
Milton Keynes UK
UKOW02n0854160915

258711UK00007B/42/P